JPR
GIVEN THE
BREAKS

MY LIFE IN RUGBY

JPR
GIVEN THE BREAKS

MY LIFE IN RUGBY

JPR WILLIAMS

with Miles Harrison

H

HODDER &
STOUGHTON

Copyright © 2006 by JPR Williams

First published in Great Britain in 2006 by Hodder & Stoughton
A division of Hodder Headline

The right of JPR Williams to be identified as the Author
of the Work has been asserted by him in accordance with
the Copyright, Designs and Patents Act 1988.

A Hodder and Stoughton Book

1

A CIP catalogue record for this title is available from the British Library

ISBN 978 0 340 92307 8
ISBN 0 340 92307 5

Typeset in Stone Serif by Hewer Text UK Ltd, Edinburgh
Printed and bound by Mackays of Chatham Ltd, Chatham, Kent

Hodder Headline's policy is to use papers that are natural, renewable
and recyclable products and made from wood grown in sustainable forests.
The logging and manufacturing processes are expected to conform
to the environmental regulations of the country of origin.

Hodder & Stoughton Ltd
A division of Hodder Headline
338 Euston Road
London NW1 3BH

To my family – my wife Scilla and my four children, Lauren, Annie, Fran and Peter, inspire me, and my three brothers, Phil, Chris and Mike, are always there for me.

CONTENTS

ACKNOWLEDGEMENTS

Special thanks go to my wife, Scilla. I continue to value her support and she has been a wonderful help in the creation of this book.

I am also indebted to a number of people for their assistance: Miles Harrison, rugby commentator at BSkyB, for his quiet enthusiasm and skill in piecing the book together – Miles is not only a fine broadcaster, he is a fine writer too; Roddy Bloomfield, my publisher at Hodder, for taking on this project and expertly guiding it through the final stages – Roddy has years of experience in the field and it shows; Jon Holmes, sports agent at SFX, for bringing us all together in the first place – Jon, like the others, is the consummate professional.

Photographic Acknowledgements

The author and publisher would like to thank the following for permission to reproduce photographs:

AFP/Getty Images, AP/Empics, Andrew Cowie/Colorsport, Don Hall, John Harris, The Telegram (Toronto), Western Mail & Echo Ltd.

All other phtographs are from private collections.

Every reasonable effort has been made to contact the copyright holders, but if there are any errors or omissions, Hodder & Stoughton will be pleased to insert the appropriate acknowledgement in any subsequent printing of this publication.

FOREWORD

by John Dawes

JPR, the Ultimate Icon

In September 1968 Wales embarked on only the second major tour in their history when they accepted an invitation to visit Argentina. That summer a British Lions tour to South Africa had been beset by injury, so the Welsh Rugby Union decided to rest its Lions for this trip to South America. Thus an opportunity was provided for some new faces to make a mark at national level, although no caps were awarded for the two Test matches played.

Among the new players selected was a certain John Williams, a fresh, baby-faced youngster who at that stage was better known for his tennis achievements – he was Junior Wimbledon Champion – than for his rugby prowess. Mind you, he was still a teenager at the time. In a somewhat disappointing tour where the strength of the Argentinians was greatly underestimated few Welsh players had an opportunity to shine. One of them was John Peter Rhys Williams, later to be known throughout the rugby world by his initials – JPR.

On returning to the UK and the domestic scene, JPR moved from his first club, Bridgend, to resume his medical studies at St Mary's Hospital for whom it was his intention to play his rugby. But such was the impression he had made in the Argentine that London Welsh showed more than a passing interest and snaffled him at short notice to play in the First XV when their regular full-back cried off injured. Some six weeks later John was selected to play in his first capped international against Scotland at Murrayfield on 1 February 1969. The rest is history.

JPR had all the requirements to become a great. He was talented, brave, committed and totally uncompromising. His impact on the game was immediate and long-standing. By 1974 he had travelled with Wales to New Zealand, Australia, Fiji and Canada. He was an outstanding member of two victorious Lions tours – to New Zealand in 1971 and South Africa in 1974. JPR was an established icon.

In an international rugby career that spanned thirteen years as a player (1968–81), JPR achieved everything possible. Triple Crowns, Grand Slams and Lions Test victories were all his.

Today, a little older and wiser but not heavier nor less committed, JPR still attends all the matches and is president of Bridgend RFC, although on his own admission he doesn't make a very good spectator. There is no doubt, however, that he is a legend and will always be remembered for his contribution to rugby football throughout the world, but especially in Wales and with the British Lions.

John Dawes

INTRODUCTION

It is hard to believe that it is twenty-seven years since I was involved in a huge controversy over the publication of my first autobiography. I had been writing it whilst still playing for Wales and planning my retirement from international rugby. Many of my team-mates, who are some of my closest friends, had written theirs and I suppose I felt that I had my own story to tell. Being fiercely competitive, I did not wish to be left out and I also wanted to do it all by myself.

They turned professional on their retirement, but I had other ideas as I already had a full-time job as an aspiring young surgeon and had no plans to be a sports writer or commentator. Maintaining my amateur status gave me the option to stay in the game but that is where my troubles started. It is almost impossible for young people today to imagine the serious consequences of receiving money from playing rugby union as an amateur when you compare this with the huge contracts and endorsements that the current professional players can now attract. Anyone involved in rugby after 1995 might think it ridiculous that there was such a breed of international player who represented his country all for the love of the game. The older ones will remember some good times though and will still be watching the videos and harping on about the past.

In making the comparison, I think that the contrast between myself and a player of today such as Gavin Henson could not be greater. We both made our way via the Bridgend and District Under-11 team, loving our beautiful game, but the paths we chose were dictated by the different decades of rugby that we grew up in. I was a diehard Corinthian, and all that I have to say about modern professionalism comes from that standpoint. Gavin embodies the glamorous modern game and receives the attention and money that people associate with a young professional. He, like me, caused controversy by writing his autobiography but for entirely different reasons. The repercussions from his book, which he wrote early in his career, spread much wider, involved many people and may have ultimately caused the break-up of the Welsh Grand Slam squad and coaching staff. Set beside that, the fall-out from my book was a small ripple. It involved only me and my family, that is unless you count all the people who have benefited from the creation of the Bridgend Sports Injury Clinic, which was born from the proceeds of my book.

This book allows me to look back with a new perspective and bridge the gap from 1979 through to my eventual retirement and to describe a life of two 'careers' – in rugby and medicine. I reflect on all the changes that have taken place in rugby and on the teams that I have played in from when I was first capped in 1969 to when I finally hung up my boots at Tondu in 2003. I also consider the recent momentous events in Welsh rugby; it seems there is never a dull moment when it comes to this sport in my country.

It is strange to think that I might never have ended up as a rugby player had I chosen to pursue my other sport of tennis. 1966 was a special year for me on the court and, as in rugby, my time in tennis spanned both the amateur and professional days.

In the world of medicine, I was fortunate to have inside know-ledge of the National Health Service straight from the cradle as I was born to two GPs in the late 1940s. I qualified in 1973 and then, after thirteen years of extra studies and exams, became a consultant orthopaedic surgeon. I have seen the best and the worst of the NHS; as it was then and as it sadly is now.

I recount the difficulties of trying to marry the demands of a challenging medical profession with my chosen sport and, of course, the needs of my loving family. I found myself playing for Wales in the days when we won Triple Crowns and Grand Slams and I see myself as being so lucky to have qualified and played when I did. Our results made it much easier to want to keep combining the two, as anything is achievable when you are part of a winning team.

I used to say that I spent half my life breaking bones on the rugby field, then the other half putting them back together in the operating theatre. Given all the breaks, it has been fun.

1
PARENTS AND CHILDREN

I SUPPOSE we should get the business of my name out of the way first. My family always call me John and my close rugby friends call me Japes but, to the rest of the world, I am and always will be JPR.

I used to get embarrassed at school when everyone had to wait for me to recite 'John Peter Rhys'. After all, it is quite a mouthful, but it had to be done because, in Wales, there are so many Williams in a class. Now, of course, my initials are my trademark. On the Lions tour of 1974, my team-mate John (JJ) Williams passed to me and I, John (JPR) Williams, passed it back; the commentators needed to differentiate between us so, suddenly, I was just JPR. After that, if I signed an autograph 'John Williams', small boys would run back, looking short-changed: 'You are JPR, aren't you? So, why haven't you put JPR then?'

People who know me will confirm that I am not a fan of lateness and so I have always regretted being born just a few hours after the close of St David's Day. It would have been pretty special to share a birthday with the patron saint of the Welsh people and, some would say, a good omen, considering the importance of St David as the great deliverer from the enemy – usually the English. This time, however, my mother was the great deliverer and, on 2 March 1949, I came into the world. It will come as a surprise to many that she was English.

My mother, Margaret, hailed from Rochdale and, all through her life, she proved the perfect example of northern English grit and

1

determination; her family worked in finance and she was shrewd with money but always generous with her time. For Mum, nothing was impossible and her stock phrase was 'I will hold the fort' – she was the full-back of the family. She studied medicine at Manchester University and qualified early at just twenty-two in 1945 because of the war. She met my father, Dr Peter Williams, who was studying in Cardiff and she must have liked him because she gave him her bacon rations.

When I was born, the National Health Service was also in its infancy and it was a very busy time for Mum. With many doctors still in the forces, including my father, she returned to her job as a GP as soon as she could and I spent a great deal of my first twelve months in a carry-cot in the back of her car as she went on her rounds. An awful lot fell on her shoulders but, throughout, she bore it with grace and a great will to succeed; I have no doubt that the perseverance and desire to win that I showed during my sporting career came from my mother. When things have been busy for me, I have often found myself thinking, 'Get on with it!' as Mum would have said. Once Dad finished his service as a surgeon in the army, he joined her in general practice in Bridgend. It was very much a family business and still is, with my three brothers, Phil, Chris and Mike, and also my wife Scilla, running it today.

I was quite a mischievous little boy and a fierce competitor too. The competitive side to my character really began to shine through when my brothers arrived on the scene. Phil was born in 1951, with Chris and Mike coming along within the next five years. We loved each other's company and we loved our sport as well; I remember we three elder boys keeping our fingers crossed that Mike, the fourth born, would be a boy too, so we could even the numbers up in our teams. One of our favourite games was indoor rugby, two-a-side on the bed, with the pillows down the middle as the halfway line. When we had been playing the real thing outdoors, my mother used to say that she could tell who had been trying the hardest by the colour of our shorts – the dirtiest belonged to the winners.

By 1952, we had moved into Ashfield on Merthyrmawr Road in Bridgend, which housed the doctors' surgery. The garden was large and could amply accommodate all our sporting needs. Conveniently spaced fir trees were perfect for drop-goal attempts, and there was even a grass tennis court. We would play long into the evenings, with our parents so busy at the practice.

I was just six months old when I was given my first rugby ball, a present from the great Dr Jack Matthews of Cardiff, Wales and the Lions. He and my father had been good friends at medical school and, when they played for the Cardiff Medicals, my dad was on the left wing, outside Matthews, who went on to be a tough tackling centre for Wales in the late 1940s. I only realised how good Dr Jack had been when I read about him after I had grown up. As a child, I loved that ball and was rarely seen without it tucked under my arm. I still have it today, a rather tatty and deflated little thing, but it sits proudly amongst my most prized rugby possessions on the shelves at home.

My dream in those days was simple – to play for Bridgend. It was the same for all of my brothers and probably every little boy in the town. We would dress up in the blue and white, cross the River Ogwr and run to practise our game at Newbridge Fields where the posts were the real size and, in addition to being child-minder, I would be team-picker and referee! By the age of seven, I was playing in real rugby games and loving it. Indeed, I spent the whole week longing for match day.

It was about this time that I encountered my first-ever sporting hero. Billy Morgan was a teacher at Trelales Primary School in Laleston and, more importantly in my eyes, was also the full-back for Bridgend. On Saturdays we would watch him play down at the Brewery Field and on Monday he would be back at school, imparting his infectious enthusiasm for the game. I idolised Morgan but one day I had to face the fact that sometimes your heroes are not always what you want them to be. As a special treat, I was taken to an away match at Cheltenham and, to my horror, Morgan was sent off. This was a much more serious proposition before the days of yellow cards. Once sent off you were out of the match for good and dismissal carried quite a stigma at the time. I could not understand it! How could he have allowed this to happen? I felt so badly let down.

Billy Morgan played a huge part in my rugby career, however, as he was the man to persuade me to move from my early position of fly-half, always the glamour spot in Welsh rugby, to full-back. In my ten-year-old mind, being asked to wear the number fifteen jersey was akin to being dropped from the team and I can assure you that I did not take the suggestion well. Morgan's opinion was that an attacking full-back would be the coming position and, in that respect, he was way ahead of his time. He did me a great favour, especially in view of the exceptionally talented fly-halves that would emerge from Welsh rugby over the next few years. My life could have been very different had it not been for his intervention.

Morgan was my first rugby mentor but the Rev. Canon Haydn Rees was the most important influence on me outside my family. In common with many Welshmen, I have made music an integral part of my life. I was a chorister and also rang the bells at my local church in Bridgend. Nolton Church was literally at the bottom of our garden and I would run across the road to choir practice after school. After a couple of years' apprenticeship, I had my big chance: a solo in the Christmas service with a 500-strong congregation listening intently to my rendering of the first verse of 'Once in Royal David's City'. It was nerve-wracking but I loved it. I knew then that I could rise to the big occasion and that an audience was to be enjoyed, not feared. I still think that was a harder test than facing a pack of All Black forwards!

Canon Rees was the man in charge at the church and a great

family friend. Coming from the Rhondda, he was so passionate about his rugby that he would sometimes watch a Sunday afternoon match on television when he should really have been polishing his sermon for Evensong. Years later, when his health was failing, he made a 400-mile round trip to Derbyshire so he could officiate at my wedding to Scilla and he even gave the rugby-playing guests from London Welsh a team-talk before the service began, exhorting them, 'All these people up here know that you're Welsh and expect you to sing. Get into that pub, have a couple of pints, and then go into the church and show 'em!'

But by far the biggest male influence on me was my father. Nobody could have been a father like my father. He spent hour after hour with his boys, helping us to hone our sporting skills, especially in the two sports that he loved so much – rugby and tennis. They were great times; Dad was competitive but a kind man who loved to laugh and his motto was 'Work hard – play hard'. Perhaps it should be mine as well.

My rugby abilities were hardened by our family training sessions on Sunday afternoons. We would all drive out to Porthcawl, a place well known for its strong breeze, and on Lock's Common, where the wind would howl, Dad would give us a barrage of up and unders. We were determined not to let that ball drop – it was simply a matter of pride. Those sessions formed the basis of my confidence underneath the high ball for the years to come. I am a great believer that there is only a certain amount of natural talent available to anyone; what makes one athlete different from another is hard slog and persistence, plus an underlying belief that anything is possible.

We were always a close family and certainly in our young lives my brothers and I followed in each other's footsteps: all four of us played rugby for Bridgend Under-15s, we all became Welsh Junior Tennis Champions and, even on the academic side, we all studied medicine at St Mary's Hospital Medical School in London. It might sound freakish but it's true. Of all our achievements, I think it was our all becoming doctors that made our father most proud, as he was a medic first and passionate about it – putting in stitches was what he enjoyed most. Over the years I gave him plenty of practice.

Three of us went on to play regular first-class rugby but, regrettably, Phil did not. When he was sixteen, he hit his head on the ground during a match for Bridgend Grammar School against Millfield. He thought nothing of it but then he started to get dreadful headaches and, after a series of tests, a small blood clot was removed from the outer membrane of his brain. Phil only ever played rugby one more time.

I loved growing up as one of our band of four brothers and now Scilla and I also have four children who, like their parents and grandparents before them, share their own passion for sport, something that seems to run through the Williams' family tree like a seam of rich Welsh coal. Now they are at the peak of their sporting lives, I am enjoying supporting them.

Our eldest daughter, Lauren, has combined her medical career with representing Great Britain as a tri-athlete in her age-group. I thought that I had worked hard to combine medicine with a burgeoning sports career but she has had to give an even greater level of commitment because of the modern day demands on young doctors. Lauren and our second daughter, Annie, both played hockey for Wales at the 1998 Commonwealth Games in Kuala Lumpur and, more recently, Annie, a physiotherapist, has had great success at the 'Iron Man' triathlon in Lanzarote. I had such admiration for her – it was a very hard competition and I could tell that others were impressed too when, for the first time in my life, I was referred to as 'Annie's Dad'! Fran, our third daughter, played hockey for Wales Under-21s in the Junior World Cup in Argentina and is now captain of her club, West Hampstead. All my children are musical but Fran is the real artiste of the family, playing the piano, organ, harp and even the trombone!

My son, Peter, played rugby at representative level. I was very conscious that being my son was going to make it tough for him and remember before one game, East Wales against West Wales Under-11s, Peter coming to me and saying, 'Dad, I'm really nervous.' 'That's good,' I replied. 'Nerves make you play well.' Yet I realised that the cause of his anxiety was probably trying to live up to his name. I was determined to encourage Peter, just like my father constantly encouraged me, but when he decided that golf was his game, I admit that I was slightly relieved because that sport could belong solely to him. I was a total novice at golf and all that I now know is down to Peter. We have a great relationship and he delights in calling me 'the old man' and laughing at my creaking joints.

Peter is now at the University of St Andrews studying geography and golf – but not necessarily in that order! For the last two summers I have had a great time driving him around the golf tournaments. He has genuine natural talent and could well have made some sort of living out of the sport but Peter knows his own mind and he has taken the decision that he does not want to be a professional golfer. Instead, he says he wants a 'proper job' that he can combine with the amateur game.

So am I relieved by Peter's decision? There is no doubt in my mind that playing professional sport is much riskier than having a 'proper job'. Thousands go for the top positions in sport and only a very few make it. Of course, I would have backed my children had they said they wanted to go down the road to professional sport but I am also sure that they would have been honest enough to make a fair assessment of their abilities before it was too late. I continually see echoes of my own life in my children's experiences. My father thought that I would be unwise to take a year off from my studies to concentrate solely on tennis and, although I suppose I will never really know if he was absolutely right, I have a strong feeling that it was good advice.

Children also keep their parents' feet firmly rooted to the

ground. At Lauren's wedding in 2002, the guests decided on an impromptu game of touch rugby behind the marquee, with Peter and one of the other lads as the captains. It was to be at least twenty-a-side, so I was looking forward to showing the youngsters that this old dog could still perform a trick or two. But, one by one, all the other players had been selected and I was left like the sad lad in the school playground without a team. I had to referee – if anything ever showed me that life moves on, it was that!

2
SCHOOLBOY SPORTSMAN

M Y PARENTS were delighted that I could begin at Trelales Primary in Laleston when I was only four. It was the one school in the area where children could start that early, which was helpful to them with their busy GP's practice. I loved my schooldays. Sport was never far from my mind and I showed signs of promise when I was awarded the Victor Ludorum for sporting achievement at the age of nine. My success on the playing fields would be central to developing my character for the years ahead.

When I was ten, I moved to Bryntirion Preparatory School; my parents had put my name down for Epsom College, famous for its medical connections, and I needed time to prepare for the Common Entrance exam. They had my best interests at heart. They wanted the very best for their children after enduring the years of post-war hardship, but, after a few months of Latin and very little rugby, I became wary of what was in store for me. I also felt uncomfortable as a day-boy surrounded by boarders and I decided that the prospect of public school did not appeal one bit. I refused to take the exam and, instead, took the Eleven-Plus and got a place at Bridgend Grammar School.

My mum would have preferred me to continue at a private school but my dad, who had gone to Pontypridd Grammar himself, felt that the state system was the better choice. There were some heated discussions over the issue but I was very lucky that when I decided Bryntirion Prep was not for me, they went along with what I wanted. They were clearly of the opinion that I was old enough to know my own mind, even though it was the first really big decision that I had ever had to make.

Regardless of where I went to school, I soon realised that I had a privileged background compared to many others growing up in the Rhondda in the 1950s. Dad was proud to be the son of a miner who had made good and he never forgot his roots but I became increasingly aware that, as the son of two local doctors, I could have been labelled as being born with a silver spoon in my mouth. On the school sports field, it gave me an extra incentive, to prove to my mates that I was tough and one of them.

In later years, when I was playing international rugby, Dad's views relaxed and he bought a Rolls-Royce. Having vowed never to become a member of the Twickenham West Car Park brigade, now he was one of them. I knew that cars were one of his great interests but I never felt comfortable seeing him driving around in such a status symbol and, if anything, it made me into an inverted snob. I have always tried to remember where I came from, right through from my childhood to the present day.

I started to play for Bridgend and District at Under-11 level and still remember the thrill of pulling on the blue and white jersey. The keenness and success of the junior side was due almost entirely to the hard work and dedication of Illtyd Williams, a teacher at Pencoed Junior School and one of the finest rugby brains that I have ever met. It was unfortunate for him that he had played rugby league at a time when players following that code were made outcasts; officially, they were not even allowed near a rugby union ground but Illtyd fought hard against any rejection and won the respect of all those at the club as the 'unofficial' coach. Having been a rugby professional, he taught me a lot about attitude and skills.

There was nothing particularly professional about the setting for our home games though, especially when we played on a pitch known locally as the Cabbage Patch. The grass was coarse and there were some very odd dimensions – the pitch was tiny, almost as long as it was wide. If the ball was kicked high over the goal line, it went into a fenced-off tennis court, so whenever there was a conversion or a penalty kick, we had to climb over the fence to retrieve the ball. We must have wasted many hours of playing time over the years.

I enjoyed the games for the Under-11s very much but, in retrospect, I doubt the wisdom of playing competitive rugby so intensively so early. In my opinion it is much better to learn the skills involved in a variety of sports at that age rather than to specialise in just one or two.

For instance, it is extremely useful to acquire the ball skills involved in soccer as a solid grounding for rugby. Gareth Edwards, Barry John and Phil Bennett were all good soccer players whose prowess was sufficient for them to be offered professional terms with the top Welsh clubs, Swansea City and Cardiff City. All sports are specific in what muscle groups they use and I am a big believer in what is now called cross-training. Running, cycling, swimming and gym work all use different muscles in each activity so, if you can play other sports, it benefits the body as a whole.

I made my entry into Under-15 rugby at the age of just thirteen at full-back – nobody else wanted that position! I always played in the year above me; I am not sure that this is necessarily a good thing either but I suppose if you survive, then it is in the end. I really enjoyed rugby at this level and we had some memorable matches against Llanelli in the cup competition called the Dewar Shield. In one round it took a marathon five games to get a victory against a Llanelli side containing Phil Bennett and Derek Quinnell – and one of the matches had to be abandoned because Illtyd Williams shouted too much on the touchline!

Since Wales had an Under-15 national side, this was also my introduction to the competitive trial system. After playing in the final trial in 1964, I was thrilled to learn that I had been picked at full-back to face England Schools. I can still remember the unbelievable excitement when I heard my name called – I was to represent my country at Twickenham! The trial had been held at Bridgend Rugby Club and my father and his friends were all gathered in the bar after the match to hear the team read out. I did not show any outward emotion but inside I was bubbling over with joy. Dad, however, surrounded as he was by his mates, was grinning from ear to ear and we hurried home to break the good news to my mother. It still is one of the happiest days of my life and remains my most cherished rugby memory, regardless of all that has happened since. No matter how much the players are paid today, money can never buy the red shirt of Wales for the first time. That Under-15s shirt is in the cabinet on my wall in centre spot.

Although I was very nervous about the match against England, strangely, I did not worry about playing in the huge arena of Twickenham. Perhaps I knew that the wind would never be as strong as at Porthcawl for those family up and under sessions! As it was, it went well and we won 11–3. Phil Bennett was now my international team-mate and he kicked a long drop-goal from nearly halfway out. Several of the young Welsh players on duty that day went on to win further honours, not just Phil Bennett and myself, but also Allan Martin.

After our next match, a victory over the South of Scotland at Galashiels, we got into deep water as we all had a few drinks and, although many of the team were big enough to pass as eighteen, unfortunately, they did not hold their drink like eighteen-year-olds. I was better than most because I had been taught to have a couple of beers but one or two certainly got out of control. Of course, word of our misdemeanours got back to the Welsh officials so, when we assembled at Newport before our successful return match with England, those who been drinking were asked to stand up. When everyone got up, I remember the chairman saying, 'Not you too, John!' At the time I was the smallest member of the team and certainly did not look older than fifteen.

As I made the transition from Under-15 to senior schoolboy

rugby, I realised that it was time for me to do something about my size, or lack of it, as then I was smaller than Phil Bennett, something that seems amazing when you think about our comparative sizes later on. Luckily, in just twelve months, I grew five inches. I eventually ended up as six foot one, reasonably tall for a player in my day but, admittedly, a midget by modern standards.

I put my rapid growth down to nature and the intensive weight-training that I started under the watchful eye of Lynn Davies, the great long-jump champion who taught at Bridgend Grammar School for a year. Lynn also made me feel taller by telling me that one day I would be a superstar. He could see something in me and the fact that those words came from him was a source of great inspiration. Nowadays Lynn, in his modest way, tries to play that comment down and talks as if it never happened but I remember him saying it and I will always be grateful. He had won a gold medal in the 1964 Tokyo Olympics and, a year later, was imparting his knowledge to me! He had no pretensions and was the ideal role model. Underneath his pleasant exterior there was definitely an iron will and, like many people who have made it to the top, he had nothing left to prove. There is a big difference between arrogance on the sports field and that kind of behaviour off it.

Lynn trained with such dedication. I shall never forget the sight of him hopping around the field with 300 pounds of weight on his back, as if there was nothing there. He was also a very fine rugby player and played for Bridgend. At school, he would regularly join in the games, ignoring the risk of injury and the fact that the senior boys love to have a go at their teachers when given the chance. This simply would not happen these days because of the legal issues connected with teachers going full on in a rugby match against pupils, but in the 1960s it was perfectly acceptable and anyway nobody ever got the better of Lynn.

The next few years spent trying to gain international recognition at Under-19 level were hard and often frustrating. One year, I played in ten trial matches and still did not get into the national side. It felt as if you had to serve an apprenticeship – selection is often a lottery and my early experiences prove it. When I finally got the call, it was almost as if I had done my time and the selectors finally felt compelled to pick me because I had been knocking on the door for so long.

Off the playing field my early ambition was to be a police detective rather than a sportsman or a surgeon. I loved to watch crime series on television and still do, so, when I first considered being a doctor, I thought about being a police surgeon, a fascinating job, combining the worst of medicine, if you like, with the best of detection. First, I had to get the right grades in the right subjects at A level. At fifteen, I decided on physics, chemistry and biology, imperative if I was going to study medicine but, unfortunately for me, I found them all boring and much preferred English, history and geography. I still wonder what would have happened had I continued with those arts subjects but I had to persevere and get on with it because being a doctor was the way that I saw my life going. Quite frankly, I would not have reached the standards required for medicine today but, in those days, it was much easier to get into medical school with a family connection, quite the opposite of what the case is now. In the end, what swayed it for me, though, was my rugby cv.

For my final year in the sixth form, I had a chance to move to Millfield School in Somerset on a rugby and tennis scholarship. It was a difficult decision to make, as I would have to leave home, my family and friends, and would probably not have much time to make many new friends at Millfield. This time, though, I had a far more positive feeling about going to a private school. What really swayed it for me in the end was that so many accomplished sportsmen and women had been through the Millfield sporting academy.

Changing my school was about to bring me right out of my shell and would be a real eye-opener for a relatively insular Welsh boy. Millfield's pupils were from all walks of life – Iranian princes, extraordinarily talented artists and children with IQs so high that they were on a different wavelength from the rest of us. The full fees were astronomical but they were paid in proportion to the parents' income and scholarships were plentiful. My parents still had to find a considerable amount of money – mine was not a full scholarship – but they did all they could to help me.

Millfield had a fine reputation for rugby, largely due to three Welshmen who had been there a couple of years before me – Gareth Edwards, Vaughan Williams and Nick Williams. The emphasis was always on adventurous play, which was great for my development as an attacking full-back. I was given the freedom to break out; throwing the ball around and having fun seemed to me the right way to play, an attitude that has stayed with me all my life.

However, I had my first encounter with rugby politics during this time, when the selection of my friend Wayne Lewis and myself to play for the Welsh Secondary Schools against England presented us with a very awkward dilemma. The problem was that the international was to be held on the Saturday after the prestigious Public Schools Sevens and, just like the senior internationals, no schoolboys were permitted to play in the week before the match. So our selection might rule us out of representing Millfield at the sevens tournament.

Our headmaster, Mr Meyer, was extremely unhappy. He confronted the selectors and was quoted in the newspapers as saying, 'Who the hell do the Welsh selectors think they are, trying to take my players from me?' As is often the case with these things, it was a big misunderstanding. Wayne and I had heard unofficially that the selectors were going to allow us to play in both matches but, after Mr Meyer went to the press, this certainly was not going to happen! Instead, the Welsh selectors issued an ultimatum, telling us that we had to choose between our school and the national team. After long discussion, we opted to play for Wales.

It was the classic club versus country argument and, as my overriding rugby ambition, even at that stage, was to play for Wales at senior level, there could only ever be one outcome. Achieving this aim was far more likely if I played for the Welsh Under-19s side rather than for Millfield but I think that it was a decision that a schoolboy should never have been asked to make in the first place. In the years that followed, I would always give country priority over the clubs that I played for – but then, I was an amateur and no club ever paid my wages. The situation can be far more complex for the modern professional player.

The whole incident left a very bitter taste and I never felt comfortable at Millfield after this. Soon though, these troubles were overtaken by a more pressing issue. I had another potentially life-shaping decision to make: should I continue with rugby or concentrate on my other sporting love? Tennis was also a major part of my life and my two favourite sports were about to go head-to-head in the battle for my affections.

3

TEMPTED BY TENNIS

1 966 was a fantastic year for sport and for me in particular. Two months after the England footballers triumphed at Wembley, I won the Junior Wimbledon tennis title – a Welsh boy took on the system and beat it. I remember watching the World Cup final with my friends at a tennis tournament in Torquay, gathered around a black and white television set, but I had little idea of the personal excitement that was to follow later in the summer.

I was only four when I became hooked on tennis, having been mesmerised by the exploits of the stars at Wimbledon on television in the early fifties. My father, a keen player himself, had been men's champion at Bridgend Tennis Club several times, so he coached me on our court at home and was obviously delighted at my enthusiasm for the game. Just like me, he could not choose between rugby and tennis as his favourite sport.

I had to be ten before I could join him at the tennis club and, even then, juniors were allowed to play only when the seniors did not want the courts. This strange failure to encourage keen youngsters still exists at many tennis clubs today – tennis was and, perhaps always will be, an élitist sport. Admittedly, this was less of a problem in Wales. In England I am sure I would have had to wait even longer to get started. It was not so daunting to play at a Welsh club, just frustrating if the adults would not come off the court!

In 1961 I took part in my first tournament. Aged twelve, I was considered good enough to partner my father in the men's doubles at the County of Carmarthen Championships in Llanelli. We went out in the first round, beaten by the eventual tournament winners, but were not discouraged. A year later, I won the boys' singles at Langland Bay near Swansea 6–0, 6–1 and, as a very tiny thirteen-year-old, was nicknamed 'The Mighty Atom' by the Welsh news-papers for beating an opponent who was almost twelve inches taller than me.

From there things went from strength to strength and, after becoming Welsh Under-16 champion, I was accepted for a place at Junior Wimbledon in 1963. This was a big step for me – there was no doubt that I had proved myself in Wales but it was going to be quite a different matter to compete against all the juniors in England in what were, in effect, the British Junior Championships. I enjoyed my first taste of the big time and I felt reassured that I could hold my own but, in the eyes of the other players, I was still a little lad up from an unknown town in Wales.

There was plenty of work to do and, whilst I continued to practise with my father, my ability had come to the attention of John Crooke who was coach to the Welsh LTA. I used to go to John's home in Shropshire where he would coach me on a swim-ming pool covered with wooden boards. My backhand was very weak and John gave me the confidence to put topspin on it, an ability I had always admired in the champions. I still enjoy seeing the top players in action on hard courts when they are able to spin their returns. John also improved my second serve which, up until then, had merely been a weaker version of my first, so I felt as if my game was really coming together.

By 1964 I was playing regularly in tournaments outside Wales and, as my brothers were now also old enough to enter the competitions, the family began to plan our summer holidays around tennis. Eventually our journeying around the country began to pay dividends and, by the end of that summer, Bridgend Tennis Club had been firmly placed on the tennis map with no less than two Junior Wimbledon semi-finalists, my friend Gerald Battrick and me. It was a fantastic achievement for such a small Welsh club.

Gerald was my tennis role model and inspiration. He too went to Bridgend Grammar and Millfield and in 1964 he won the Junior Wimbledon title. We all wanted to be like Gerald and his success filled me with a belief that perhaps I could do it too. He became a regular in the Great Britain Davis Cup team but tragically died a few years ago in his early fifties from a brain tumour. At his funeral in Bridgend, the whole of British tennis turned out to say farewell.

I was defeated in my 1964 Junior Wimbledon semi-final by another future Davis Cup player, the now entrepreneur David Lloyd. Playing at Wimbledon was always an enjoyable experience. It was just amazing to be there and to feel the power of the Lawn Tennis Association at first hand. It was thrilling to walk past the ivy-covered walls and the courts where, only a few weeks earlier, John Newcombe and Roy Emerson had entertained the vast crowds. As juniors, we did not play on the show courts but we did use the same dressing rooms as the star names. The locker rooms and the facilities were palatial compared to those we used during the rest of the year. The baths were huge and I remember soaking there for hours after long matches. Towards the end of the week, there were fewer and fewer of us and we lived like kings. One of my strongest memories was that we were all issued with free Fred Perry tennis gear, so we at least looked the part.

My character on the tennis court was starting to form and, en route to the semi-final at Wimbledon, I played an opponent who completely lost his temper, slinging his racket about and shouting abuse. I kept calm and took the third set 6–0. I let my opponent's temper ruin his game and, according to the *Daily Mail*, it was my 'serene disposition' that won the day – I was a different animal on the tennis court! It was rather against my nature but I felt that coolness was a good psychological weapon. With the infamous exception of John McEnroe, most of the top players have been this way – Sampras, Borg and now my current favourite, Federer, who is almost ice cold. My father had also made it very plain to me that temper tantrums were not going to be part of my game and I made sure I took his advice.

Dad never wanted me to be a professional tennis player. He thought that sport was meant to be fun and to play for money tainted its purity. He was also very keen on making sure I got some professional qualifications and, in our family, that meant medicine. I was not quite so sure and, for a while, my successes made me wonder about playing tennis seriously. Eventually though, I realised that I had the whole of my life to think about, not just my time as a young sportsman and that studying medicine had some distinct advantages. At medical school, I could still play rugby, with some tennis in the summer as well, whereas, if I chose tennis, I would have to exclude the other two completely.

Anyway, I was becoming rather disillusioned with the life of a tennis player. In those days, only the very best players travelled to exciting far-flung places and, in my mind, the lifestyle was not all that great either, wherever you found yourself. It was boring and predictable off-court, the same old faces and endless gossip. Not just that, I felt that I did not fit in. Many of the competitors were either children from wealthy families or the offspring of top British players, and those whose parents could afford the fees were sent to Millfield. Of course, at this point I did not know that I too would finish my schooling at Millfield, I just knew that, by and large, there were not many others like me on the tennis circuit. I felt quite inferior, the English juniors all seemed so self-assured, and this was a strange reversal of roles for me. At grammar school I had been teased, sometimes envied, because I was the son of the local doctors and therefore assumed to be well off but, in the world of junior tennis, I was definitely considered to be at the lower end of the economic and social scale.

So by the time of Junior Wimbledon in 1966 I had come to the conclusion that my decision not to pursue a serious tennis future had definitely been the right one, but that left me with another problem. I did not want people saying that I had given up because I could not make it in tennis – I was far too proud for that. No, I would really have to prove myself and to exit in the semi-final was not going to be good enough for me this time.

I went to Wimbledon as third seed. The weather was fine all week, everything went smoothly and I reached the final where my opponent was the top seed and hot favourite for the title, my old adversary, David Lloyd. I remember being very laid back before the match. My father visited me in the dressing room and was absolutely flabbergasted when he found me sitting calmly reading the *Beano*. Dad was always nervous before whatever sport I played but I went the other way. I felt that I was in a much better position than David as I had nothing to lose except perhaps my pride. He was the oldest player in the competition and was only eligible to play because they had extended the age limit. To tell the truth, I am not sure that David really wanted to return to junior level again because he had spent all year playing full-time senior tennis at home and abroad. As one of the most talented young players in the country, he was sponsored under the 'Barrett Boys' coaching scheme run by John Barrett who, of course, took over as the voice of BBC tennis after the death of Dan Maskell. Lloyd was to be a playing advertisement for the scheme, showing how much he had improved in his year as a Barrett Boy. Everyone expected great things from him in the final.

Content to be the underdog, I went out on to the court and broke his service twice to win 6–4, 6–4. It was over so quickly! I did not really believe I had won and all I can remember thinking was how I would not be able to jump over the net at the end. Even when I was presented with the huge cup, I still did not take it on board and it was not until I saw the reports in the papers on Sunday morning with my name in print that it began to sink in that I was the 1966 Junior Wimbledon Champion.

A few weeks after my triumph, I started at Millfield for my final year at school. This meant that I had plenty of opportunity to play against my rivals from the circuit but I was no longer an unknown quantity. Being an outsider had given me an extra edge, a little more aggression and pride, as I convinced myself that I was as good as the others, in spite of all their coaching and the circumstances of their birth. Now I was part of their establishment and although I was learning their strengths and weaknesses, to my detriment, I was letting them get to know mine. When I lost to John de Mendoza in the Queen's Covered Court Championships in January 1967, my spell at the top had finished.

At the same time I had to concentrate on my school work as I had accepted a conditional offer to study medicine at St Mary's Hospital in London later that year. Unfortunately, for most of the summer when I should have been studying, I was out on the courts and this was reflected in my disappointing A level results. Thankfully, and by modern-day standards luckily, I was still able to go up to St Mary's in the autumn to spend the year as a first MB (Preliminary Medical) student.

The tennis continued and I still had some good wins left in me. I represented Great Britain at the Canadian Centennial Junior Open in Ottawa and played some of the best tennis of my life. On my way to the final, I beat Dick Stockton and Alex 'Sandy' Meyer. At the time their names meant very little to me but they both went on to become world top ten players. I won the tournament and was incredibly proud to add an overseas title to my achievements but, surprisingly, when I got home, there was hardly any coverage of the event in the press. Just imagine that happening now if a British boy had done so well abroad!

Despite that victory, there were definite signs that my best days in tennis might be over. I felt it was right to move on but I do sometimes wonder what might have been had I continued, especially in the light of a later comment by Dan Maskell, which I treasured, that I had all the attributes required to become a regular in the Davis Cup team. True enough, I have always played better as a team member than competing solo.

At St Mary's, I played mainly for pleasure; for more serious competition, I represented London University. The team included some of my old friends from the junior tournaments and we had a lot of fun as we beat most of the stronger counties and better club teams. My first match for London University was up in Oxford and, although the weather was shocking and the match abandoned, we had a marvellous day in the pub. That day set the seal on what became known as the Old Purples – our merry group, named after the London colours, still survives today. The OPs are no longer playing matches but it is great to get our families together and relive the old times. In May 2005 we met up in France, an emotional reunion because we paid a visit to the battlefields of the Somme. It was an incredibly moving experience and one that I will never forget.

My serious competitive tennis was slowly drawing to a close during that first year at St Mary's. It had to, because rugby was starting to establish itself as the number one sport in my life and, even on one of the most famous days in the history of tennis, rugby was the dominant force for me. In April 1968 the first professional tennis tournament took place – the British Open in Bournemouth – with the great Ken Rosewall and Pancho Gonzales in the draw, along with other stars of the game, and me! In the first round, I came up against the Australian Davis Cup player, Bob Howe, and gave him a contest, although I eventually lost. I even received a cheque for £20, great news for a student, but straight afterwards I had to rush to Bridgend, 130 miles away, to play in a crucial fixture against Newport. The Welsh selectors were at the game and I knew I had to be there. That night, I made two try-saving tackles on Stuart Watkins, the Welsh international winger, and was chosen to go on tour to Argentina with the full national squad. That game set me on my way with Wales and I still find it hard to believe that I did it on the back of a professional tennis match.

There were times when tennis was my first love but I never wanted it to be the sole object of my existence. Now, I feel that things might be different and, if I were a teenager in 2006, I would definitely choose tennis over rugby. I appreciate that this revelation might knock a few people sideways but I think that I would be bored stiff by the monotonous training professional rugby players are subjected to these days. Whatever the sport, I much preferred playing to training. When I was growing up, the tennis circuit seemed the tedious option but at least, if I was making the decision now, I would be able to take part in matches every day.

I have always continued to watch tennis with great interest and, like everyone else, was excited by the emergence of Tim Henman. In one sense, you cannot knock him; he has been to the semi-final at Wimbledon on four occasions, a fantastic achievement in itself, and he was very unlucky when the rain came to ruin his greatest chance of making it to the final the year Goran Ivanisevic took the title. But I do feel Henman has underachieved, considering that he is probably the best exponent of the volley in the world. His ground strokes have also been secure, so there is no lack of talent, but there is a lack of a killer touch. Perhaps he has never possessed that overpowering desire to win that a player needs to make the last push for the big title. On occasions Henman looks as if he is thinking, 'If I win, I win – but, if I don't win, I don't.' It is like tackling on a rugby field – you either want to put your body on the line or you do not, and I do not think Tim Henman does. It is not something that can be coached, it comes from inside.

One young man who looks as if he does have the competitive zeal to succeed is Andrew Murray. By and large Henman is a grass court player, with his serve and volley technique, but Murray, who has grown up differently on the clay courts in Spain, looks as if he has much more to offer. He needs to bulk up and must clearly work on his fitness but I have high hopes for him.

One thing that has struck me about Murray's young career is that his mother, Judy, has been very heavily involved. There is no doubt that she has been central to his success but, from experience, I feel it is important that she takes more of a back seat as time goes on. This does seem to be happening now that she has taken on the role of manager, with others fulfilling the job of main coach. My father was always there for me, supporting from the sidelines, but he could not resist the lure of the dressing room. This continued beyond tennis days, into my time with Bridgend and Wales. The lads always got on well with him but there were occasions when, understandably, I was not entirely comfortable with him being there – certain things have to belong solely to the player.

I sincerely hope that Andrew Murray is the man to end the long wait for a British men's Wimbledon champion. It would be great for the nation and great for the sport. Britain's failure to produce a champion since Fred Perry is down to many factors, the key ones being a perpetuation of the game's upper- or middle-class image, a lack of encouragement for juniors, a scarcity of facilities, particularly indoor courts, and an absence of decent competition for those setting out in the sport. The longer it goes on, the more psychology comes into it. British players start to feel they have gone as far as they can and are destined never to win a major tournament. Of the current British players, Murray is the strongest contender to succeed at the top tournaments, and one day soon, he will undoubtedly have the Wimbledon title in his sights.

The Lawn Tennis Association and local authorities have a responsibility to encourage young tennis players by providing the right environment, that is one that stops them from going abroad to train and play. Just look at the interest in Wimbledon. Surely some of this can be harnessed? Tennis is big elsewhere around the world and millions watch regularly on television. I feel very frustrated that, given we have a tournament of the magnitude of Wimbledon, we cannot maintain the public's interest all year round. I feel that tennis is a sport worth backing.

4

LIFE AMONG THE EXILES

S o, had things turned out differently, I could have been a tennis professional, but I am sure that I would have hated to have been a full-time rugby professional. One of the best things about my time in rugby was the knowledge that, whatever happened on a Saturday, I could always go back to work on Monday and concentrate on my real job.

The co-existence of rugby and medicine ultimately made me a better player and a better doctor but, these days, I think it is almost impossible to be a medic and expect to hold down a professional rugby contract. During the 1991 World Cup, when the game was still amateur, England's full-back, Jonathan Webb, had a locum paid for by the RFU to take the pressure off his work as an orthopaedic surgeon. It would be unheard of today. When it comes to the long years involved in medical training, there are very few individuals now who combine the study with professional rugby. Argentina's Felipe Contepomi is one of the few to go against the trend and run his medical studies alongside his involvement at club and international level. I admire him greatly for this. Another example of a modern doctor trying to combine the two careers is Billy O'Driscoll, the son of the former Lions and Ireland flanker, John O'Driscoll. He finished his medical studies and took a year off from house jobs to see how he fared in professional rugby at Saracens.

These men will have another career to fall back on if their rugby does not go to plan but, for the majority of modern players, the talent scouts have been out looking for them long before they leave school and many do not go on to higher education. This concerns me because, in reality, very few really cash in on their sporting success and never have to worry about working again. Yes, rugby professionals earn a decent wage from the sport but it is certainly not enough to retire on and, in many cases, is less than the money they would have earned had they seen through their education. When their sports career comes to an end, either through advancing years, loss of form or injury, players often find themselves in much less well paid jobs and without the necessary academic qualifications to maintain their standard of living.

Some rugby clubs are gamely trying to address this problem and provide learning schemes as part of their rugby academies but, in nearly all cases, as soon as the young player is offered a full-time contract, studying has to take a back seat as the available time must be devoted to playing, travelling, resting, training and training some more. In my view, players should only train for two hours each day – academic study or a part-time job would be an excellent distraction from the monotony of rugby. I know that my opinion is unlikely to be shared by the surfeit of coaches who are all trying to justify their existences but it is an issue that really should be given greater consideration. Many young soccer players get into trouble with drugs, drink and betting because football is all they have. We never want this state of affairs in rugby.

My medical training began at St Mary's, Paddington in October 1967. Although my time at Millfield School had built up my confidence, I was understandably nervous about going up to London but I did, however, have one very useful contact at the hospital already. I had played rugby against the United Hospitals side in London and met the St Mary's first-team captain, Murray McEwen, a lucky encounter for me since his position was one of the most prestigious in the medical school. Murray sought me out on my first day and showed me around the place, imparting all sorts of useful advice, like how to get into the Nurses Home after midnight!

Whilst I enjoyed making new English friends, it was easy to join up with other exiled Welshmen – our accents stuck out a mile – so I did not lose the Welsh in me. Even my digs in Kilburn were with a delightful Welsh couple and as my room-mate, Phil Evans, came from Pontardawe near Swansea, it was like a home from home. My landlord, Bill Maddocks, had been a pillar of Maesteg schoolboy rugby and had been awarded the MBE for his services to youth clubs, whilst his wife treated us like sons, cooking us huge meals and turning a blind eye to the food being pinched from the fridge late on a Saturday night.

I was quickly into my studies but to start with there were, of course, all the fun and games you would expect from students new to a hospital environment. I vividly recall a clinical demonstration when one fresher was shown how to remove a leg plaster with an electric saw – a pint of blood in a transfusion bag had been hidden inside the demonstration cast so when the saw reached halfway, blood spurted everywhere and the 'patient' screamed horribly. The poor student almost fainted. He really thought that he had hit flesh and there seemed no way to stop the bleeding with the rest of the leg encased in plaster. I was lucky that squeamishness never affected me too badly but, for some, the first sight of blood on a large scale is too much to take.

Everyone at St Mary's was rugby mad and with good reason. In the 1950s they had been one of the country's top club sides with an impressive fixture list. At first, I thought that I would be playing for the Second XV for quite some time. Young aspiring players generally had to wait until the older students qualified before they could be elevated to the Firsts, and their elders were determined to show them that senior rugby was a far cry from schoolboy stuff – which it certainly was. There was great camaraderie and a strong team ethic at St Mary's, something that has always appealed to me.

In football, eleven individuals can be a good team and this is why you can buy success in that sport. You just cannot do the same in rugby because, if the players do not get on together, they are much less likely to put their bodies on the line for each other.

In fact I broke into the first team quite quickly but it soon became apparent that I needed a better standard of rugby than the hospital side could provide. Frustratingly, many of the senior players were losing interest as they came up to qualifying and, without them, the team was in the doldrums. I had played one or two games for Bridgend before going to St Mary's but had not taken this any further, mainly because it seemed ridiculous to be travelling back and forth to Wales. I also knew that I could not expect just to walk into the Bridgend side as they already had a good full-back in David Griffiths, the vice-captain of the club. But I realised that if my rugby was to improve, I had to find more top-class games in addition to my weekend rugby at St Mary's.

So I started taking the train to Wales on Wednesday afternoons for mid-week matches at the Brewery Field. Neither the hospital nor the rugby club were particularly happy about my tight schedule and, of course, I had several hairy moments. One day the train stopped only half a mile from Bridgend station because of workmen on the line. As time was ticking on, I decided to get out and finish my journey on foot but, unfortunately, the sides of the track were too steep for me to climb up with all my kit so I had to walk along the track itself. My mother, who was meeting me at the station, was horrified to see me – and the train, which had restarted and was following me up the track, not too far behind!

The matches for Bridgend were part of the Floodlit Alliance, a tournament brought in by the WRU in which only tries counted. These games, together with the rule change under the Australian dispensation, which meant you could not kick direct to touch outside your own 25-yard area, really helped me to develop as an attacking full-back. When I was selected, aged nineteen, for the

Welsh squad to tour Argentina in the summer of 1968, after only a handful of games for Bridgend, I felt that my strategy had proved successful and I am sure that I would not have been picked to play for Wales so early had I continued to play solely for the medical school.

Although we lost the Test series to the Pumas, the trip had fulfilled at least one of its objectives, to be a testing ground for the younger Welsh players, and I for one returned home stronger for my time spent in Argentina. There had been plenty of defensive work – the locals nicknamed me 'Canasta' or 'Basket' so you can see how many high balls came my way! Sometimes, however, there were not only rugby balls to contend with, as the volatile home crowds would hurl bottles and fireworks down onto the pitch to intimidate us. We had heard stories that a referee had been shot just a couple of months before and, in the light of our experiences, we could quite believe them.

The party was led by the experienced John Dawes and the initial impression he made on a lad barely out of school was of an individual who could command instant respect. I certainly had no idea at that stage of the huge impact that he would have on my rugby career or, indeed, how close our friendship would become. That summer, John helped me immensely and our fireside chats at the country club near Buenos Aires proved invaluable in developing my skills and planning my future in rugby. If nothing else, his suggestion that I should join London Welsh changed the course of my life.

I made my debut for London Welsh in 1968, following a late phone call from John one Friday night, asking me to play as injury cover for their regular full-back, Gareth James. I was due to appear for St Mary's the next day and, for an intrinsically loyal person like me, switching clubs at such short notice was quite a big thing. They were not at all happy about it at St Mary's and there was also my loyalty to Gareth, a good friend of mine, to consider. It was rather a sleepless night but I never regretted my decision to say yes to John.

In those days, London Welsh were renowned as an exciting, stylish side and had a reputation for fifteen-man ball-handling rugby that was a complete contrast to the dour game that had taken hold elsewhere. As a result, rugby fans came from far and wide to watch them play, and not just the exiled Welsh either. There would regularly be crowds of four or five thousand at Old Deer Park, which was considered big business in the amateur seventies.

London Welsh played that way out of necessity as, unlike their counterparts back in Wales, the club could not call on the miners and steelworkers of the valleys. The relatively light front row would struggle up front against big packs and a confrontational game was never going to be in their interests. So Welsh's game was based on continual support of the ball-carrier and being able to give and take a pass – even the forwards were mobile and threw the ball around. It was the key to a successful attacking game then, just as is still the case now. Anyway this liberating style of play was highly enjoyable and no less successful, especially when played on firm pitches in the good London weather.

When I started training under the direction of coach Roger Michaelson, I was amazed at the overall fitness of the team. Those were some of the hardest training sessions that I have ever experienced. The majority of the squad were school teachers who spent most of their day on the playing fields or in the gym and it showed. I was only just out of school but sometimes I found it a struggle to keep up with them.

It was not just the kind of rugby that London Welsh played that attracted me; in fact, the whole set-up there suited me far more than that at many Welsh clubs. In Wales all the first-class sides regularly played mid-week matches under floodlights but at London Welsh mid-week games were few and far between because there were no lights strong enough to play under. That was fine by me and it attracted other international rugby players to the club, too – we had all week to recover from a hard game at the weekend. The internationals were also lucky that the club had tremendous reserves who could step in and play so well that we were hardly missed at all. In comparison, most clubs back in Wales had a squad of players for a first team only, meaning that there could be a heavy burden on the top players.

Even the setting at Old Deer Park was impressive. The old clubhouse had been replaced with a brand new complex costing £100,000, not much money by modern-day standards but a small fortune then. One thing had not changed, though – the beautiful position of the ground, alongside Kew Gardens, with the famous Chinese Pagoda jutting up between the uprights at one end.

After my debut against local rivals Richmond, our visitors were home stars, Llanelli, and I landed a penalty goal to draw the match. As the kick was from somewhere near the halfway line, I gained immediate acceptance from the highly critical Old Deer Park crowd who, before that, had been rather suspicious of me, a long-haired upstart who had replaced Gareth James, one of their favourite players. I had known Gareth since tennis days, when we played for Wales together. Like me, he had been shortlisted for the 1968 tour of Argentina, so I had taken both his national and club place in the space of a few months. Despite that he is still a good mate and my son's godfather.

Playing for London Welsh improved my fitness and developed my attacking game immensely. I lost count of the times when we won games with last-minute tries by charging out of defence. I would switch the angle of attack with Gerald Davies, a ploy that served us well in the years ahead. Our policy was to run all our own penalties and even to attack when the opposition missed their kicks at goal by running back at them. We had huge belief in ourselves.

It could only help my embryonic international career. The team was packed with men who were, or were on the verge of, playing for Wales, not just Gerald but also John Dawes, John Taylor and

Mervyn Davies, to name just a few. With such a strong core of exiled Welsh internationals, London Welsh were very successful and our flamboyance was borne out by the fact that we won the Middlesex Sevens crown three years in a row. Down in Wales, we were accused of being airy-fairy and not tough enough but what we did at this time pointed the way for the national team over the years that followed.

In my view, no one was more influential than our outstanding captain, John Dawes. John was a very clever man, a teacher with a first-class honours degree in chemistry. He was the brains behind much of our attacking play, as was highlighted in that famous Barbarians versus New Zealand game in 1973. Although he himself did not have great pace or strength, as a midfield general he kept the forwards and backs running because of his ability to give and take a pass at speed. In fact, I have never seen a better passer of the ball in that key position.

John Taylor was a world-class back-row forward but could play in the back line as well. I remember him moving to full-back during a game against Bath in 1975 and he was so good that people suggested that he could easily play the following week in that position in the international against England. He epitomised what London Welsh stood for and the emphasis that we placed on flexibility and improvisation.

There was a great team spirit at the club, especially when we went down to Wales for our national squad sessions. In those days, Welsh training was only on a Sunday so Dawes, Taylor and I would set off straight after our Saturday afternoon match and often stayed with my parents in Bridgend. After a few pints at the local men's club, we would talk tactics long into the night. My mum was in her element with all her 'extra boys'; even at my dad's funeral, despite being distraught and quite unwell, she was pleased to see John Taylor and John Dawes – they reminded her of such happy times.

The long journey back to London after Sunday training was always hard. We were shattered and, as there was no M4, we had to drive cross-country, packed into John Dawes' little Mini. A much-loved stop was the Lamb and Flag at Kingston Bagpuize on the Farringdon to Abingdon road. There was real ale from the wood and magnificent game pie, pheasant and duck, just what we all needed. We really used to look forward to it, although I think big Mike Roberts probably enjoyed it more than anyone as he had one of the largest appetites I have ever come across. It was so good there that we would often end up staying until closing time.

In 1971 an amazing six of the London Welsh team were selected for the successful Lions tour of New Zealand: John Dawes as captain, John Taylor, Mike Roberts, Mervyn Davies, Gerald Davies and myself. With Geoff Evans making it seven when he joined us later as a replacement, it was a proud moment in the club's history – and one in the eye for our detractors.

The following year the club went on a very different type of tour, as we broke ground again by visiting Sri Lanka (or Ceylon as it was then), not the most obvious place for a rugby trip. The game there had been promoted by Europeans working on the tea plantations and, despite having to play in very high temperatures and humidity, we won our matches quite easily. One thing I will never forget was the reaction of the local supporters when points were scored; it was very strange. Tries were being run in at will but there was only ever any applause when 50 or 100 points were posted on the board. We were puzzled until it dawned on us – they were far more used to watching cricket!

It was a fascinating trip, with one unforgettable train journey from Colombo to the tea plantations up country. Even though it was only about seventy miles, it was uphill all the way and we knew it would take an age to get there in a rickety old carriage so, in the honourable tradition of rugby tourists, we made sure we had a good stock of drinks on board. Halfway up the mountain the train ground to a shuddering halt and we rushed into the driver's cabin to find that he had passed out on the floor – he had been helping himself very freely to our beer! Mike Roberts and Jim Shanklin had to take over as rookie train drivers and nervously steered us the rest of the way to Kandy.

Those were great days but after John Dawes retired in 1973, there was a general downturn in the club's fortunes. Mervyn Davies left to play for Swansea, Gerald Davies went to Cardiff and Tony Gray returned to his native North Wales. Their boots were never really filled by those who played after them and it was clear that the glory days of London Welsh were over. At the root of this decline was the upsurge of Welsh nationalism in the 1970s. Quite rightly, there was far more pride in Wales and what it had to offer and far fewer people were leaving the country to seek jobs and education in England. Because of this, the club began to rely more and more heavily on English-born players with sometimes dubious Welsh parentage and I think our team spirit seemed to diminish – after all, we could not really be called exiles any more. The English fly-half Neil Bennett joined the club on, I think, the back of having driven once through North Wales!

I was not enjoying it as much but I stayed at the club during those transition years and left only when I headed back home to work in Cardiff in 1976. Although I was ready for the change, I went knowing that I owed London Welsh a great deal. If I had not spent my formative years at Old Deer Park playing risk-taking rugby alongside John Dawes, John Taylor, Gerald Davies, Mervyn Davies and the others, I suspect that I would never have developed at Bridgend in the same way.

Sadly, London Welsh are now a shadow of what we were in the early seventies when we played with a swagger and strode around England and Wales as one of the top clubs. Recently, they even forfeited home advantage against Harlequins so that the match could be played at The Stoop to maximise revenue – how sad is that? And what a dangerous precedent to set. Perhaps they will never get out of National League One and into the English Premiership – so why not offer something different and turn the clock back to recapture that 'exile' spirit of old? I would love to see the club playing with only Welsh-qualified players and I believe it could be done as vast numbers of Welshmen are now finding themselves either working or studying in London. It would be great to see London Welsh being exactly that again. What is nice to know is that my family still feels at home at Old Deer Park. All three of my daughters attend matches and my nephew Huw, son of Chris, is playing for the Druids, the London Welsh Seconds, whilst studying medicine at St Mary's. In my family at least, it seems that some things never change.

5

RED JERSEYS, WHITE COATS

I AM and always will be a Welshman first. Representing Wales was what I dreamt of as a youngster so when the call came to pull on that red jersey, the sense of pride that I felt could never be surpassed. As a wonderful bonus, it led to Lions selection, recognition that can be attained only if you play well for your country.

For thirteen glorious years, from 1968 to 1981, I shared in an unforgettable period in the history of Welsh sport. To be born at a time when I could play rugby with the exceptional Gareth Edwards, Barry John, Gerald Davies, Phil Bennett and the rest was fortuitous in the extreme – men like this come along very rarely and for them to arrive within a few seasons of each other was remarkable.

I have always felt that it is a misconception that we were the greatest ever national team to play the game. If you judge greatness by success on the field, then we were not even the best of our era! I played for Wales against New Zealand five times and did not win once. It is also true however that, at our height, Welsh supporters would come along to internationals not hoping for victory but expecting it, and wondering by how many points, so I think what really earned us our special place in the history of rugby was the way that we played. It was our unforgettably exciting style, more than the winning of the Grand Slams and the Triple Crowns, that has meant that the Welsh teams of the 1970s will always be revered.

After my performances on tour, I was hopeful that my first Welsh cap would not be too long in coming. It is impossible to forget the feelings surrounding that first cap against Scotland at Murrayfield in 1969. When the news of my selection came through, my family and friends treated me like royalty, although I recall that the Welsh media were somewhat less enthusiastic. I had, in effect, come from nowhere, with just St Mary's and a short spell at London Welsh under my belt but, thankfully, I was in London at the time and so did not feel the full force of the Welsh journalists' scepticism, which seemed to centre on my alleged inability to kick. Walking down Edinburgh's Princes Street on the morning of the game amidst the massed red of the Welsh supporters, my nerves were undoubtedly building. It was a new feeling for me; when I had played David Lloyd at Wimbledon, less than three years before, nothing had been expected. This was totally different and I knew that the whole of Wales would be watching and expecting a great deal from their new full-back.

I need not have worried: when the first whistle went, I felt suddenly calm and my mind cleared. I distinctly remember deciding to run with the ball the first time that I touched it. I wanted to show everybody what I could do and how I thought the game should be played. From then on, the game disappeared in a flash, as most debutants will confirm, but the most important thing was that we won and, that night, I celebrated with Mervyn Davies, who had also made his international debut. The irony for both of us was that our mentor, John Dawes, had been left out at the start of the 1969 Five Nations, but his time would come again.

The next victory, against Ireland, was also never to be forgotten – my first time at the Cardiff Arms Park as a player and the fulfilment of that part of my childhood dream. When I had attended matches as a spectator with my father, for some strange reason I had imagined that only the crowd would be able hear all the noise and the singing – but how wrong I was! The atmosphere down

there on the pitch was unbelievable and completely beyond anything I had ever experienced before. The ground was like an
amphitheatre and the volume potentially quite frightening if
you were not used to it. It seemed to throb around you, almost
like a giant heart beat.

Unlike in Argentina, however, I felt completely at home. At the
Cardiff Arms Park the crowd was backing my every move – it was an
addictively exhilarating feeling. In my next game Wales could only
manage an away draw against France but with my first taste of Paris
came the knowledge that I would always love playing rugby in that
city. It quickly became my favourite Five Nations venue outside
Wales because of the amazing atmosphere generated by their crowd
and the positive response to the stylish way the French team
wanted to play the game. With such firm ground, the urge to
run the ball was powerful and one of the best runners of the time
was the great Jo Maso, now the French team manager. After the
match, I remember him strumming his guitar in the cosmopolitan
bars of Paris. I sang along to my heart's content, thinking that this
was the life!

Although a Grand Slam in my debut season was no longer a
possibility, there was still the prize of the Triple Crown to aim for,
something that carried just as much weight in those days, in part
because France had not yet been admitted onto the International
Board. We finished with a rousing win over England to take that
Triple Crown and I felt I could not have wished for a better way to
end my first season of caps.

It has been said that the 1969 Triple Crown was the birth of the
great Welsh age but I disagree. I think we still had a lot of maturing
to do at that stage. England were a poor team and we had not had to
play very well to beat them. The real benchmark was going to be our
summer tour of New Zealand that year and, in my first encounter
with the All Blacks, I realised that they were as hard to beat as you
could possibly imagine. They gave us a brutal hiding in both Tests

and some harsh words were said on the plane journey home, with young Mervyn Davies telling the forwards that, unless they bucked their ideas up, we would go nowhere – you could see then that Merv was future captaincy material. Although we had been well beaten, we now knew exactly what had to be done if we were to become the team that we thought we were capable of growing into.

If the heavy defeats by the All Blacks were not enough, the New Zealand press rubbed it in further by branding us the scruffiest side ever to tour down under, purely because one or two of our players grew moustaches. How times have changed on that front – in 2005 the Kiwis had a go at Gavin Henson for shaving, albeit his legs! We restored some pride when we beat Australia and Fiji on the way home but I will remember our stay in Fiji most for the 'interesting' post-match reception at the palace. It was searingly hot and we gratefully accepted a drink of the local kava to cool us down. The only problem was that it tasted just like mud; in fact, it was so awful that when our tour manager, Ivor Jones, drank the first cup, he could not help spitting it out in front of the King. The room fell horribly silent and, in the face of the increasingly disapproving expressions from the royal entourage, we had no choice but to gulp away, nodding approvingly but desperately hoping that there would be no refills. When we arrived back at Heathrow, still wearing our gifts of Fijian flowered skirts, the expressions on the faces of our wives and girlfriends had to be seen to be believed – especially those who were there to meet the forwards with their big shoes and socks sticking out from underneath their 'dresses'!

Thankfully, my devotion to rugby had not affected my studies too much and I had rounded off my first year at St Mary's by passing the first MB. Much of that second year was spent in the dissection room. We grew quite attached to our 'companions', laid out on the table before us, and loved to speculate about how they had lived their lives. My group 'owned' a little old lady with hardly a single muscle in her body but a marvellous pair of lungs. We could tell she had never let a cigarette pass her lips, in complete contrast to the fine specimen of a young man on the next dissection table. Although he had marvellously developed muscles, his lungs were as black as the coal tips back home in Wales.

It was shocking to see what effect smoking can have on the body. I have never enjoyed being around smokers but I think that everybody has the right to smoke in their own space, as long as they do not interfere with anyone else. I, more than most, know that the damaging effects of smoking have put a big strain on the resources of the National Health Service over the years but if you were going to ban smoking on this basis alone, then you should not allow people to drive cars.

By far the best thing about the dissection sessions was a blonde fresher called Scilla who worked at the adjacent bench. Despite this proximity, we were not even on chatting terms and I did not dare pluck up the courage to speak to her as she seemed so preoccupied with her work and her boyfriend Murray McEwen, the captain of the hospital rugby team who had so kindly shown me around on my first day.

The ice was finally broken with Scilla through a practical joke. My friend Neil knew how much I liked her so he faked my signature on a Valentine's Day card; there was also a card from her to me – supposedly. For a moment, I toyed with the very welcome idea that she might have sent one but then realised that it was too ludicrous, something that was confirmed when I arrived at St Mary's and saw the expectant look on Neil's face. Then he told me about the card that I was meant to have sent to Scilla and my heart began to sink – how on earth was I going to explain this schoolboy lunacy to her without scaring her off completely?

Typically, I bumped into her the very next day. She was obviously embarrassed because she thought my card was serious. Once I had explained the joke, an awkward silence followed but

I plucked up enough courage to ask if we could meet up for a drink some time. She agreed, rather half-heartedly and, hoping to impress, I told her that our date would have to be in a fortnight's time as I had Welsh squad training and a rugby international to play the following week. I should have saved my breath, Scilla had never even seen a rugby ball until she came down to St Mary's from Derbyshire.

Our first drink turned out to be a bit of a disaster, too. After our rather inauspicious start, I wanted to change the atmosphere and take her to the City Barge, a pub on the River Thames with a peaceful garden overlooking the water. Unfortunately, we never found it as I got totally lost, driving around in circles and taking dead-end roads to warehouses and boathouses. We ended up in the George and Devonshire at Hogarth Roundabout and, instead of enjoying the gentle lapping of the River Thames, we fought to make ourselves heard above the noise of the traffic. Perhaps that was the only good thing about the date because I could not think of anything to say anyway.

We did discover that we had one thing in common at least – our birthdays were on the same day, 2 March. As students, we needed little more excuse than that for a party, so we arranged our joint celebration for a Sunday evening and invited the whole second year, about ninety people. It was a tremendous success, nearly everybody showed up and we were still in good form when we strolled into the anatomy lecture theatre on the Monday morning, straight from the party. The best bit about that night was that Scilla and I were at last a couple and she even started to take an interest in my rugby. This meant that she volunteered to copy the notes for me of the lectures I missed when on the New Zealand tour, writing comments across the top of the page like 'Congratulations on your try against Taranaki' – they looked quite strange beside the key points of the Embden-Meyerhoff pathway.

That tour meant that I missed a fair part of the summer term so my workload at St Mary's was starting to concern me. Despite cramming all through the holidays, I did badly in the autumn exams and seriously began to wonder how I would cope with the second MB, a big hurdle because I had to pass the exam before I could start clinical work. Students were given two chances at the exam but, if you failed the second time, you were kicked out of medical school. In the circumstances, I knew that I had no choice but to devote myself pretty well single-mindedly to my studies and play only enough rugby to keep my mind fresh.

As it turned out, though, my rugby was a huge help. I have always believed in Parkinson's Law that 'work expands to fill the time available', and it would have certainly been easy for me to spend more time sitting at my desk and to end up doing less. Rugby was an important diversion and I used it as a reward for the hard hours spent studying. Instead of doing one thing badly, I ended up doing two things well and it paid off; I passed the second MB, doing very much better than I or my lecturers had ever thought possible – not for the first time or the last.

After the Easter of 1970, I proudly exchanged my long white lab coat for the shorter coat that is the trademark of a medical student on the wards. With a brand new stethoscope dangling around my neck, I was beginning to feel like a doctor but the first few months for us junior 'dressers' (the equivalent of tea boys in office jargon) were shattering. All that time spent learning biochemistry and anatomy seemed totally pointless when we were confronted with real live patients. The enormity of our lack of knowledge was frightening and it seemed inconceivable that we would be dashing through the wards like the housemen in only three years' time.

On the wards, we were organised in 'firms', headed by a consultant, with a senior registrar, registrar and houseman. As juniors, it was our duty to interview the patients, help the housemen, take blood samples and prepare presentations for ward rounds. Those poor patients were bombarded with a barrage of questions, most of which must have seemed totally irrelevant to their complaint. A gentleman admitted for a hernia repair would be asked his whole family history, what his father died of, how many pints he drank a night and if he had ever had whooping cough as a child – and all these probably three times over. No wonder they needed a pre-med before going to theatre!

In those days, what you made of your time on the wards was entirely up to you. You might spend hours clerking patients (i.e. taking their medical history) and learn less than if you spent a quiet half-hour looking up a certain condition whilst, on the other hand, you could learn more about multiple sclerosis by remembering someone your own age, crippled with the disease, with whom you had talked on the wards. I think that I learnt most on the wards with the consultant; this is where you develop your patient management skills and it is the key period in the study years.

Our responsibilities started to increase more than some of us had bargained for and, suddenly, we found ourselves delivering babies. Every student needed twenty deliveries under his or her belt, so to speak. The first birth that I witnessed was bad enough but my first delivery was a terrifying shock. True, it was breathtaking and miraculous that there could be a little living creature as the outcome of it all but it was so bloody. I had an unexpected mixture of feelings, a cross between awe and repulsion, and my ability to cope with the squeamish side of the job was tested to the full.

Hospitals always have been and always will be full of characters and this was certainly true of the midwives I worked with. One night midwife was a formidable individual, weighing in at around eighteen stone and with one blind eye. The story was that she had been injured when clamping the cord of a patient with secondary syphilis as some blood spurted into her left eye . . . but with her, there were bound to be stories. She did put the fear of God into us and we felt sure that she made some of the mothers deliver out of sheer fright.

* * *

Our first away match of the 1970 Five Nations was against England and it was a chance to see if we had learnt from our New Zealand experiences. It was to be my first visit to Twickenham since my Under-15 debut against the England Schools. I went into the game as Wales' front-line goal-kicker, alongside our young captain, Gareth Edwards. I had mixed feelings about this, as I knew that goal-kicking was not my strongest suit and I never liked doing it anyway because I felt it affected my concentration on the other aspects of full-back play. When I failed to convert a try from Barry John, I started to worry – were England going to win the match because of my mistake?

Everything changed when Ray 'Chico' Hopkins, who had replaced the injured Gareth, put me in for my first try for Wales. The fact that it was against England and we were in danger of losing made it all the sweeter. Then, with time running out, Chico levelled things with a magical try of his own. It now seemed that everything depended upon my conversion. Gareth and I had already missed six kicks between us, whereas England's Bob Hiller had been deadly accurate, so the pressure was really on. I put my head down, struck the ball well and watched with relief as it sailed through the posts to a great roar from the Welsh contingent in the crowd. A magnificent forty-yard drop-goal from Barry John sealed the win so, in the end, my conversion did not matter as much but I was pleased because it had shown a triumph of nerve and I took immense heart from it.

I was beginning to appreciate that, as an international rugby player, I was very much open to the public gaze and that this could be both a positive and a negative experience. After our next game, a defeat by Ireland, it was reported in the newspapers that there had been a big post-match argument between Gareth Edwards and myself over the goal-kicking. I was supposedly upset that he had not given me the kicks – well, at least the media now thought that I could kick! The whole thing was ridiculous; the next story was that there had been a punch-up in the dressing room and then it got even sillier because we were accused of having stolen each others' girlfriends! It was complete rubbish, of course, but it did serve as a salutary lesson for me on how the spotlight can turn on and against you in those moments of failure when people are scrabbling around for someone to pin their disappointment on.

Gareth lost the captaincy after the Dublin defeat but, quite honestly, he was too young to be skipper then. In my opinion, he is the greatest player of all time but, even when he was older, he was never the best team leader. In his place the inspirational John Dawes took over and, with his return to the helm, and Clive Rowlands in charge as coach, I felt that Wales were capable of taking a big leap forward in the next Championship.

Indeed, we started well in 1971 by winning our home matches against England and Ireland with ease, although my involvement in the remainder of the tournament was seriously jeopardised by an unfortunate collision with Gareth Edwards in the England game. I kicked an up-and-under and followed the ball downfield but, when I got there, I ran into Gareth and, unluckily, his head jerked backwards, leaving me with a depressed fracture of the cheekbone. A successful operation meant that I was fit to play against Scotland a few weeks later, something that I will be eternally grateful for as that game turned out to be one of the most famous matches the old Championship has ever witnessed.

Despite an encouraging start by Wales, the Murrayfield crowd screamed their team on for two quick tries. It seemed that Scotland would be well placed for a win but their captain, Peter Brown, who had been kicking his goals all day, unaccountably missed the second conversion. I remember thinking at the time that it could prove to be a costly miss because instead of being 6 points behind, we were trailing by only 4. In the gathering gloom and with time fast running out, Wales forced a line-out well inside the Scottish half. Our lock, Delme Thomas, all muscles and energy, leapt high and the ball was spun out to the three-quarters. I came into the line and passed it swiftly to Gerald Davies and, as the Scottish full-back Ian Smith was not far enough across, it was easy for me to see that a man of Gerald's ability was going to have no difficulty in scoring in the corner.

All now depended on John Taylor. The kick was far from easy but JT looked like the calmest man in the ground when, with his around the corner style, he took aim and seemed casually to flick the ball on its way. A deathly hush fell as the previously raucous spectators held their breath . . . and then the silence was shattered as the touch judges raised their flags. It has since been said that it was the greatest conversion since St Paul's and I would certainly not disagree. We had done it or, should I say, JT had done it. I was so sure that he would get the kick and my feeling sums up the great spirit and confidence that the players in that team had in each other. There have been very few other occasions when I have been just as sure about a conversion. My rosy version of this story is slightly clouded by John's later admission that he was in fact a bag of nerves!

After three victories, there was just France between us and the Grand Slam. I had now matured sufficiently as a player to be sure that I did not want to let the chance slip and Wales were in no doubt that it would be hard. Paris was where we had come unstuck in 1969 and we knew that the French would keep pounding away on our line all afternoon. As I pulled off a tackle on their right wing, Roger Bourgarel, I recall thinking that it was only serving to delay another attack. Then, France went wide again, and I could see that Bourgarel was going to pass. Instinctively, I went for the interception, something I never used to do – I always preferred taking man and ball. Possibly because of the previous tackle, Bougarel had decided not to take me on again and, suddenly, I was in possession, running towards the distant French line. I realised that our prop, Denzil Williams, was managing to keep up with me – in fact, the shock of seeing him on my shoulder had nearly made me stop – but

I also knew he was not best placed to take the pass. With their opposite centre and wing coming across at great speed, time was running out when, at the last second, I caught a glimpse of Gareth Edwards out of the corner of my eye.

How he got there I will never know. With great relief, I jinked infield to check the defence and threw the ball to Gareth, who went full tilt for the corner and just made it. He had been suffering from hamstring problems – we said it was probably rust after spending so much time in the water fishing – but Gareth being Gareth made sure he was there when it mattered, injury or no injury. The Grand Slam was ours and it heralded an unforgettable evening of celebrations. Mervyn Davies and I took charge behind the bar in the Winston Churchill pub in Paris for the perfect end to our Grand Slam season. With us as barmen, the glasses never ran dry.

What was particularly satisfying about that Grand Slam-winning side was that many of us, especially in the pack, had been recovered from the debris of the New Zealand tour two years before. Jeff Young and Mike Roberts were perhaps unsung heroes alongside the more famous back row of Mervyn Davies, John Taylor and Dai Morris but they were absolutely critical to our success. The backs performed with great precision and style under John Dawes' leadership but Wales' trump card was, without doubt, our outstanding half-back pairing of Gareth Edwards and Barry John. For many of us, our reward for the Grand Slam was the chance to return to New Zealand to beat the All Blacks as British and Irish Lions and underline the talent that lay in that Welsh side.

6

LIONS RAMPANT

T o be a Lion is the highest accolade for any British or Irish rugby
   player; possession of that famous red jersey confers member-
ship of a very select club and presents a unique challenge. It was the
absolute pinnacle of my playing career because, with the Lions, I
took on the best that the rugby world could offer and won. Even
Wales, at the height of their success, could not achieve that and,
because of this, those series victories in New Zealand and South
Africa rank above other wins. But, being a Lion is not just about
rugby matches; those long tours created a fellowship with other
players from other countries that the passing years have not
diminished. This depth of feeling was one of the reasons why I
was so angered by the 2005 series against the All Blacks, a tour that
besmirched the glorious legacy of the Lions.

   Thirty-four years earlier, the British and Irish Lions were about to
embark on another famous tour to New Zealand, the greatest rugby
nation in the world. Before 1971 the Lions had never won a series
there, a daunting prospect for those in with a chance of selection. I
was optimistic about making the tour party but nothing was
certain. Of course, I had tried to second-guess who would be in
the squad but this did not give me much comfort, there were still far
too many unanswered questions. Did I have enough experience?
Would being Welsh count against me? Our Grand Slam earlier that
year should have paved the way for the selection of many of the
Welsh boys but there was a fear in some quarters that too many
'Taffs' on the plane would be a bad thing. They said we were bad

travellers and that our homesickness and clannish mentality could have a detrimental effect on the touring party.

Despite this, a strong Welsh flavour had already been created. John Dawes was an inspired choice as Lions captain and the first Welshman ever to hold that position, whilst Carwyn James had been appointed as coach two years before. Carwyn was an amazing man, intellectual, dapper and always his own person. He would never be without a cigarette or, it seemed, a gin and tonic. Carwyn had thrown himself into his coaching role and no stone was going to be left unturned with him in charge. He spent hours in South Africa House in London, poring over the newspaper reports of how the Springboks had beaten New Zealand in 1970. He even visited Manchester United Football Club and, rather daringly considering the times, Wigan Rugby League Club to analyse their training methods. He had the most amazing rugby brain that I have ever come across and, from my medical background, I could see that he was not only a coach but a psychologist as well. Under his direction, the lazy ones would train twice a day whilst the over-committed would be given the day off. He understood every single one of his players.

When my selection letter arrived from the Home Unions Committee, I was as thrilled as when I found out about my first cap for Wales. Remember, I was still a student at St Mary's and hearing the squad announced on the BBC One o'Clock News made it even more special. Quite rightly, Wales' success in the Five Nations had been recognised, with just over one third of the party coming from my country – in fact, six of the thirty Lions players came from London Welsh alone.

I just could not wait for the tour to begin. I was so desperate not to get injured beforehand that I even held the banister every time I climbed upstairs. We were not allowed to participate in any rugby games for four weeks before departure so, to maintain my fitness, I took to the squash court with John Dawes and John Taylor. How modern players would love to have that kind of rest period before such an important tour.

Before leaving for New Zealand, we were herded off to East-bourne for a week of training and getting to know each other. It was the traditional start to the Lions tour but I felt that it had already outlived its usefulness. Meeting up with the other players was worthwhile as once on foreign soil we would need to put up a solid front, but the common fear that we might get ourselves injured during the training sessions was overwhelming. To this day, I am not a fan of pre-tour get-togethers. Modern team-bonding exercises borrowed from the world of business leave me a little cold to say the least. Instead, I would advocate allowing enough time to acclimatise in the country where you will be playing your rugby.

En route, we stopped over in Hong Kong. The intention was for us to get some rest but Hong Kong is really the last place to have a quiet night in! Most of us found it irresistible after all that pre-tour tension in Eastbourne but in Hong Kong I was to learn a big lesson. The combination of a night out and jet lag meant that I woke up late the next morning and found, to my horror, that the bus to the training ground had already left. I was sharing a room with the Irish forward Sean Lynch, an amazing character who was quite unfazed by our lateness. Whilst I was really upset and had started to panic, Sean's response was to order a full breakfast. He took his time and enjoyed every lingering mouthful but his calm only made me even more anxious and agitated. After what seemed like an age, we ordered a taxi and rolled up at the training ground a good half an hour late. When the Lions tour manager Doug Smith spotted us, he tore into me and gave me the biggest dressing down that I have ever received – in front of all the other players too. I was trembling after he had finished and the rest of the squad, sensing how shaken I was, stayed perfectly quiet. That was it; I was never ever late again for a training session with the Lions, or any other team for that matter.

Next stop was Australia, for a couple of warm-up games against Queensland and New South Wales. We lost in Brisbane but the defeat pulled us together and made us all the more determined to fulfil our true potential. After a victory in Sydney, John Dawes said that we had won 'because we had to' – and this became our motto. For the Welsh players who had suffered humiliation at the hands of the All Blacks on our tour of 1969, the resolve to settle that score was becoming a crusade. Doug Smith was also incredibly enthusiastic about our chances and, from the outset, predicted that the Lions would win the series 2–1, with one match drawn. We could not wait to find out if he was right.

When we walked off the plane after the short journey over the Tasman Sea, we were certainly not treated like losers by the New Zealand public. Interest in the tour was at an unbelievable level and we were given a fantastic reception at the airport. After a traditional Maori welcome, our choirmaster John Taylor gathered us together and we responded in full voice. We were ready for our first match on Kiwi soil.

We started the tour well and, of our early victories, it has always been the match against King Country that stands out in my mind. Their side contained the immortal All Black captain Colin Meads, as much a legend then as he is now. The photographs of him working on his farm with a sheep under each arm had created an image of a man so powerful that he could not be conquered. In 1971 he was nearing the end of his international playing career but that victory over Meads and his team still imbued us with a confidence that never left us for the remainder of the trip.

The spirit that was building within the squad was amazing. Three and a half months on tour was a long time to be away from loved ones and it was vital to forge strong friendships with your team-mates, particularly with the other men competing for your position. You had to support them and they had to support you. To start with, we used to let our hair down mid-week but that meant the Thursday morning training sessions were killers as Carwyn would really push us hard; he never laid down the law about our socialising but he certainly never made any concessions to it either. After the first few games, we had a players' meeting and decided to make Saturday night our official party night, cutting out the heavy mid-week celebrations until we split into two teams as the Test matches approached. It was not as if we were not being treated like adults; Carwyn himself had decreed that we should have wine with our meals – something that, believe it or not, was a major step forward for a Lions tourist in those days.

As the tour went on, I was appreciating the skills of our fly-half maestro, Barry John, more and more. It was not just BJ's ability to run a game; his immaculate goal-kicking was strengthening my claim for the full-back spot in the Tests. My main competitor for that position, England's number fifteen, Bob Hiller, was also a splendid kicker but I was confident that the place would be mine if Barry kept slotting the goals.

It was clear, however, that the Lions would need much more than accurate goal-kicking to beat the All Blacks and in the match against Wellington our back line clicked, scoring an incredible nine tries. It was the best display of running rugby any British side had ever produced because of the quality of the opposition, and the only Lions performance that I have seen to match it since was the match against Free State in 1997.

The Welsh winger John Bevan scored four of his seventeen tries on tour in that Wellington match. He was the strongest wing of his generation – the Jonah Lomu of his day – although a little slighter of course! Bevan could hand off defenders or go straight through them and it seemed amazing to me that he was not seriously injured during that tour. It did reinforce my belief that the harder you go into a tackle, the less likely you are to get hurt. Not too long after the tour, John left to try his hand at rugby league, a game for which he was ideally suited and at Warrington he was a great success.

Gerald Davies was of course a very different sort of winger. Gerald had arrived on tour a fortnight late because of exams and immediately announced his presence with two tries in the game at Timaru. He could beat a man off either foot and more regularly than any other player that I have ever seen. Just as importantly, he was never a greedy player and would pass if a team-mate was better placed than him to score. He was quite simply a genius.

During the next match in Otago, I crossed for my first try in a Lions shirt. I was never a great try-scorer or indeed celebrator of the event when it came along. I think that the try-scorer just happens to be the last person involved in the movement. That said, I confess to a warm glow after this one. The New Zealand public were beginning to take notice of our ability to score tries, although they seemed confident that our hopes and our forwards would be squashed by the hard men of the South Island.

The match against Canterbury had always been seen as a key point in the tour. They were New Zealand's leading provincial team at that time and the game was only one week away from the First Test. It turned out to be a downright bloodbath. Our management must have seen the writing on the wall because Barry John was withdrawn at the last minute to avoid possible injury. Irishman Mike Gibson took his place at fly-half and I was to share the kicking duties with him.

Canterbury seemed to think it their duty to prove to the whole of the country that the Lions could be beaten. Not only that, they seemed to take it upon themselves to make sure that many of us would not, or rather could not, feature in the Tests. In the absence of Barry John, the Scottish prop Sandy Carmichael became Canterbury's main target and he was so severely punched that both of his cheekbones were broken. Sandy was not a man to be easily intimidated and he bravely returned to the field when really he should have stayed off, considering the extent of his injuries. The after-match photographs showing the horrific state of his face have entered rugby history.

Nine of our players needed medical attention and our dressing room was, in Carwyn's words, 'a casualty clearing station'. Having seen a few of those in my time, I was inclined to agree. But we won and if there had been any doubts over our togetherness, there were none after this match. As John Dawes had said in Australia, 'we won because we had to'. In the aftermath, the heat was turned up when the All Blacks coach Ivan Vodanovich suggested that the First Test would now be a second Passchendaele as we had been asking for trouble by lying on the ball. We were furious – it was a pitiful reaction from their coach to what had been the worst advertisement for the game that anybody could remember.

Understandably, the tension grew and grew during that week before the First Test in Dunedin but, come the morning of the match, our mood was considerably lightened by a telegram from two jokers who had toured New Zealand on the 1959 Lions tour, Tony O'Reilly and Andy Mulligan: 'VICTORY WILL MAKE US RELEVANT AS DINOSAURS STOP WILL PRESS FOR WELSH AS UNIVERSAL LANGUAGE IN COMMON MARKET STOP' and so it went on. We reflected on just how close these great players had come to Lions glory of their own, so not only did the cable provide some welcome relief, it focused our thoughts on the fine line between success and failure. It was time to make the 1971 Lions into winners.

When the game finally started, it seemed that the ball actually belonged to New Zealand but, crucially, they could not score. The Lions defence was magnificent and, at times, we were just holding on until Barry John could find some way to kick the ball out of danger. To make it even more difficult, scrum-half Gareth Edwards went off after only six minutes with a recurrence of his hamstring injury. Barry did not have his best goal-kicking day but he was our saviour when it came to getting the ball to safety. We hung on and recorded a famous 9–3 victory. To his great credit, Colin Meads came into our ecstatic dressing room to offer his congratulations. As the captain of an All Black side that had won seventy per cent of possession, I thought he was noble in defeat.

New Zealand reacted to their shattering loss by making changes, including the call-up of Laurie Mains, the goal-kicking full-back from Otago. Mains, who went on to coach his national side in the 1990s, was exactly what the All Blacks had missed in the First Test and he made us pay for the penalties that we conceded in the Second.

My most significant moment of that match in Christchurch was the bit that I cannot remember! Midway through the first half, I found myself struggling at the bottom of a ruck, feeling rather peculiar. I had no idea what I was doing there or indeed what day it was. On automatic pilot, I set off to cover the space created by my absence at full-back but the All Black scrum-half Sid Going had already aimed a beautiful kick to where I should have been. I just managed to cover it and then I did another automatic thing – I ran with the ball! After selling a dummy, I passed to Mike Gibson, who in turn set up Gerald Davies. Gerald had quite a run to make but we knew he would do it. That did not seem to stop me following him though; it was as if I was in a trance and, just after he had dotted down, I collapsed over the line, still concussed. After a second, I dusted myself off and trotted back to the halfway line, still not quite sure what had happened.

We eventually lost 22–12 and our tackling was as poor in that Test as it had been good in the First. Mentally and physically, we had got it wrong and the rest of the tour was going to be as much a test of our coach, Carwyn James, as it was a test of ourselves as players. Carwyn immediately emphasised the positives; he said that at least we had finished strongly and scored a good try towards the end. He even concluded that 'we had lost a match but won a series'. Once again, his absolute confidence was inspiring. We were also given a day to relax together, getting back the spirit of the tour, and that was a marvellous tonic as we did anything but play rugby or commiserate over our loss.

A week in North Auckland at the Bay of Islands before the Third Test was a welcome respite from the goldfish bowl that is New Zealand during a Lions tour. There was much less media attention in those days but, even so, it was good to be away from all the press scrutiny. The weather was fine and it was an ideal place to prepare for what was certain to be the most important game any of us had ever played in. We made several changes for the match in Wellington. Gordon Brown of Scotland came in at lock for the first time in the series and England's winger, David Duckham, and the Welsh forward, Derek Quinnell, were also picked. The selection of Quinnell was vital. He played Sid Going out of the game, constantly getting to the All Black number nine, and was also a key member of our line-out, along with Brown and the new pack leader, Willie-John McBride of Ireland.

John Dawes won the toss and decided to play with the fierce Wellington wind at our backs. The management had been on to the local meteorological office before the game and the forecast was for the wind to ease during the second period. Our plan was to amass as many points as possible before running the ball into the wind after the interval. And what a start we had. After only three minutes, Barry John scored a drop-goal and, six minutes later, we added a try by Gerald Davies. Gareth Edwards was playing a blinder and he made another try, this time for Barry. Before New Zealand knew where they were, we were 13 points to the good and the crowd was silenced. In the second half, Laurie Mains scored a try for the All Blacks but, as the wind dropped, our determination to finish the job increased and our defensive powers returned. We won 13–3 but, most significantly, now we could not lose the series.

There is one other reason why I will never forget that afternoon. Bob Burgess, the All Black first five-eighth, or fly-half as we term it, was double tackled and fell to the floor unconscious. For one awful

57

moment, we feared that he had broken his neck. A stretcher was called for and, after an interminable delay, one eventually arrived but the ambulance crew, the trainer and the referee all just stood around looking at him. I went across and suddenly realised that not only was Bob still unconscious, he was turning blue. Although I was only a medical student, I knew something had to be done so I rushed forward and felt inside his mouth. Sure enough, his tongue had slipped back, cutting off his air passage. I turned him on his side and pulled his tongue out of his throat with my finger. Once his tongue was held forward, his colour picked up. I was furious because it seemed such a basic error on the part of the first-aid team who had stood by so idly. In these situations, it is imperative that a person is turned onto their side to make sure there is no obstruction. I realised no one wanted to risk aggravating any possible serious neck injury but, once the patient starts turning blue, you have to act. The human brain needs its oxygen supply to be cut off for three minutes only before irreparable damage is done.

Bob Burgess was one of the few All Blacks whom we had got to know socially on the tour. He seemed to spend more time with us than with his own team-mates at the after-match functions and so we were especially relieved to hear that he had woken up in Wellington Hospital after the game with no long-term injury. My friendship with Bob was rekindled when he flew halfway around the world to recount this story in the *This is Your Life* television programme that was recorded in my honour in 1979. It was another twenty-six years before I saw him again on the 2005 Lions tour to New Zealand and it was very special to share some memories of our 1971 tour, although his recall of that fateful day was a little sketchy!

The Lions knew that if we avoided defeat in the Fourth and final Test we would make the history that had been our aim all along. The British press on tour were jubilant and brought us champagne to celebrate. We had enjoyed a very good relationship with them, and the New Zealand journalists for that matter, but, unfortunately, this rapport is increasingly a thing of the past. The tabloid press, especially, are just out to sell newspapers and the tastier the story, the better it is for them. It leads to an air of mistrust; blind eyes were frequently turned in our day and that, I am sure, would never be the case today. There were also no more than a dozen journalists from home covering the 1971 tour. Compare that to the hundreds in the media pack when the Lions go abroad now.

When we arrived in Palmerston North for our next match, it seemed that some people thought that we had already taken our place in the history books. Every Lion had a chauffeur-driven vintage car to collect him from the airport and take him around streets lined with well-wishers. It was amazing that they had found the time to organise this in the space of the few hours after our Third Test victory. Perhaps they had expected us to win after all! The locals gave us the impression that they were more concerned about us beating the Springboks on our next tour in 1974 than whether the All Blacks would beat us in the final Test of the current series. We were, however, being lulled into a false sense of security.

In retrospect, I felt that our preparation for that final Test in Auckland was not as good as it should have been. Instead of being determined to drive the point home with a convincing win, we seemed content to go out onto the field and accept a draw. On arrival at Eden Park, it was clear that the New Zealand crowd wanted their side to show the Lions who really was the boss and their team responded accordingly.

In the second half I found myself in the middle of the field, just inside New Zealand territory, with virtually no support around me. I thought I might as well take a shot at the drop-goal, something I had been practising with Barry John and Bob Hiller all through the tour, but the idea would probably never have come into my head had I not for some reason said on the bus that day that I would drop a goal. My bold pronouncement had led to uproar because drop-goals were not seen as part of my repertoire! I hit it perfectly though and it was still rising as it went over. I knew as soon as I had put boot to ball that it was there and, when I think about it now, it still makes me chuckle. I waved up to the non-playing lads in the stand and I could tell that they were as stunned as I was. For twenty glorious minutes, I really thought we were going to win and that I had scored the clinching points.

I was wrong. New Zealand scored one more penalty goal to give a final score of 14–14. We had not played well; I think too many minds had been centred on going home but at least we had won the series 2–1. What was truly remarkable was that Doug Smith's pre-tour prediction had come true, even the one drawn game. Carywn James insisted that Doug had also said that Arsenal would win the FA Cup that year, Evonne Goolagong would take the Wimbledon singles crown and Lee Trevino, the Open golf!

7

WORK AND PLAY

THE Lions tour had meant a serious reorganisation of my medical studies because, unlike in previous years, when the tours with Wales had been shorter, there could be no suggestion of me just catching up after a four-month absence. Instead, I had to drop back six months, as I would only be allowed to sit MB finals with a full three years of clinical experience behind me. I was not concerned, though – it seemed a small price to pay for the chance of a lifetime and I intended to maximise the opportunity both from a rugby and a medical point of view by staying on afterwards to do my elective (an optional three-month period at a different hospital) at the General Hospital in Auckland.

As I stood at the airport and waved off my companions of the last four months, I was regretting my decision. I felt orphaned. I was envious of the reception they would find when they got home. In Wales they would probably declare a national holiday! It was going to be a very different experience in Auckland, with rugby post-mortems at the hospital and New Zealand bitterness over the series loss. When I did eventually return to Britain, I was in for a big surprise. Waiting at Heathrow were many of my London Welsh colleagues and other friends who had travelled up from Wales. I was overwhelmed that John Dawes had even arranged for some of the official functions to be postponed until I could join in. It was a marvellous gesture that was typical of the attitude of the squad. Every one of us had contributed to the success and John made sure that we all shared in it.

Amidst the social whirl of dinners and parties, including a civic reception in Bridgend, I came to appreciate the full implications of what we had done and what it had meant to the British people. If anything, the significance of our win has grown with every passing year; four times the Lions have returned to New Zealand and four times they have come home beaten. I find it odd that the longer time has gone on, the more famous we have become. Like the England football boys of 1966, nothing would make us happier than to see our achievement equalled.

As the Lions will not return to New Zealand until 2017, I suppose we will have to put up with it. Whatever else happens, that 1971 team will always stand the test of time. The back line was outstanding: Gareth Edwards and Barry John, the best half-back combination to have played the game; Mike Gibson, the best centre ever; John Dawes, the best passer of a ball; and three wingers, Gerald Davies, John Bevan and David Duckham, amongst the greatest finishers to grace a rugby field. And, of course, they were under the direction of the greatest coach of all time, Carwyn James.

After that experience, ordinary lectures at St Mary's were always going to be a bit of an anticlimax. I am sure that when I finally got home I must still have been a bit too cocky. Luckily, it was wasted on my student friends who immediately cut me down to size. After such a long absence it was very good to be back amongst them again.

There was one more reunion still to come. Since the summer of 1969, Scilla and I had gone our separate ways but, soon after my return from New Zealand, we met up again. With our shared birthday approaching, I could not resist the obvious temptation of suggesting that we share a few drinks together on 2 March. At that point Scilla was engaged to an American that she had met during her elective in the United States, so imagine my amazement when she telephoned to break off the engagement after our night out! Soon after that we decided to get married.

With all this happening, I felt that I should begin to think seriously about getting myself qualified; if I had not gone to New Zealand with the Lions, I would have been taking finals with the rest of my year in the spring of 1973 but my time out from studying meant that I did not have enough clinical experience for the final MB. As an insurance policy, I decided to take the external exams set by the Royal College of Surgeons and the Royal College of Physicians on obstetrics, medicine and surgery.

Whenever I had a viva, or oral exam, I admit that I sometimes tried to use the influence of my rugby achievements. I was very proud of my British and Irish Lions tie and it did match my three-piece suit, but I cannot deny that I secretly hoped it might be a talking point and give me a little leverage in the interview. My policy had mixed results. During the medicine viva, the examiner latched on to it immediately, firing questions at me about rugby and the Lions tour. I thought all was going well until, at the end of the interview, he led me to the window. Oh no, I thought, here comes the tree speech – a euphemism for letting you know gently that you had failed. 'See that tree over there?' the examiner would say. 'Well, go away and learn something and come back when the leaves are brown.' We stood together at the window. 'See that tree over there?' he asked. 'Do you happen to know what it's called?' Then he smiled and said, 'I just wanted to know if you had any other interests than rugby.' I was astonished – it was such a mean trick – but he had not wanted to know anything about medicine, so I must have done better than I thought.

My third and final exam was surgery, in March 1973. The pathology museum at the Royal College of Surgeons was the awe-inspiring venue for the anatomical viva and, once again, my Lions tie did not seem to be doing the trick. The examiner showed me specimen jar after jar, and fired question after question at me. In the final pot was a spleen and when I turned to leave the room, he called after me, 'Make sure you don't end up with a ruptured spleen with those tackles of yours!' He had known all along! I found out later that he would have loved to ask all about my rugby but, as I was in line for the Gold Medal, he had to limit the questions to medical matters.

This was very welcome news for me. Although I did not get the Gold Medal, just hearing that I had been in the running for it was enough to cement my ambition of becoming a surgeon. It had taken six years of my life to replace Mr with Dr. Now I would need seven more years of study to replace Dr with Mr and become a Fellow of the Royal College of Surgeons.

I am convinced that the Welsh team of 1972 would have gone on to take a second consecutive Grand Slam but the Championship that year was severely truncated by the decision of Wales and Scotland not to play in Dublin because of the troubles in Northern Ireland. We won the three matches that we did play but, when the WRU suggested that the game against the Irish be played at a neutral venue, Ireland said it was Dublin or nothing. On a personal level, I would have been willing to go, knowing that we would have had high security, but there were genuine concerns at this time and others in the squad felt it was too risky.

It was the game against Scotland in Cardiff that year that stood out for me. That was the match in which Gareth Edwards scored his famous 'try in the mud' when he slid into a corner of the Arms Park and into the red shale of the dog-race track that used to surround the pitch. It is a memorable moment for many but not for me as I am afraid I was no longer at the ground to witness it. Earlier in the game, I had been underneath a high ball when it seemed like the whole of Scotland descended on me and knocked me clean out. Unwisely, I carried on and, shortly afterwards, mistimed a tackle on their winger, Billy Steele; his knees hit me square in the face and the world began to spin again. When I came round for the second time and opened my eyes, the colour of my team-mates' faces said it all –

they were grey and my upper jaw had caved in. This time there was no alternative but to leave the field and, when I was stretchered off, the crowd could not quite believe it. They had never seen me really injured before and, as the stretcher was almost clear of the pitch, apparently my foot moved slightly, prompting some supporters to claim that I was signalling that I was OK and would be back on in a few minutes!

Instead, I was on my way to the Cardiff Royal Infirmary. It was deserted when I arrived – Wales were at home after all – and after having X-rays taken, I listened wistfully to the rest of our win on the radio, wishing I could have been part of it. The facio-maxillary specialist, Mr Russell Hopkins, arrived as soon as he could, that is, straight after the final whistle at the Arms Park. At least my gum shield had saved my teeth but Mr Hopkins gave me a stark choice: he could either reduce the fracture under a full general anaesthetic or have a go under a local anaesthetic. Rather than taking clinical matters into account, my decision on the most suitable treatment was based solely on the fact that I wanted to make the after-match dinner so, as I knew that a general anaesthetic would mean an overnight stay in hospital, I opted for the local and readied myself as Mr Hopkins pulled my jaw straight and put on a metal brace to keep it in place. Then, after the pain, came the good news – he told me I should have some alcohol to assist my recovery. It was the first time that I had heard of a prescription for gin and tonic but I was definitely not complaining as I joined my victorious team-mates at the Angel Hotel. I admit that I had no trouble with dosing myself with G & Ts that night, although the steak was a little more difficult to manage.

The end of that 1972 season marked the retirement of Barry John at the age of twenty-seven and, to a certain extent, it was the end of an era. Playing with Barry gave you so much confidence; he was the conductor of our orchestra and such a calming influence. Like Gareth Edwards, I believe that Barry was the best ever in his position, so his departure from the international scene was a sad moment, not only for Welsh fans but for rugby supporters in general. If you loved rugby, then you loved watching BJ.

But Wales did have a ready-made replacement, although he was a very different man. If Barry had been the extrovert, then Phil Bennett was the introvert and, although it must have been an immense challenge to replace Barry, Phil would grow into the role perfectly and prove himself to be a great player in his own right. Benny was part of the Llanelli team that beat the 1972 All Blacks at the start of their tour later that year and, just over a month later, he played against them again, this time for Wales. A Welsh victory in that match would have been our first over New Zealand since 1953, and just over ten minutes from the end, I really thought that I had scored the try to give us a famous win. There were forwards all over me but the referee, Johnny Johnson, ruled that I had made a double movement when grounding the ball and disallowed the score. I still have the photograph of that 'try' at home and I am as convinced today as I was then that it was good. We sickeningly lost 19–16 and my third chance of beating New Zealand in Welsh colours had evaporated.

8

SOUTH AFRICA HEAD ON

S CILLA and I were married in May 1973. Naturally, the wedding day was chosen with rugby fixtures in mind – the first Saturday after the Middlesex Sevens, the old finish to the domestic season, and just before Wales' tour to Canada, a slot of about ten days and just enough for a wedding and a quick honeymoon. We had no choice, we wanted to invite our rugby friends as well as our guests from the medical world. Whilst I was away in Canada, it was lovely to be able to send her postcards addressed to 'Mrs JPR Williams'.

Our first jobs after qualifying were as house surgeons back at St Mary's. They were demanding positions, requiring us to be on duty every other night. Fortunately, we were on the same on-call rotas so, on Saturdays, Scilla could cover for me if London Welsh had a home game or if we were playing against another London club. It was still tough, fitting my rugby into a fast-moving medical career, and working the long hours was leaving me exhausted. When I assisted on renal transplants, they did not even start until after midnight and usually took four to five hours to complete.

I was just not able to give as much time to rugby as I had in the past, missing several squad training sessions with Wales and roughly one in three matches for London Welsh. There were some compensations, however, as when I was out of the game with a posterior cruciate ligament injury sustained against London Scottish in January 1974, I could get my knee seen to by the exceptional physiotherapy department at St Mary's. When you are in hospital for 120 hours each week, you do have the time to find the right place for your treatment! Because of that injury, I missed Wales' game against England at Twickenham but, as it turned out, it was a good one to miss, as Wales lost for the first time in over a decade against the old enemy. What I had not bargained for was the trouble I had in getting a ticket for Twickenham. In the end Clive Rowlands, in his last match as Welsh coach, got me in on his pass and I had to sit on the steps in the aisle of the stand. I watched in dismay as England took the honours. My replacement, Roger Blyth, had a very good game, although I did feel that perhaps I could have anticipated David Duckham's side-step to stop their winning try. Having played with and against Dave so many times, I knew he tended to go off his left foot.

In general, though, Welsh rugby was on a high and I was selected for my second Lions tour, this time to South Africa.

All those involved in the 1971 Lions tour to New Zealand could not wait to get to South Africa three years later – it was a case of one down, one to go. Australia were not the force then that they are today, so it was the Springboks who posed the other big global challenge. We felt that we had proved nothing unless we could follow 1971 up with victory in South Africa. The All Blacks had never won a Test series there and we wanted to show the world that the Lions could.

My participation in the tour, however, was in serious doubt because of the knee injury that had kept me out of the England game and was more serious than I had let on. I kept the Lions management up-to-date on my recovery and, when it came to the crunch, I assured them that I was fit to tour. I would need the first two weeks to complete my rehabilitation but the length of the trip allowed for this and I was certain that I would be fine when my time came to play. It was a great credit to the management that they took my word for it and I am sure that my being a doctor and able to explain everything in detail convinced them. These days, however, my view is completely different and I am sure that I would have ruled myself out of selection. Nowadays overseas tours are much shorter and players have to be totally fit if they are to take their places on the plane – although one notes that on the 2005 Lions tour to New Zealand several members of the squad who were carrying injuries still travelled.

In 1974, two Irishmen were chosen to take charge of the Lions, with Willie-John McBride selected as captain and Syd Millar as coach. I thought they were excellent choices; they had both been at Ballymena, as well as representing Ireland together, so we knew that they were on the same wavelength. Welshman Alun Thomas was the manager but, as good as the Lions preparations were, they were overshadowed by the threat that the trip would be cancelled altogether.

As we assembled at the Britannia Hotel in London, we were greeted by angry demonstrators protesting about the existence of the apartheid system in South Africa. I knew what to expect. I had played against the Springboks twice during their tour of Britain in the 1969–70 season and on both occasions the games had been marked by protests designed to prevent the rugby taking place. Before the London Counties versus South Africa match, the Twickenham pitch had had to be painstakingly cleared of the tacks that demonstrators had hidden in the grass and they had followed this up with flour bombs at Cardiff Arms Park for the international against Wales. In 1974 the government became involved, with Denis Howell, the Minister for Sport, meeting with the Home Unions Committee to set out the official opposition to the tour. There was intense pressure on us, both as individuals and as a group, to pull out entirely. The situation was uncomfortable, to say the least.

I remember feeling resentful that we were being used as pawns in a political game of chess. Nobody wanted openly to defy their own government but there was a sense of 'Why us?' I was certainly not condoning what was happening in South Africa, far from it, but at the time there were many other places where human rights were being violated – in the Soviet Union and South America, for instance – and there had been no large-scale demonstrations against the British athletes or gymnasts visiting those countries.

We were intelligent people and we had thought deeply about the issues involved. My close friend, John Taylor, did rule himself out of the Lions squad for political reasons; a brave decision and one that was consistent with his withdrawal from the Wales versus Springboks game four years earlier. Many thought that this would have put his international career in doubt but JT had already toured South Africa with the Lions in 1968 and he felt that he could not play against them. He tried his best to influence me and, whilst I accepted everything that he had to say, I also felt that I could not form my own opinion until I had actually been there to witness the situation at first hand.

It was the general view of the tour party that we would be doing more good by going to South Africa and winning, than by staying at home. We wanted to show the whites that they were not all-powerful and that black people would have to be accepted into their sports teams. When the Lions arrived and saw how badly the black South Africans were being treated and how willingly they became our supporters, it made us even more determined to beat the Springboks.

Due to the demonstrations, we were in effect billeted in our London hotel for three days, coming and going through the back entrance for training sessions. The secrecy and the deliberate mis-leading of the press about our movements gave us a tremendous tour spirit right from the start. It was interesting to read the newspapers one morning to find that we had apparently sneaked out of Heathrow the previous night to avoid one last confrontation with the government, when we were in fact eating our bacon and eggs in the hotel restaurant. But it was a great relief when the plane finally did take off – it was almost as if we were escaping our own country.

We arrived in Johannesburg to a tumultuous reception as many South Africans had never really believed that the tour would take place. Instead of the pre-tour training week in Eastbourne, the management took us to Stilfontein to acclimatise at altitude. It was not only good for our lungs, it was good for our minds as well and just what we needed after the political storm back home.

The effects of altitude were immediately obvious and, for several days, we struggled to find our breath and felt light-headed. Ken Kennedy, the Irish hooker, was also a doctor and together we devised special breathing exercises aimed at getting more air into the lungs. We must have looked like a group of pregnant women at their antenatal class doing their elementary breathing! We also took blood samples from the players, before and after our training week, to evaluate the changes that were taking place in our bodies so high above sea level. These revealed that some of us were quite anaemic and England's Tony Neary and Johnny Maloney of Ireland were put on iron tablets and extra steaks. On the training paddock, Syd Millar and Willie-John McBride were developing the powerful forward play essential for beating any South African side. Get at them there and you get to the heart of Springbok rugby – the strength of our forwards would prove to be the major asset of that Lions squad.

We began with three fairly comfortable wins but then, in Port Elizabeth, we had our first taste of the physical confrontations to come. The match against Eastern Province was a brutal affair. We heard later that they had been sent out to soften us up, much in the same way that Canterbury had in 1971, but they had not bargained for our teak-tough forwards. There were plenty of willing volunteers when the going got tough. I did not particularly like this type of rugby but it was imperative that the Lions showed early on in the tour that they were not going to be intimidated. The confrontational atmosphere was not confined to the pitch, however, as there was also an uncomfortable display of anti-British feeling in the crowd. One small boy supporting the Lions was slapped in the face by his schoolmaster for showing his allegiance to the 'wrong' team. It was another sign of things to come.

After a massive 97–0 record victory over the South-Western

Districts in Mossel Bay, we moved on to Cape Town for the game against Western Province, billed as the unofficial Fifth Test. It came just a week before the First Test, also to be played at Newlands. We won again but Western Province ran the ball at us the whole time and the watching Springbok selectors decided to include the hard core of that team in their First Test side. South Africa clearly wanted to keep the ball away from our forwards and attack out wide.

Unfortunately for their selectors, the weather that week was atrocious, it never stopped raining. When we arrived on the day of the Test, Newlands was in a terrible waterlogged state and, to make matters worse, the traditional curtain-raiser game ruined the pitch. In such conditions, it was ten-man stuff all the way, or rather nine-man, because the ball hardly ever got past our scrum-half, Gareth Edwards, who, along with the pack, controlled the match. The Springbok forwards were pushed back yards in the mud and then Gareth would kick the ball downfield to rub it in. I almost felt sorry for their forwards – I did say almost! The nature of our 12–3 win sent panic through the country. The South African press tried their best to destabilise us and criticised our rather limited forward approach but, in international rugby, you have to find the easiest way to put points on the board in a match and then carry on doing it.

Aside from our style of rugby, our mere presence in the country was stirring up trouble. We had our first taste of South African anti-apartheid demonstrations at the game with Southern Universities when students kept running onto the field in an attempt to stop the match. The way they were dealt with by the police was appalling – and these were white demonstrators. We shuddered to think what they would have done to them had they been black. The only consolation was that their government's hard-line policy was now on display to the rest of the world.

It was so important to keep winning and, even when a flu bug tore through the squad, we managed to dig deep and dog out a win on the highveld against Transvaal. I did not dare take my temperature and my legs felt like lead but that day I realised how much stamina and cussed self-belief there was in that Lions side. We were not going to let the team, nor Willie-John, down just because we were not feeling too good. In some ways I think this was the most important win of the tour.

The Second Test was at Loftus Versfeld, South African rugby's spiritual home. To an overseas player this ground is the most formidable of all the Test venues because it is in the Afrikaans heartland. Everything about Loftus was different from Newlands: the high altitude, the dry climate, the springy turf singed by the sun and the perilously high open stands towering over the pitch below. The Springboks were convinced that they would get back on track there and, certainly, the odds should have been stacked in their favour.

I vividly remember arriving at the ground. We were in the middle of one of our favourite songs, 'Flower of Scotland', when the bus suddenly ground to a halt. Not a single member of the squad moved until we had reached the end. They were not going to interfere with our singing and tell us when to get off the coach. We were building a confidence within the team that was unshakeable but the Springboks seemed to be in a very different frame of mind. The locals were upbeat but their team were not; they had been virtually imprisoned in their hotel in Pretoria for the three days before the Test and had been forbidden to read any newspapers or have any communication with the press. I know their management were trying to generate some team spirit of their own but I am sure it only served to lower the South African players' morale.

In the Test match, it was the Lions who played with freedom on the hard ground, running in five tries, including one beauty from our flying winger, JJ Williams. We were proving that we were a side who could play all types of rugby and in the second half we threw the ball around as if it was a sevens or charity exhibition match. It finished 28–9; the sight of the sun setting over the stand, gradually shading more and more of the pitch, with the crowd growing quieter and quieter, is an everlasting memory.

Now we were 2–0 up in the series and could not lose. The South African public felt their national team was in danger of falling completely from grace and there was a growing body of opinion that, because of the defeats, multi-racial teams should be allowed to represent the country in the future. It was as if the white people could only begin to question apartheid when it was suggested it might be affecting their rugby side. Would the loss of the two Tests worry the South African Rugby Board into making some positive move towards integration, we wondered. And was there a chance that, at last, we might come up against some non-white players in the match versus the Quaggas, the South African Barbarians? It came to nothing, though, and the talented black flanker, Morgan Cushe, did not make it into the side and nor did any other non-white players. Another disturbing aspect of the Quaggas game was the verbal and physical abuse directed at the referee, Ian Gourlay. It was quite disgraceful and at full-time several of the Lions players had to escort him off the field to prevent him suffering serious injury from the so-called fans.

This kind of abuse was not an isolated incident. In Bloemfontein, our tour liaison officer, Choet Visser, was branded a traitor in his own city because he had become a friend of the Lions. The South Africans seemed to have an amazing ability to turn on their own when things were going against them. At the end of the tour I gave Choet my Lions tracksuit and the dirty old headband that I had worn to keep the long hair out of my eyes. Our friendship grew and Scilla and I became godparents to one of Choet's granddaughters. Sadly, he died in 2005 but I will never forget him or, indeed, the way he was made to feel by his fellow South Africans.

By the time of the Third Test, the Springbok selectors were frantically chopping and changing and it seemed that common sense had evaporated. The most ridiculous choice for the Port

Elizabeth match had to be the number eight, Gerhardus Sonnekus, as scrum-half. If anything, the selection method was even crazier – the three candidates were put on show at a training session the week before and one was chosen purely on his performance that day. What a desperate way to go about selecting a Test team.

Despite this, that Third Test turned out to be the best contest of the series and even Gareth Edwards was having his kicks charged down. But, just before half-time, Scotland's Ian McGeechan kicked a beautiful ball downfield and into touch a fraction short of the Springboks line. To our delight, they chose the short line-out and all that Gordon Brown had to do was to put his hands up, catch it and fall over for a crucial try. 'Broon from Troon', another man to pass away recently, was nothing more than an overgrown school kid who loved playing and simply could not believe that he was in the same team as his all-time hero, Willie-John McBride. Broony kept us laughing right through that tour and all the way up to his 'last supper' at the Grosvenor House Hotel in London a couple of years ago. He was a charming man and a heck of a rugby player who always rose to the big occasion.

At the interval, we knew that the Springboks were going to come at us hard with one last almighty effort but, with our now infamous code 99 call, we were prepared for anything that they could throw at us. If foul play broke out and one of our players was in danger, then on the call of 99, we would all rush in to defend him. This way, no player would ever be isolated and the referee would have to blow up because of all the confusion.

In Port Elizabeth the 99 call went out after a vicious attack on Bobby Windsor and a nasty brawl erupted with players from both sides throwing punches. Since I had farther to run to get there than anyone else, there was no doubt about my intentions. Today I am not particularly proud of my actions but at the time we felt it had to be done, otherwise we would have been trampled on. As I arrived, I took aim and put a player by the name of 'Moaner' van Heerden on his back. Thirty-one years later I met him on the train from London, on his way to a South Africa versus Wales match. He was going to Cardiff to present the jerseys to the Springbok players and when he saw me, he came over and said, 'Do you remember who I am?' I had to confess that I did not but he told me that he had played in that Port Elizabeth Test so we chatted away. When I got home, I was desperate to check his name in the match programme and then the penny dropped – 'Moaner' was the man I had punched in 1974. He had not mentioned it all the way from Paddington – how polite is that!

After things had settled down, JJ Williams scored another couple of tries, his second being especially satisfying for me as it involved a mismove, which I eventually came back into, handling twice before sending JJ over the line. It was a try that not only confused the Springbok defence but the television commentators as well: 'It's John Williams who passes to John Williams, who is now going to pass back to John Williams – what a try from John Williams.' Or words to that effect. That was the moment when I became JPR.

So, comfortable winners by 26–9, the series was ours. History had been made again and it seemed only right to chair Willie-John off the field because, as our leader, he deserved the greatest credit. It was typical of him to insist on being put down – he was not one to take all the glory – and he made his feelings quite clear when he gestured up to the rest of the squad sitting in the stands.

Willie-John was the old campaigner on that tour and we looked on him as our father figure. He would take himself off to lie on his bed and smoke his old pipe in his string vest. Everyone knows the story about Willie-John and the hotel manager, a classic and one of my favourites, which bears repetition. After the Third Test we had allowed our drinking to get the better of us and this had led to the rearrangement of some of the hotel furniture. The hotel manager found Willie-John and complained. 'Mr McBride, your players are running amok and causing a lot of damage.' Of course, Willie-John just calmly puffed away on his pipe. 'Are there many dead?' he enquired. When the manager returned a few minutes later to announce, 'Mr McBride, your players are getting worse – I have sent for the police,' Willie-John took another deep puff on that pipe and replied, 'Tell me, Mr Manager, how many will there be?'

We never quite played to the same standard for the remainder of the tour but we kept on winning, including victory over the mighty Natal. Many people there had been incensed that their players, and especially their captain, Tommy Bedford, had been overlooked for the Tests. I must confess, I did little to improve their mood. About halfway through the second half, when Natal were holding us extremely well, I fumbled a high ball and was bundled into touch by Bedford. I think I was annoyed with myself as much as anything but, when I felt my hair being grabbed, I really lost my cool. I lashed out at Bedford and rabbit-punched him. Then I looked around and the horror of the situation suddenly dawned on me. The spectators close by were going mad and I thought the whole crowd was going to attack me – they were shouting and screaming, and one man was beating me over the head with a stick. It was unbelievable! When the game was restarted, all kinds of objects rained down as the crowd went berserk again. Tangerines were a traditional missile for South African rugby fans but when beer cans and bottles landed on the pitch, Willie-John stepped in and gathered us in a huddle. It was really quite frightening to be out there in the firing line.

I thought that the repercussions of the crowd unrest would dominate the after-match focus but, instead, the criticism centred on me. I was described by the press as the biggest thug ever to tour South Africa and well known for my violent nature in British rugby. That seemed very unfair to me – tough, yes, but violent, no. My problems did not stop there either. Tommy Bedford's wife marched up to our table at the after-match function and accused me of all sorts of crimes. This really upset me because I had spoken to Tommy in the dressing room and he appeared to have accepted my apology. I know that I should not have hit him but, bearing in mind all that the Lions had suffered throughout the tour, I feel there was a serious loss of proportion in the treatment of me.

Even when the tour was over, during a spell of tennis coaching I undertook in Durban, the South Africans would not let the subject drop. Scilla was also working in Durban at the Addington Hospital and she received numerous threatening letters and anonymous phone calls to inform her how awful I was. People would stop her and say, 'Oh, you're JPR's wife, are you? It's surprising you haven't got a black eye!' or 'What's it like being married to a thug?' A cartoon appeared in a local newspaper, showing me punching a patient with my doctor's bag whilst making a house call. This really upset the doctors at the Addington and a group of them wrote to the paper, warning that the Medical Defence Union would sue if it happened again. The only positive thing to come out of it was that the whole furore really sorted out our true friends from the hangers on.

The Lions management were solidly behind me and demonstrated their support by making me captain for the Eastern Transvaal match. Our opposition had a reputation for violence themselves so I suppose, on the back of the Bedford incident, it was a bit provocative in return. But I thought that it was a massive vote of confidence and I was immensely proud because I was only twenty-five and, at that stage, had not led my country or even my club. I am also eternally grateful to the Lions who played under my leadership that day; there was not a single punch or trace of bad gamesmanship during the entire match. People may think that I have double standards because I was so angry when John Ashworth took to the field for the All Blacks just days after he had raked my face in the game against Bridgend. For me, it is simple: what I did to Tommy was in the open, no lasting injury was incurred and I apologised immediately. This could not be said about what Ashworth did to me.

We had now been in South Africa for nearly three months and had won every single one of our twenty-one tour matches. The twenty-second and final game was the Fourth Test in Johannesburg but, to use a tennis term, it was a dead rubber. We did not really have the right attitude and it was obvious that many of the lads were tired and already thinking of home. Rather like in the Fourth Test against the All Blacks in 1971, our approach was more about making sure we did not lose than going out in style and, once again, the result was a draw. A team's attitude can dramatically alter the outcome of a game and I was always the sort of person who could not accept a compromise – it was all or nothing with me. Having said this, I think we should have won that Test. I thought that I had put Fergus Slattery in for a try right at the end, but it was disallowed and, after ordering a five-yard scrum, the referee blew up for full-time before the ball came out. It was a controversial end to a controversial tour and we narrowly missed out on a perfect record.

Still, we had won the series and achieved exactly what we had set out to do, to beat the Springboks in their own back yard. At our farewell party it was a great honour for me to present Willie-John McBride with a silver salver from the players. It was an emotional moment – maintaining that unbeaten record right to the end had been physically and mentally exhausting. On our triumphant return home, we found that we were no longer vilified and that the political cloud hanging over us seemed to have lifted. Indeed, the squad was invited to 10 Downing Street to have dinner with the Prime Minister. It was a far cry from sneaking out of the back door at the Britannia Hotel!

The issue of apartheid was at the forefront of our minds all the time we were touring South Africa and, sadly, for many years afterwards the people of that beautiful country continued to be torn apart by racism. In 1974 I saw it for myself; a great many things disturbed me but I have never regretted going. I am older and wiser now but, given the same circumstances today, I would make the same decision and in the same manner. I would take the government's views into account but base my decision on what I thought was right as an individual. For professional rugby players, however, the position is more complicated. They also have a duty to their employer and, had I had been a professional in 1974, then I would probably have done what my employer advised.

Importantly, the Lions did play two non-white sides during the tour, the Proteas in Cape Town and the Leopards in East London. Although we saw plenty of promise, we also knew that these games were a token gesture because genuine integration was not happening at club level. We had hoped to expose South African rugby standards and, in doing so, make their sporting teams change for the better and I still believe that our presence did help to move things along in the right direction. Morgan Cushe, the black flanker who did not play against us for the Quaggas, did appear in a representative game at a later date but it was clear to me in 1974 that things would have to change very dramatically if South Africa was ever to take a full part in international sport again. The Lions returned there in 1980 and there had been little progress. Perhaps the politicians should have backed up their words by not trading with South Africa, rather than leaving it to sportsmen or women to make the big stand.

Apart from a single visit in 1989, I did not return to South Africa again until the 1995 World Cup and when I saw Nelson Mandela on the pitch with the victorious Springboks, it confirmed that apartheid had eventually been confronted. Regardless of colour, every South African was delighted for the Springboks to win the Webb Ellis Trophy that day, whereas in 1974, the black population had all supported us. When I went back in 1997 to watch the Lions tour, I was treated like a king and a hero because of what we had achieved on the field all those years ago. But in my view the real heroes were those who never got the chance to play the sport they loved merely because of the colour of their skin.

Back out to face the All Blacks after serious injury in the infamous 1978 meeting with Bridgend at the Brewery Field.

A family of doctors – my mother with Phil, Chris, Mike and me. Doctor number six, Dad, is behind the camera.

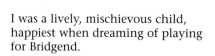

I was a lively, mischievous child, happiest when dreaming of playing for Bridgend.

Right: Dr Jack Matthews, my rugby hero, gave me my first rugby ball. I realised how good he was when I read about him after I had grown up.

Below: Trelales Primary School Under-11s rugby team. Billy Morgan, the man who persuaded me to move to full-back, is pictured top left.

We all wanted to be like Gerald Battrick, my tennis role model, seen here in 1973 at full stretch.

The 'Mighty Atom' in action.

Pro-celebrity tennis with two great players, Rod Laver (*left*) and John McEnroe (*right*), and the equally great motor-racing driver, James Hunt (*second right*).

My son Peter gets to grips with the rugby posts at an early age, with a little help from Dad.

John Dawes was the best passer of the ball in midfield that I have ever seen.

Immortal All Black captain Colin Meads is, typically, in control of the ball.

Crossing the line against England at Twickenham in 1970 for my first international try.

Gareth Edwards – simply the best of all time.

I loved to run with the ball – in action on the Lions tour to New Zealand in 1971.

Scilla and I get married, 1973 – 'flanked' by my best man, John Taylor, and Scilla's bridesmaid, her sister, Melanie.

9

DAYS OF GLORY

WALES' new coach for the 1975 season was John Dawes and his choice of Mervyn Davies as captain signalled the return to the exciting ways of the 1971 team. We topped the Championship table once again, and a defeat by Scotland was the only frustrating blemish on a more than solid season. A world record crowd of 104,000 watched us in the game at Murrayfield but I was never a great fan of playing there. It was not only because of the fervency of their supporters but the openness of the stands, which made it very difficult for a full-back to judge the flight of the ball. The wind would swirl it all over the place and that losing day was no different on that front.

The good news for Wales was that we were moulding a formidable outfit, with new stars such as JJ Williams, Steve Fenwick and Ray Gravell now part of our back line. In the pack the Pontypool front row of Charlie Faulkner, Bobby Windsor and Graham Price were on the scene too. Who will ever forget Graham's magnificent run to score the try that sealed the win at the Parc des Princes in 1975 as one of six new caps that day? Allan Martin and Geoff Wheel were becoming established second rows who complemented each other: Martin the jumper, Wheel the enforcer. We also had flankers of the quality of Tom David, Trevor Evans and Terry Cobner.

There were no egos in the squad and everybody was on the same wavelength. Above all, we were like a club side and an event in the final match against Ireland in Cardiff illustrated that perfectly. We were winning at a canter when Gareth threw a sloppy reverse pass and allowed the Irish number eight, Willie Duggan, to score a late consolation try. Merv tore a strip off Gareth but I went even further, saying, 'How dare you let them cross my line?' Gareth was a little taken aback but immediately apologised. I knew he would have no problem with me talking to him like that. He was a great – he knew it and we knew it – and great players can take honesty. I and the rest of the team had been hurt by his loss of concentration.

We all knew that what was required to become a Grand Slam team again was time to develop an unshakeable winning mentality. On tour to Japan that summer, and then against Australia later that year, we achieved our victories by establishing control in the pack and then the backs would ruthlessly kill off the opposition as they tired. John Dawes felt we still had a lot more to give and kept our feet firmly on the ground but there was a sense that 1976 was going to be another important year for Welsh rugby.

No other jersey in Welsh rugby means as much as the number ten. The brilliance of Barry John had rendered superfluous any debate about who should occupy that position but, after he retired, the selectors seemed to take their time in deciding on his regular successor. Despite some fine performances in the first couple of seasons post-BJ, Phil Bennett seemed to have slipped behind John Bevan and David Richards in the pecking order when the squad for the 1976 Five Nations was announced. The situation left me feeling uneasy. To my mind Phil was the best of the three, although I knew how very good John Bevan was, having played with him at secondary school level. As players we knew we could not select the Welsh team but there was general relief when injuries to Bevan and Richards meant that Bennett was reinstated in the side to start at Twickenham.

That match against England is sometimes referred to as JPR's match. I know that I played pretty well and scored two tries for the first time in an international – that always guarantees you the headlines – but in my view the 'heroism' was overplayed because of the blood that was streaming down my face as I went over for the second score. These days I would not even have been on the field, I would have been in the blood bin. I already had eight stitches above my right eye, a souvenir from a club game against Bath the week before, so I looked like some kind of war hero with another piece of embroidery under my left eye after the international. The problem was that the new sutures did not hold. My father was always the best at dealing with my lacerations but he had not been allowed into the Twickenham dressing room and, unfortunately, the wound kept oozing. After celebrating the victory with my family out in the West Stand car park, I had to dive into the gents to get some tissues to stem the bleeding. It took so long that the boys on the team coach thought that I had stayed with Scilla, so they gave up on me and headed off into town. Instead, I had to get a lift in Scilla's little Fiat and the blood continued to drip down my face even at the dinner.

Wales seemed to be unstoppable that season against the Home Unions and we scored over 60 points in beating Scotland and Ireland to set up a Grand Slam match against France in Cardiff. I was expecting a much closer game as the French, with an unyielding side packed with great players – Jacques Fouroux and Jean-Pierre Romeu at half-back and a back row of Jean-Claude Skrela, Jean-Pierre Rives and Jean-Pierre Bastiat – were on course for a Grand Slam of their own. It turned out to be an uncompromising match, typified by Mervyn Davies playing through the pain barrier after a stud had punctured a blood vessel in his calf muscle.

The game was reaching its tense climax when I saw the French winger, Jean-François Gourdon, sprinting determinedly towards our line. I knew that I had no margin for error; he had to be prevented from scoring to keep Wales' dream of the Grand Slam alive. I quickly considered the options and, when Gourdon was a couple of metres short, I shoulder-charged him – if I had tackled him around the legs, he would definitely have made the try. Instead, I shuddered into him and he flew into the air, the ball coming loose from his grasp. Nowadays, my challenge would be considered illegal, France would get a penalty, perhaps even a penalty try, and I would get a yellow card, but in 1976 the spectators in that corner went berserk with jubilation. I instinctively raised my arms in triumph, not because it was the final whistle but because I knew that we had in effect won the Grand Slam. Sure enough, a few minutes later, we had our prize.

I think it is pertinent that only seventeen players were used by Wales to win that Championship in 1976 and so there was a real sense of unity and purpose to drive us through the competition. Mervyn Davies was a wonderful captain and, despite his nasty leg injury, he fulfilled his skipper's duties by again leading our riotous celebrations in Cardiff. It still seems inconceivable that, less than a month later, he would be lying in hospital in the same city fighting for his life. When he collapsed with a brain haemorrhage during the Cup semi-final between Swansea and Pontypool, it shocked the whole nation, put an end to our Grand Slam euphoria and, of course, finished Merv's rugby career.

It was a terrible thing to happen. With hindsight, there had been a warning sign four years earlier when Merv had complained of feeling unwell during a game for London Welsh and had then collapsed in the showers. On that day I and my team-mate Bob Phillips, who was also a doctor, immediately recognised the seriousness of the situation, so we sent Merv straight to the local hospital in Roehampton. The tests indicated infection but, in view of what was to happen later, it was potentially the wrong diagnosis. The only positive to be gleaned from it was that at least Merv had all those extra years of rugby – he would undoubtedly have been told to stop playing had the doctors detected the possibility of a haemorrhage.

As soon as I saw the news of his collapse on the television, I remembered the previous incident at London Welsh but it was still a massive shock. I spoke to my friend Rob Leyshon, a neurosurgical registrar in Cardiff, before setting off to see Merv. I knew he was in good hands medically but it was devastating to think that he would never play rugby again. Not only had Wales lost a fine captain but so too had the 1977 Lions. The sheer quantity of work that Merv got through on a rugby field was unbelievable and, because of his enormous stamina, he never knew when he was beaten – which was not very often. Thankfully, he carried this approach through into his life in general and I am absolutely sure that is why he made such a strong recovery.

The flanker, Terry Cobner, was the new captain and he led us against a gutsy touring side from Argentina later that year. We only just managed a narrow win, courtesy of a last-minute penalty awarded for a dangerously high tackle on me. The reaction of the press to that Pumas game was to call for retirements from the senior players, including Gareth Edwards and me. How fickle! It was only six months since we had won the Grand Slam but I suppose it was just indicative of the measure of expectation that we had built up in Wales at that time.

Meanwhile, my first challenge on the long road to becoming a Fellow of the Royal College of Surgeons was to pass the notoriously difficult Primary exam. After the Lions tour, I had moved to Hillingdon Hospital but I decided to transfer back to St Mary's as an anatomy demonstrator to give me some extra experience. Unfortunately, my plan did not work and, after failing the exam for the second time, I felt down. What was I going to do with myself for the next six months until I could try again? But, as is often the case in life, good things can happen when you are at a low ebb and I saw a job advertised for a casualty officer at Battle Hospital in Reading. Suddenly everything clicked into place; medically it would give me invaluable experience, as the hospital dealt with many of the motorway accidents on the M4, and geographically it would fit in very well with my rugby too. I could still get to London Welsh but would be even closer to Wales.

I have so many incredible memories of my time in Reading but none more vivid than of my first night on call. I went in at about five o'clock, hoping for a quiet time as a young medic with opening-night nerves, but three hours later I was plunged into a drama. A boy was brought into the hospital with a head injury after a fall at Scouts. At first it seemed a fairly routine job but then he developed a bleed. One pupil was fixed and dilated and the other was starting to go, so we knew we had to operate immediately. There was no referral in those days, the nearest specialist centre was in Oxford, so we had no choice but to get the book out and perform an operation. The senior registrar and I held the instructions with one hand and operated with the other; we had to drill basic burr holes into the skull to release the pressure caused by the bleeding. This could never happen now because we would need a CT or MRI scan, with the child being transferred to the unit in Oxford and, given this scenario, there is a high likelihood that the boy would die. Instead, he walked out of the hospital after two weeks and I will never ever forget the joy on his mother's face.

Life was never dull in that busy casualty department – I always felt the name of the Battle Hospital was very apt. One Saturday evening a coach load of rowdy football fans burst in with several supporters who had been injured in a football-related fracas. The atmosphere became so menacing that I decided I had to do some-thing and, standing on a chair, I ordered those who were not in need of any treatment to get out. It says something about my reputation as a rugby hard man at the time that, having recognised me, they left rather meekly. I would never get away with that now!

Having begun my move up the M4 towards Wales, I was anxious to complete my journey and get back home after a nine-year absence and in June of 1976, I finally passed the Primary exam to become a senior house officer in the surgery department at the University Hospital of Wales in Cardiff. I was determined to do well in my new post; a lot of people had applied for the job and I did not want anyone to think that I had got it only because I was a well-known rugby player. This was the other side of the coin – although rugby undoubtedly opened doors for me, it could sometimes get in the way when I was trying to prove myself as a doctor.

It was good to be back in Wales. I started to play for Bridgend again and my involvement with the Welsh national side was far more straightforward than when I had been living as an 'exile' in London. Life at the hospital in the operating theatre and on the wards was interesting too, but doubly busy, as I often had to make two ward rounds, a working round and then an autograph round afterwards.

Until our new home at Llansannor was ready to move into, Scilla and I lived in hospital accommodation at East Glamorgan Hospital where she was working in the paediatric department. It was a strange house and, because of its deficiencies, we lived almost exclusively in the upstairs bedroom. On Sunday afternoons, we would close the curtains and settle down to watch *Rugby Special*. I am sure that our neighbours thought we were newly married! After these odd arrangements, it was rather a relief when we finally moved to the Vale of Glamorgan in November 1976 and we have lived there ever since.

The club game has been the heartbeat of my rugby life. As a player, I felt honoured to wear the colours of St Mary's, London Welsh, Bridgend and, in my twilight years, Tondu. Later, as president of Bridgend and as manager of Tondu and then the doomed Celtic Warriors, I experienced the club game from another angle. After nearly five decades of involvement, I have an unbreakable bond with the Welsh clubs. I try not to sound like a relic from the past, saying, 'It was better in my day,' but on this issue, I firmly believe that it was. Nothing in rugby has made me sadder than the demise of the Welsh club system.

In Wales, we had the strongest tradition of club rugby in the world. The name of its rugby club identified that town or city, putting it on the map and creating a focus for the people. For instance, Llanelli is a relatively small Welsh town but it is known the world over because of the rugby club. The traditional big four were Cardiff, Llanelli, Newport and Swansea, with a host of other clubs constantly vying for a place on that pedestal. Each team seemed to have its own personality. Llanelli were well known as a running side but then so were Bridgend and we loved to show them that they were not the only ones who could score tries. In complete contrast, Pontypool was a forward-dominated club and, for a while, this style took them and their players to the top. I know that some people criticised the clubs for being parochial but I strongly believe that, over the years, this was Welsh rugby's great strength and not its weakness.

I returned to Wales in 1976 a very different person from the one who had left nine years before. Although I was now a senior house officer at the University Hospital of Wales and an established Welsh rugby international, one thing had not changed – I still wanted to play for Bridgend. By going back to what I already knew I suppose I was leaving myself open to accusations of being boring but I did not care. I knew how I felt. I never once considered any other Welsh club.

I knew what to expect at Bridgend but the players were not quite so sure what to expect from me. It was easier with the older team members who already knew me from my previous spell there, and soon I was back in the thick of it, with them taking the mickey out of their new 'star'. Some of the younger players were a little more wary; perhaps they thought that I was going to try to pull rank. I hope they soon realised that this was very far from the truth. I know that I was probably always a bit arrogant on the field but, off the pitch, I was quite retiring.

Despite being back in the town of my birth, it was like starting from scratch again. I knew the best way to win everyone's trust at the club was through my rugby but, unfortunately, my first match back against Saracens turned out to be something of a disaster. Playing with a Welsh club in London on a weekend away from home with the attraction of the bright lights was totally different from playing against them for London Welsh. With the exiles, I had never had much difficulty in beating Saracens but, playing for Bridgend, we lost and, rather unfairly I thought, the critics heaped much of the blame on my shoulders.

After that initial setback, we settled down as a team. The squad accepted me and I began to make a valuable contribution both on and off the rugby field – for a start, my presence was adding between 500 and 1,000 spectators to the gate. It meant a great deal to be back at 'my' club and when, in May 1978, the chance to be Bridgend team captain for their 1978–79 centenary season came up, I was incredibly excited. To captain Bridgend at such an important time was something I wanted to do very badly.

On the medical front, my last stepping stone to the final FRCS exams was a three-year surgical registrar rotation job at the hospital in Cardiff, starting in July 1977. Although it was the ideal position for me, it fell at the wrong time, clashing badly with the Lions tour to New Zealand and so, after much deliberation, I had no choice but to rule myself out of the trip. I had been very lucky up until then as I had already been on two Lions tours but this time there was no way around the clash between my medicine and the rugby. There was also a new pull on my conscience – our first daughter, Lauren, had just been born and our new family simply could not take four months with me on unpaid leave.

Phil Bennett took over the captaincy for the 1977 Five Nations when a defeat in Paris cost us another Grand Slam. France were the one European side who could live with us then and the destination of the Grand Slam seemed to depend on who was at home when the two nations met. The relative importance of the Grand Slam had been growing throughout the decade, something that I feel was largely down to those epic matches between ourselves and the French. The 1977 season finished with a Triple Crown at Murrayfield when Phil Bennett scored what BBC commentator Bill McLaren described as 'the try of the Championship'. The move started well inside our half and Phil finished it off underneath the Scottish posts by falling in exhaustion and turning to look in triumph at his equally tired but victorious team.

Wales were desperate to wrestle power back from the French and, as in our two previous Grand Slams seasons, we set off with victory over England in 1978. The Twickenham weather was dreadful but Gareth Edwards had a great game, killing the English forwards with his expert kicking. Despite my excellent record against the English, I never particularly liked playing at Twickenham because the grass was kept so long then – it was like running through a field and especially so on that damp day.

The poor weather also played a part in our next match against Scotland in Cardiff. It was freezing this time but, considering the conditions, there was plenty of attacking intent from both countries. Scotland had some great players and in the centre was Jim Renwick, one of the most underrated players of the decade, although I could never understand a word he said in his strong Hawick accent! We won but, by the time we got to the dinner in the evening, the snow was coming down fast. The following day, with traffic at a virtual standstill, the Welsh players were advised that it was too risky to set off for home in the blizzard; instead we were to stay put and sit it out at the Angel Hotel. There were no complaints as it was just like being on tour – but in Cardiff, with my wife. We knew that our baby-sitters were in for a long night but nobody had realised quite how long! Many of us were marooned for several days and Scilla and I only made it home after hiking the last two miles over fields as the lanes around Llansannor were still impassable with ten feet of drifted snow. The irony was that the Scottish players, who had so much farther to travel, had reached home on the day after the game – the eastbound M4 had suffered from very little snow – but we could not manage even a few miles.

We went to Dublin with the chance for the Triple Crown now firmly fixed in our minds. Ireland had the same ambition and, at Lansdowne Road, they had a distinct advantage – it was one of the most hostile grounds that I ever experienced. If anything, the crowd was more uptight for that Triple Crown decider than any other game I could remember and the atmosphere reached boiling point when I dumped Ireland's star player, Mike Gibson, on the floor. Mike had chipped the ball over my head and, as I thought he was bound to score, I decided to obstruct him.

Georges Domercq, the French referee, should really have awarded a penalty try so, when nothing came, the Irish crowd went mad and I have to confess that I thought I was going to be lynched on the spot. A continual stream of abuse was directed at me for the remainder of the game and, when I miskicked on my line to allow Ireland in to score and draw level at 13–13, I was almost certain that it was not going to be my day, or Wales' either for that matter. Luckily, I was wrong as JJ Williams scored a winning try for us, albeit with a hint of obstruction in midfield, which did little to dampen the Irish rage.

I felt dreadful about what had happened with Mike, especially as it had involved such a great player and a good mate of mine. As soon as the game finished, I made sure that I went straight into the Irish dressing room to apologise and we sorted it out in a friendly way. The press were less forgiving and, when I talked about it to them later, I admitted to committing what was perhaps rugby's first high-profile professional foul, if that was possible in the amateur era. Even if it was not 'professional', it was premeditated – that I do know. Perhaps I should not have let myself become more embroiled in the furore by saying things that fanned the flames but I was only giving an honest answer to a direct question.

Even now, when I go back to Ireland, people are keen to talk about the incident. My reply is always that there are very few players, whatever the times, who do not realise when defending that three points conceded is better than a try and a conversion. This is not to say that I do not regret my actions. This incident, along with the punch on Tommy Bedford during the 1974 Lions tour, are the two instances in my career when I did not act honourably on a rugby field and I still feel guilty about them. If anything, the Mike Gibson foul was much worse because I was not acting in retaliation as was the case in Durban.

The upshot of the controversial win in Ireland was that, once again, we had the chance of a Grand Slam and, once again, so did France – but we would be playing in front of our own fans in Cardiff. Although the match had all the makings of an epic and the crowd was fully charged, I thought that this one turned out to be rather an anticlimax as, once we got ahead, the French seemed to lose heart. It was our third Grand Slam of the 1970s and, as they are never easy to win, securing three in the space of only eight years was a substantial achievement for the whole of the team. What we did not realise at the time was just how our success would stand out in the years that followed.

Phil Bennett scored two tries in that match, his last appearance for Wales, and with Gareth Edwards retiring after that game too there was talk in the media of me starting to be the old man of the side. It was now ten years since my first tour with Wales and, because I had started in international rugby so young, I think a lot of people were under the impression I was well into my thirties instead of being only twenty-nine. I certainly felt that I still had a lot to offer. The tour to Australia that summer would be a great opportunity to unearth a new breed of talent and I wanted to be an integral part of that process.

In spite of my enthusiasm for the sport, that trip turned out to be one of the most deflating of my career and I was forced to confront the fact that some in the game were simply not fit to uphold rugby's moral code. For the First Test in Brisbane, we were offered the services of an Australian referee, Mr Burnett. There was nothing unusual in that as home-based officials were the norm in those days but it was customary for the visiting side to be given the choice of three or four names. We immediately smelt a rat when only one name was put forward, especially as Burnett had not endeared himself to us when he wore Queensland socks to referee our match against Queensland earlier in the tour! During the game, the Queenslander had also made his allegiance quite clear. When, at one scrum, Burnett ordered, 'Our put in, not yours,' we knew we were in for trouble. He took pleasure in smiling when he penalised us, which happened fairly frequently and, when we lost, I remember feeling wrung out by the whole shoddy experience.

By the time the Second Test in Sydney came around, the lack of protection from the Australian officials had contributed to serious injury problems for the Welsh squad. The upshot was that I was asked to play on the flank and, despite the circumstances, I rather enjoyed my role in the back row. After all, I had been rushing in, hitting rucks for years and the rest of the lads knew how delighted I was to be at last amongst the pack for real. That Welsh number seven jersey is one of my favourites, whilst playing that game gave me a foretaste of where my future lay at St Mary's B and Tondu after my international days were over.

Our injury problems continued to mount during this match and we actually ran out of substitutes and had to finish with only thirteen men on the field. Shamefully, not all of those injuries seemed to be accidents. When the Australian prop, Steve Finnane, broke Graham Price's jaw, it appeared to us that he had just decided Graham was too good for him. I thought it was a disgrace, an act of pure violence. If this was not bad enough, our troubles were compounded when the Australian fly-half, Paul McLean, was awarded a drop-goal even though it obviously went wide of the posts. The officials' mistake was confirmed to us after the game by some apologetic Australian photographers who had perfectly captured the miss on film. Considering all that was stacked against us, I think we did well to lose by only 2 points.

I found the whole experience incredibly dispiriting. Although we were not blameless at times, it was the Australians' desperate attempt to achieve a better status in the world game that had led certain individuals to act in this way. Gamesmanship or, less politely, cheating was creeping into the game more and more, but if I had hoped to have seen the last of it when I left Australia, I was to be sadly mistaken.

10

THE UNACCEPTABLE FACE

I N the autumn of 1978 New Zealand came on tour to Britain and
Ireland and it prompted us to speculate that, in the year of our
Grand Slam-winning team, perhaps this would be the time for
Wales to beat the All Blacks. But who would lead the Welsh against
them? My room-mate for the last ten years, Gerald Davies, had
called it a day after the Australian tour and, with Phil Bennet and
Gareth Edwards gone, it was obvious that I was in with a chance of
captaining Wales for the first time. I knew that, to some extent, I
would have been made captain by default but I would have been
pretty upset had I not been given it. I was skipper of Bridgend at the
time and, when the press informed me of my appointment, I think
it did come as something of a relief.

It was not just a new captain that gave Wales a fresh look. The
Cardiff half-backs, Terry Holmes and Gareth Davies, stepped up, as
they had in the Second Test in Sydney a few months earlier. As
captain I felt it was vital to remind them of all the good work that
had been done on tour and to insist that they forget about who
they were replacing and play their own game. To their immense
credit, they did just that and, 12–4 ahead at the start of the second
half, a famous win seemed within our grasp.

New Zealand had eroded that lead to only two points when, with
a few minutes to go, a line-out was called inside our half. There had
been barging at just about every line-out that afternoon but for
some reason the English referee, Roger Quittenton, suddenly saw fit
to blow the whistle and award the All Blacks a penalty. At full-back,

I was not in the greatest position from which to argue but I could tell that my forwards were mystified. Brian McKechnie strode up and, sure enough, sent the ball through the posts to give the All Blacks a one-point victory.

There was no live television interview for the captain in those days when, no doubt, I would have been shown a replay of the incident, so I had to wait until the next day to see the match footage. When I did, I could not believe it. The All-Black lock, Andy Haden, had clearly 'fallen' out of the line-out by faking a push. The more I watched it, the more farcical it looked – it was not even a good pretence. Roger Quittenton had been conned and his sub-sequent reasoning that he had penalised Geoff Wheel for barging into Haden's fellow lock, Frank Oliver, smacked to me of a cover up. Oliver did not even try to win the ball and, as the others fell away, poor Geoff found all of his support gone and merely put his arm across to try to balance. What made it even more disappointing was that a week after the match a patient of my father's told him that he had seen the All Blacks practising this trick at their base in Porth-cawl in the run-up to the Test. If that's true, I wish I had known it at the time – we would not have contested the line-out and would simply have given them the ball!

I last saw Roger Quittenton in 2003 and, understandably I suppose, he was not keen to talk about the incident when I tried to broach the subject with him. The image of that line-out still haunts me and whenever I see it or read about it, I know there is a lot of upset there. It was the day when Wales should have beaten New Zealand. Although I admit that to a certain extent it was our own fault we lost – we were the better team and should have put New Zealand away long before Haden's infamous dive.

If I could not lead Wales to victory over the All Blacks at Cardiff, at least I would have the opportunity to have another crack at them at the Brewery Field. Bridgend's centenary year was to be celebrated with a series of special rugby matches, none more significant than the fixture against New Zealand in November 1978 – the biggest game in the club's history. It was to be the first visit of a major touring side and our chairman, Gerwyn Rowlands, talked of a dream at last being realised.

I had only been made club captain that season – just ahead of being given the Welsh captaincy – and the Bridgend appointment had certainly not been a foregone conclusion. The other candidate was Meredydd James, the prop, who had been playing for Bridgend for some time and, even though I had been back in Wales for a while, Meredydd knew much more about the current players than I did. It was also a little awkward that my father was president of the club and I was aware that others might view the outcome as 'fixed'. But at Bridgend the players picked the captain and, after a nerve-wracking wait and a close count, I was thrilled to learn that I had been chosen.

I think that I was a pretty successful skipper. The Bridgend captaincy was a very 'hands on' position and I was often involved in selection matters and club politics. When it came to tactics on the field, however, I let my fly-half run the game, along with the inside centre who at that time was Steve Fenwick – a great man to have in your side. The pack leader was in charge of the forwards and I just held a watching brief from full-back.

I had always had strong views about having the right psychological approach to sport and now I had a chance to make a real difference to how the team played. My style was to calm players down before a game, to avoid them getting too worked up when they ran onto the field. I wanted them to think about their contribution and their opponent in a rational way. Going mad before a match is counter-productive because it leads to a loss of discipline and therefore penalties. I was always quick to rush in to sort out any flare-ups and my team-mates knew that I would try to see everything that was happening on the floor and that, if the referee did not spot something, I would make it my business to tell the player. However, the biggest test of my leadership skills and one of the most unpleasant moments of my rugby life was just around the corner.

Despite a notorious defeat by Munster in Limerick, New Zealand had gone through the rest of their tour unbeaten, winning the Grand Slam for the first time by beating all four Home Unions. In Wales, Cardiff, West Wales and Monmouthshire had also tried to lower the Kiwis' colours and failed. I had captained the national side in the Test defeat and, although I had seen more entertaining All Black teams, these tourists were proving as hard to beat as any of their predecessors. The build-up to Bridgend versus New Zealand began days before the tourists arrived. The whole town was decked out in the club colours of blue and white and, even at the hospital in Cardiff, all those miles away, there was a sense of excitement. It was as if we had the whole Welsh nation behind us.

Of course, there was tremendous competition among the squad to be in the team. We were scheduled to play at Neath five days before the New Zealand game and I remember being very worried in case any of our players should be injured in the appalling winter weather that was sweeping the country. In the event, I was the only person to suffer an injury on the sodden pitch and had a real battle to get myself fit in time. Incredibly, the terrible weather actually worsened as match day approached and it threatened to ruin the occasion. All pitches in South Wales had been turned into quagmires and at one point our ground had been under water. It was a blow to us because we wanted to run the ball but we were a good club side and we still felt that we were in with a fair chance, given that the pitch had drained well.

As 11,000 fans streamed into our modest ground at the Brewery Field, there was a feeling the like of which I had never previously experienced, a mixture of bursting pride and massive anticipation. Graham Mourie, the great New Zealand flanker, led his team in the Haka just before the kick-off. I have always loved the Haka and I can never understand why people get so worked up about it. It is just a challenge to the opposition and all a player has to do is respect it. If you react to it or are confrontational, then you play into the All Blacks' hands, so I had carefully thought out our response in advance – we just clapped politely and, I felt, defused it completely.

Bridgend set off at a tremendous rate and soon had a chance for an easy goal, which would have been a great psychological bonus for us. I first asked Steve Fenwick to kick it, knowing his excellent big-match temperament, but our outside-half, Ian Williams, wanted to take it instead. As Williams had really only been selected because of his kicking, Steve persuaded me this was the way we should go but Ian missed that kick and, ever since, I have regretted not sticking to my guns.

At this stage, the game had been a hard-fought but, in my mind, fair contest. Afterwards, some people claimed that Bridgend had been over-hyped and had been looking for provocation, whilst the All Blacks accused us of all manner of foul play – kneeing and punching in the scrum and late tackling. Certainly, my usual captain's request for coolness on the field had been stretched to the limit but I still believe that my players were there to play rugby, not to look for violence.

It was the New Zealanders who changed the nature of the game into something more sinister. With the score still 0–0, a ruck formed and the All Blacks won the ball on the opposite side from where I was lying on the floor, pinned down with my head sticking out. The ball was some yards away when I felt the first kick to my face. This blow did not do much damage but then a second kick came in and I knew immediately that it was going to be bad – I could feel the studs near my right eye and then my cheek bone clunked but held firm. Luckily for me, I had broken it before and the callus that had formed had made it stronger than normal. Then, I felt the studs move down to my upper jaw, shooting my gum shield out. My teeth stayed intact but something had to give and, suddenly, I was aware of a gaping hole in my cheek, all the way through to my tongue. It was a horrible feeling.

The referee, Laurie Prideaux, did not seem to react but I knew instantly that I had to get off the field as quickly as possible. Blood was pouring out of my face at a terrific rate and, when I got to the medical room, it was far worse than I could have imagined. One of the branches of the facial artery was severed and, in the end, I lost about two pints of blood. Of course, I was being treated by not just any old medic, as my father was not only the club president, he was also the club doctor. Despite the distress he must have felt at seeing me like that, I suppose he went into professional mode and I remember he was very calm. Thirty stitches were required to mend the wound. Dad stitched from the outside and a local dentist stitched from the inside with my brothers assisting where possible.

Medically, I probably should not have gone back onto the field of play; I was feeling light-headed and my face was starting to swell badly but I knew how much my team-mates relied on me and, in my mind, the best way of getting my own back was by scoring some points. Dad was of the same mind. After he had finished patching me up, he told me, 'Get out there,' in opposition to my brothers who were trying in vain to dissuade me. The other players were amazed when I returned – I must have looked dreadful. I had worked out from the crowd noise that the All Blacks had scored; in fact, they had taken a 7–0 lead in my absence but we managed to pull it back and trailed only 10–6 at half-time. We felt that, despite my injury and the terrible conditions, we were still in with a chance of a famous win.

Unluckily for us, the wind blew up into a howling gale during the second half and, even though we tried our hardest, we found it too difficult to get out of our territory. We conceded a silly try near the end and lost 17–6. The final whistle seemed rather an anticlimax but the crowd, who had vociferously voiced their displeasure at my injury throughout the game, gave us a rousing send-off. It was as if we had won, which I suppose we had in a sense; we were the moral winners, leaving the field with our honour intact.

Not having seen the incident, I thought that it might just have been an accident but I was disappointed that not one person from the All Black squad had apologised or even asked me how my face was. Regardless, I was gracious to the New Zealanders in my captain's speech at the after-match dinner and congratulated them on their victory. As I spoke, though, blood started to run down my face again and I had to pause to wipe it away.

At this point, my father, who had been getting increasingly upset, came forward to make an impromptu address to the gathering. He directed his words at the All Blacks' manager, Russ Thomas, and his captain, Graham Mourie. 'I know you won't have anything to do it with it, Russ, or you, Graham, but there are one or two members of your party I wouldn't wish to associate with. Being hammered when the ball is nowhere near should not be part of any game of rugby . . . I rather pushed all my four sons into rugby but I don't think that I would do that again after today's experience.'

When they heard this, about ten of the New Zealand squad walked out of the dinner. Although I was reported as leaving the reception as well, I actually stayed for a drink with the remaining All Black players and my overriding feeling was that I hoped the whole sorry business could just be forgotten. When I saw the television news footage the next day, my mood changed. The pictures made me feel sick. It was abundantly clear to me that the All Black prop, John Ashworth, had raked me once and then come back for a second go when he saw who it was on the floor. I realised then that, even if I had wanted the incident to be closed, it was not going to go away.

There was great pressure for me to speak out as journalists camped out at the end of my driveway. At first, I felt that, as the evidence was irrefutable, I did not need to say anything – John Ashworth's actions had been plain for all to see. Then the Director of Public Prosecutions got in touch to see if I wanted to press charges. I wrestled with my conscience for a few days – many people thought that I should take a stand and make it a test case – but I still felt that somehow it would besmirch the game and that, as an amateur player, it would not be appropriate. I still do not know if I was right or wrong but, in the end, I resisted the pressure to prosecute.

The newspaper headlines that week were incredible, even by modern-day standards – 'The Face of Rugby at War' (*Daily Mail*), 'Black Villainy' (*Daily Express*) – and, in the midst of such a media furore, I did say some things that I now regret. I was quoted as saying that I would probably retire at the end of the season because, if rugby had deteriorated to this point, there was no more fun in playing. I said that I did not want to play against the All Blacks ever again and added that, if I had a son, then I doubted whether I would let him play rugby. Emotions were running very high. My father had calmed down a little but, when he was interviewed by the newspapers, he said that in his view I was lucky not to have been blinded, which was perfectly true. He also felt that the All Blacks had been receiving unwarranted protection from British referees on the tour. It certainly seemed to me that John Ashworth should have been sent off at the very least.

Despite the fuss, all I really wanted was an apology and an assurance from the All Blacks that Ashworth would play no part in the one remaining match on the tour, the game against the Barbarians in Cardiff, set for the Saturday after the mid-week Bridgend game. Again, I was destined to be disappointed by them. I could not believe my eyes when I saw Ashworth come on as a substitute against the Barbarians. It was truly a kick in the teeth for Bridgend, Wales, Great Britain and rugby in general, and it hurt more than the stamping and the stitches in my mouth. When the Arms Park crowd booed him as he ran onto the field, Ashworth just lifted up his arms triumphantly in a gesture of defiance, as if to say, 'Yes, I did it to JPR but there's nothing anyone can do about it.'

In my mind, the episode in Cardiff made the management as guilty as their player and, after all the complimentary things I had said about them, I felt incredibly let down. They had either chosen to ignore the incident or condone it. During their tour the All Blacks had made speeches about how they wanted to play rugby football so their sons and other youngsters would want to take up the game, but I am afraid that they lost a lot of credibility in my eyes and those of many others. In the end Graham Mourie was the only member of the squad who ever apologised to me. He wrote to me just before his team flew back home and I have always respected him for it. We are still friends today. My face healed up well but I was left with a huge scar down my right cheek, something that looked more like a duelling injury from days gone by.

Now, if I was not to captain a win over New Zealand in a red shirt or the blue and white, then I could at least try to lead Wales to another Grand Slam in the 1979 Five Nations. After we started with a win at Murrayfield, all things seemed possible. It had been ten years since my debut on that ground and the public discussion of my kicking skills, so it was rather satisfying to show that there was life in the old boot yet as I kicked through for our new cap, the winger Elgan Rees, to score. But the forwards won that game for us, as they did against Ireland a fortnight later on the occasion of my fiftieth cap. My Grand Slam ambitions were ended in Paris, though, when we lost by a point. It was so annoying, New Zealand and now France had beaten us by the narrowest of margins and stood in the way of what would have been the perfect season for Wales. We were left with the consolation of a Triple Crown match against England.

I had decided that this final game in the 1979 Championship would be my last for my country. The decision to retire was based on how busy my life had now become, with my advancing medical career and a young family to support, but a separate and more sinister matter was overshadowing my departure. During the course of that season, I had been writing my first book and a journalist, John Reason from the *Daily Telegraph*, was convinced that I must have breached my amateur status in doing so. Of course I knew that my former Welsh team-mates, Gareth Edwards, Phil Bennett and Mervyn Davies, had all been professionalised through writing autobiographies and working in the media and I was only too well aware that, if I took any money from my project, I would join their ranks. Sitting in our stone cottage in Llansannor, it was time for Scilla and me to make a decision that would determine the future direction of our lives.

In those days, rugby union players walked on eggshells; there was no halfway house between amateurism and professionalism. You could lose your amateur standing if you worked in journalism or were paid for coaching and, once that had happened, any formal involvement with a rugby union club as a player, coach or even fixtures secretary was over. In such uncompromising circumstances, there was not really that much for us to discuss. Scilla knew very well what rugby union meant to me.

I knew that I would have to proceed very carefully to avoid jeopardising my precious amateur status. The first step was to ensure that I received no money from the sales of my book and, to start with, the publishers could not understand why I did not want to take part in the nationwide promotional tour or why I was so uninterested in their sales predictions. Once I had told them about my intentions for the money, however, they fully supported my decision.

The book proceeds were to be used to set up the Bridgend Sports Injury Clinic Foundation to promote preventative schemes for avoiding injury. With my medical background and a collection of nasty rugby injuries myself, it was very close to my heart and the prospect of putting something back into the sport was exciting. The three members of the Trust were myself, Gerwyn Rowlands, the chairman of Bridgend RFC, and Cadfan Davies, the deputy director of the National Sports Council. Gerwyn and Cadfan were stalwarts of the Bridgend club, men whom I respected and trusted implicitly to organise the transfer of the funds. Setting up the Trust was far from straightforward and the intricate paperwork and legal correspondence was beyond my scope. The other two trustees did a fantastic job liaising with the Charities Commission and Ken Harris who, in particular, dealt with all the legalities. Once I had signed the affidavit promising to release the money from the sale of the book, I left it to them and the Charities Commission.

The only problem was that such a complicated process took time and people obviously thought that this gave them licence to gossip. John Reason's allegations were widely reported, although some newspapers were more careful about what they said than others.

It was a serious problem and, understandably, the situation caused grave concern amongst the Welsh hierarchy. On 28 February, less than three weeks before the crucial Triple Crown game, I was summoned to attend a committee meeting at the Welsh Rugby Union. I knew that I had done absolutely nothing that might alter my amateur status but it was clear that I would have to discuss it with Bill Clement, the secretary of the WRU. The day before that meeting I remember a visit from a legal friend at London Welsh who advised me, rather worryingly, that, for a rugby player, I was in uncharted territory – but I also knew I was in the right.

Going into the committee room at the Cardiff Arms Park felt just like taking the viva exams at medical school but, this time, I was, rather surreally, captain of Wales and in the middle of the WRU offices. Convincing Bill Clement of my position took no time. I explained that I had not received any advance from the publishers and that all royalties would go to establishing the Sports Injury Clinic Foundation I was going to set up in Bridgend, and this would protect my amateur status for as long as I wanted to continue playing at whatever level. My intention to play on after eventual international retirement was the bit the WRU found hardest to believe. To my great relief, I was completely exonerated and so, when I left, all that was on my mind was swapping rotas with my fellow medics so I could concentrate on getting ready for the last big game.

When I walked out of the meeting, however, I received a phone call from the University Hospital to tell me that Scilla had been admitted to the antenatal ward and was in early labour – I am sure the anxious events of the previous few days had had a lot to do with the unexpected onset of our second daughter's birth. Thankfully, things went smoothly and Annie was born on the next day – 1 March – managing to do what her father could not and come into the world on St David's Day!

I arrived just too late for the actual birth because I had been in the middle of an appendix operation at the East Glamorgan Hospital but, when I got there, the midwife wrapped Annie up and handed her to me. Those precious moments in the delivery room, looking at her mass of dark spiky hair, put all my problems into perspective but, outside the confines of the hospital, the question marks surrounding my amateur status did not recede and I was becoming increasingly fed up with the slurs on my character.

I decided that enough was enough. I had had a gutful of the innuendo in the newspapers and, having been given the all clear to play by the WRU, I took my lawyer's advice and sued for libel. I realise now that when the majority of people threaten to sue to clear their names they do not go through with it but I have never been like that – backing down from things when they get difficult has never been my style. It was not just that; as Welsh captain, I felt it was necessary to go to court to defend not only myself but the name of Welsh rugby and the sport in general. Having made a stand, I was content to let the lawyers get on with it, whilst I played rugby for Wales for one final time.

Against England, that script did not quite go according to plan either and, after sixty minutes, I was carried off the field. I could not walk because of a badly gashed calf muscle, the result of an accidental stray stud. I would have given anything to have completed the match but it was touching to be recognised by the players and the crowd who gave me a standing ovation. Somehow it felt appropriate that my wound was attended to by Dr Jack Matthews, the same man who had given me my first rugby ball as a little boy. My leaving the field seemed to unleash the Welsh team and England capitulated in the face of the onslaught that followed. It was as if my fellow players had been affected by all the publicity surrounding my retirement and wanted to get on and play with me out of the way. As I watched admiringly from the stand, Wales won 27–3, our biggest win over the English since 1905.

It should have been a triumphant final night but, instead of partying with the rest of the team, I had to retire to my room by nine o'clock because my leg was so painful and swollen. Being stuck in the hotel with a crying newborn baby was not what Scilla and I had intended to mark the end of my international career and, to cap it all, I had to do an interview with the French newspaper, L'Equipe, in the bathroom because it was the only place to find peace and quiet! My leg had been seriously infected by the Arms Park mud and the wound broke down a number of times. Eventually, the thing that did the trick was the famous 'Eusol' (Edinburgh Universal Solution) – a sort of bleach used in Edinburgh, the birthplace of antisepsis – but I still have a huge scar to serve as a memento of that stressful time.

11

BREWERY FIELD
SPECTACULARS

W ITH international duties behind me, I could concentrate on captaining Bridgend to our first-ever Schweppes Welsh Cup final in April 1979. As I intended to retire from rugby completely at the end of the season, I desperately wanted to go out with a trophy.

First though, we had to win the important semi-final against Llanelli. Eleven thousand fans travelled over to the neutral venue in Swansea to see Bridgend win and set up a Cup final in Cardiff against our equally well supported neighbours, Pontypridd. It makes me very sad to look back at those days and think how support for clubs such as Bridgend and Pontypridd has diminished over the years. We used to have traditional Easter Monday matches at Pontypridd when both sets of supporters met up for wonderful afternoons out. Many Bridgend people had moved down to the coast or the Vale from the Rhondda Valleys and there was a general feeling that Bridgend and Pontypridd had more in common with each other than Bridgend had with Cardiff, Llanelli or Aberavon.

With so much local honour at stake, it was an eagerly awaited final between two proud historic rivals. Bridgend were confident but I wondered whether it would be a close game, as, earlier in the season, Pontypridd had beaten us twice, one of the wins being their first at the Brewery Field in seventeen years. I need not have worried. In the Cup final, the Bridgend pack dominated proceedings, just as they had done in the semi-final, and the Pontypridd captain, Tom David, was forced to admit afterwards that his forwards had been outplayed. Steve Fenwick played a blinder and scored 15 points to give Bridgend an 18–12 victory.

What a way to celebrate the end of Bridgend's centenary season! Lifting the Schweppes Cup at the Cardiff Arms Park was one of the highlights of my career. The added twist for me was that my father had been to Pontypridd Grammar School, so it was extra special to be able to lift the trophy for Bridgend. Hundreds and hundreds of people were waiting for the team bus when we got back to the town that evening and we partied long into the night. I thought it really was the perfect climax to my rugby career.

For a while after my retirement I was quite content to throw my sporting energies back into tennis and squash but old habits die hard and, by the end of my first year away from rugby, I knew that it would take very little to entice me back. I had simply not appreciated what a big part the sport had played in my life and I needed to be on the field again. Bridgend were defending their Schweppes Welsh Cup title and the new captain, Meredydd James, persuaded me to return for the 1980 final. After proving my fitness in a match against Cross Keys, I made my return to the Arms Park where we beat Swansea 15–9, the experience being made even more special by the presence of my brother Chris on the wing.

In the spring of 1980 I presented myself for another serious encounter in Edinburgh, not at Murrayfield this time but at the Royal College of Surgeons for the tough final Fellowship exams, which enabled me to swap the title of Dr Williams for Mr Williams FRCS – a pretty hefty achievement for me as I was never considered to be that bright compared to the other aspiring medics in the early days at St Mary's. I am certain that I only passed because I believed that I could, an attitude of mind that I have carried into many aspects of my life. I am incredibly proud of my medical achievements because I had to work so much harder for them than I did at rugby, which always came more naturally to me. In my post-exam euphoria, I needed more than the letters after my name as a souvenir of my time in Edinburgh, so I brought home two lovely little kilts for Lauren and Annie. The girls wore and wore these, even when they started nursery school, and they became a kind of trademark for them. A Welsh rugby international dressing his daughters in Scottish male national dress might have seemed strange to some but I have always had a lot to thank Edinburgh for.

By now I was realising that announcing my international retirement at the end of the 1979 season was not the most measured decision that I had ever taken, and after my return for Bridgend an idea was germinating – what about an international return for Wales in the autumn? Not just that, as the All Blacks were due, could I get back for one last crack at them? During the summer, I trained in the grounds of the Rhydlafar Hospital as hard as I had ever done – I knew that, at my age, I would have to do far more than before to keep in shape.

Not everyone shared my optimism over a recall, however, and there was still a great deal of controversy over my book. My libel case was still waiting to come up, but at least the WRU was totally satisfied that all the money from the sales had gone to setting up the Bridgend Sports Injury Clinic Foundation that I had created to be the beneficiary. I managed to put this out of my mind because I was far more concerned about whether I would be called up for the game against the All Blacks. Never before during my previous fifty-two caps had I felt so uncertain over a squad announcement but I was sure that if only I could train with Wales, I would be able to convince the selectors that I was serious about this new challenge. When I heard the news of my inclusion, I was as delighted as the day when I learnt I was to win my first cap.

My enthusiasm took a knock when I turned up to training to find a shocking standard of fitness in the squad. In my view, only Terry Holmes and I were international-match fit and I became severely concerned over our chances of success. When it came to the day of my return, there was none of the drama that had hung over my last appearance at the Arms Park for the England game a year and a half earlier. Instead, I was just glad to be there, living out a sort of *Boy's Own* dream. I was kept busy in defence but the opportunities to attack the All Blacks were rare and, at the end, I felt strangely distanced from the defeat. I think I had known deep down that we did not have a chance and, although I was pleased with my own performance, I was extremely unhappy with the way the team had played. Had it not been for myself, Terry Holmes and the nineteen-year-old debutant Robert Ackerman, we would have lost by 50 points.

The WRU clearly had the same thoughts as I did and, in response to the poor performance, a letter was sent to the players demanding higher levels of fitness. Wales had regressed badly in the two years since that last narrow defeat by the All Blacks and the spirit of the team was a total contrast to the sides that I had been involved in. I felt that the media and the public were quite right to be depressed but I had not returned for a one-off game and I wanted to be part of another Five Nations Championship in the New Year. I was encouraged by the way my body felt and it was as if I had never retired. I was relishing the next game against England, the new Grand Slam champions.

The English had beaten Wales in 1980 when our flanker Paul Ringer had been sent off in what could best be described as a battle, not a game of rugby. Watching from the stands, it had been the most horrible atmosphere that I had experienced at Twickenham and there were suggestions that the match in Cardiff was going to be no different.

My return for the England game inevitably created a talking point. I had not been on a losing side against them in ten previous internationals and I was quite comfortable to answer questions on the subject because I genuinely felt that this fact played on the minds of the English players. Back in the 1970s, I was convinced that some opponents would stand off me and not tackle because of my hard-man reputation. Presence does count for a great deal in sport. Of course, nothing gave me greater pleasure in a Welsh shirt than beating England, not because I possessed any hatred – after all, my mother is English, so is my wife and so are many of my best mates – but I think I had become a little more nationalistic than even your average Welshman because I had lived and worked outside my own country for so long. After a while, not losing to them became something of a crusade. I have never been one for records but, as my unbeaten run against England will probably never be overtaken now, it is quite satisfying to recall it. Overtaking Gareth Edwards' total of fifty-three caps for Wales certainly did not bother me but I passed this landmark when I ran out in Cardiff.

As had been predicted, it was a gruelling contest, with England throwing everything at us to avoid a ninth successive defeat at the Arms Park. We won the game right at the death only thanks to a late Steve Fenwick penalty after England's centre, Clive Woodward, had been tempted into an off-side position by a dummy pass from our scrum-half, Brynmor Williams. These 'fake' passes are now illegal and even today some English fans claim a sort of victory. Whenever I hear that I am quick to point out that, the year before at Twickenham, Elgan Rees had scored two tries to England's three penalty goals and so, by modern scoring methods, Wales would have won that game 10–9!

After the relief of victory over the English, I found my international career coming full circle as I travelled up to Murrayfield to take on the Scots. On the ground where I had won my first cap, I was to wear the red of Wales in a capped game for the last time. There was no victory in 1981, though, and it was a nightmare end, with our forwards being hammered and the backs having bad ball all day. My choice of boots for the match made matters worse for me. I had been experimenting with the soft studs that had been introduced by the sports equipment firm adidas to prevent laceration from the more traditional sharpened aluminium variety. I saw myself as a bit of an injury-prevention guru at the time, what with the new clinic, the much-publicised stamping injury that I had received from the All Blacks at the Brewery Field, not to mention my gashed leg at the Arms Park in my so-called retirement match. I had been undecided about which boots to wear and, as it turned out, those soft studs were to be my downfall. I slipped, got caught in possession and looked generally slow.

In the aftermath of the defeat, I was, for the first time in my career, left out of the side, together with the rest of the backs bar Gareth Davies, although, remarkably, the pack managed to survive the selectors' cull. My reaction was to train even harder as sulking was not my style but I admit that my international pride had been badly pricked. I gratefully remember that, when he heard I had been left out of the side, my old friend John Taylor drove down to my place and we polished off a crate of bitter to drown my sorrows. I was able to gain a reasonable perspective on the situation quite quickly, I think. After all, I had always accepted that sooner or later the bubble would finally burst and I will never regret returning to international rugby for those last few games.

I found it difficult to watch the next game in that 1981 Championship against France as I was too wound up to concentrate on what was happening on the pitch and I think it took me a good year to rid my system of the disappointment. I was lucky in many respects as I had so much else in my life – work was always busy and I enjoyed having more time for my family – but I think it was not really until I drifted into veterans' rugby with the St Mary's B side that I finally put my rejection by Wales behind me. For a man who had originally said that he would stop playing as soon as his country no longer wanted him, playing with the veterans was a great turnaround but I realised that it was a marvellous second chance at rugby. We had some fine wins as well, beating the Irish

College of Surgeons in Dublin and the Paris University Club – they became my new Five Nations Championship trips!

The player I felt most sorry for after the Murrayfield disaster was our skipper, Steve Fenwick. In my opinion a captain should never be dropped mid-season as it is bound to affect morale. It was the first time he had been dropped too and the fact that we were in the same boat spurred us on towards another goal: getting our club side, Bridgend, to the Schweppes Cup final again later in 1981.

Sadly, we could not make it a hat-trick as we lost to Cardiff in the final – my final match for Bridgend. It had been a memorable run of success from an all-round team full of good blokes and I had especially enjoyed those last two Cup runs without the distraction of Welsh squads or any captain's duties. Steve Fenwick was the leading light of the team. A great player who did not take himself too seriously, he was always up for a laugh and, with a few quips, would help to set the right tone in the dressing room. Those Bridgend players, supporters and committee members had been my extended family. I had much to thank them for, just as I had been so grateful to London Welsh in the early part of my career.

My Welsh jersey days were not entirely over in 1981 as I played in the inaugural World Rugby Classic tournament in Bermuda in 1988, along with some great old faces and some not quite as great old bodies! The old Pontypool front row turned out again and we won the trophy. I loved it, especially as it was England that we beat in the final. The former English scrum-half, Steve Smith, said that the match brought back a load of bad memories of previous losses against Wales and, very satisfyingly, I managed to preserve my unbeaten record against the Red Rose. My brother Chris had a great game alongside me and, thanks to fate, I sped in for the final score to finish England off. I had to smile as it did feel like 'twas ever thus!

12

SENIOR REGISTRAR

W ITH international rugby finally behind me, I was ready for a new challenge. As my long-term ambition was to be a consultant in orthopaedics, the next step was to find a position as a senior registrar in that field. I applied for a six-month fellowship in sports medicine and knee injuries under Dr Doug Jackson in Long Beach, California. It was too good an opportunity to miss. Dr Jackson was an expert on knee injuries and was blazing a trail in the up and coming world of knee arthroscopy, a technique that uses a small flexible fibre-optic light to see inside the knee joint. Most importantly, he taught operative arthroscopy, looking into the knee and operating at the same time, a revolutionary procedure although the technique is common-place today. In 1981 knee arthroscopy was still in its infancy in the UK and, even then, was only used as a diagnostic instrument rather than an operative technique. I knew that if I could get the job, I would be in the right place to see the whole of this exciting new field developing.

Of course, I would not be the only person interested in such a prestigious fellowship so, to catch Dr Jackson's attention, I shamelessly played on my sporting achievements, hearing he had been a top basketball player at college. Instead of a normal cv, I chanced my arm and simply sent him a paperback copy of my first autobiography. If he had required details of all my surgical training and research, it would have backfired badly as they had taken me so long to achieve, but luckily Dr Jackson shared my love of sport and accepted my application to be one of his post-graduate fellows. Not for the first time, rugby had eased open the medical door.

Many people thought Scilla and I were either mad or very brave even to attempt a trip to America with three children, one of whom, Fran, was only due to be born three weeks before our departure. There was no payment attached to the honorary post, just the promise of a hospital apartment, so we had to find enough money to cover six months of travel and living expenses. There was a certain irony in having to ask for contributions from medical companies and charities when I had not long since transferred £30,000 from the sales of the book into my Sports Injury Clinic Foundation to retain my amateur status.

Eventually, we scraped together enough money but that was certainly not the end of our difficulties. We hoped that Fran would arrive early, as our older girls had, but she arrived punctually on her due date, leaving us with little time to finalise our travel arrangements. Trying to book a return air flight that included a baby not yet born was, I recall, not an easy task and there was also a tight deadline for getting her onto our passports. We must have had some seriously negative thoughts because I remember we made our wills before departing and Fran was christened just the day before we left.

Our time in California turned out to be a wonderful adventure. Of course, living in a small hospital apartment with no garden and searing heat and smog was often a challenge but, without the pulls of club and international rugby, we were able to spend far more time together as a family than we had ever done before. I was much more of a normal dad to our lovely daughters, possibly for the first time in their lives, and, with weekends off, we travelled widely up and down the west coast of America, enjoying the scenery but also the air-conditioning in our ex-rental car. That car was a life-saver but I recall that getting the insurance to drive in America was a painful struggle. In desperation, I tried the line, 'Do you know who

I am? Try looking in the *International Who's Who!'* But this cut no ice, especially in the United States. It took a bit of female soft-talking from Scilla before the insurance was granted.

One of the most fascinating aspects of my work was attending American football matches in case of injury to the players. I covered the games every Friday night and found it such a change from rugby. Sitting on the sidelines watching for injuries relieved some of the tedium of the sport itself. I could not see the attraction of a game that went on for over three hours and was punctuated by constant time-outs and stoppages for television advertisements. (It took me time to realise that the adverts were only there to fill up those gaps.) I do not think that I would have ever played the game had I been American but it was certainly an experience watching it at first hand.

Our main research topic at Long Beach was the anterior cruciate ligament or the ACL, one of the main stabilising ligaments in the knee joint and one very commonly injured in sport. Many people first became aware of this injury when the footballer, Paul Gascoigne, famously damaged his ACL in the FA Cup final in 1991. However, the correct diagnosis of a torn ACL can be difficult, even by the most experienced doctors, so we were trying to identify an investigation to help make diagnosis easier. These days most knee injuries, particularly in sportspeople, will be examined using an MRI (magnetic resonance imaging) scan before treatment. It is hard to believe that only twenty or so years ago, MRI scanning was not readily available, even in the United States. Instead, we had to rely on CT (computerised tomography) scanning of the knee.

For a detailed study of the anatomy of the ACL, I often needed cadaver specimens. One day, I was stopped by the Los Angeles Police Department for speeding; I held my breath and anxiously hoped that they would not decide to take a look in the boot of the car where there was a freezer box of human 'bits' – something that would have taken some explaining to the American Highway Patrol. In time, our team produced enough material for a paper on CT scanning of the cruciate ligaments in the knee and I was able to present this to the British Association of Radiology on my return home in 1982.

Those six months in America changed the course of my career forever. Not just that, it had been a much-needed time-out for our family and had given us a new perspective on the world. As with so many things, the Americans are twenty years ahead of the rest of us but, whilst it was certainly an advantage to see such revolutionary methods, I did not leave the United States thinking that they had a better medical system than ours. Then and now, healthcare over there has a far more private outlook and many of the hospitals that are available to the less well off are not very good – the more you can pay, the better the treatment you get. I cannot agree that this is the way to run a health system and when I returned home I was grateful to be part of the National Health Service.

Back from my fellowship in California, I was even more determined than ever to work my way up the ladder to a consultant post in orthopaedics. Advancement at the hospital in Cardiff was not an option – there were far too many people in front of me in the pecking order to become a senior registrar – but, in 1981, there was a job going at St Mary's, Paddington. I remember that I was rather hesitant about applying to my old college, even though I had loved my time there as a young medical student. When I had worked there, I was just a houseman who took orders from the senior registrar and consultant, so now things were very different – I was applying for a very prestigious orthopaedic senior registrar job at the famous St Mary's. It was a daunting prospect.

I was interviewed by George Bonney, a giant of a man who had terrified me as a student and houseman but, with my trip to America to talk about, I must have impressed him because, amazingly, I got the job. I travelled back to Wales feeling that a completely new phase of my life was around the corner and wondering how on earth we would make it work. We had lived in London for six years as students but what would living there be like now that we had three little children? This was no Long Beach adventure, it was real life and it was going to turn our world upside down.

Fran was now eighteen months, Annie was three and a half and Lauren five and a half, so we had to find a good school as well as decent family accommodation. We decided to keep our house in Llansannor as a way of getting away from London on weekends off and so the girls would remember 'home' as Wales. Luckily, someone at London Welsh put us in touch with the Euro MP Gwyn Morgan who had a house to rent in Teddington whilst he was in Brussels. Teddington was ideal; we knew the area very well as we had bought our first little house there and we quickly settled back in. It seemed incredibly cosmopolitan to us, compared to our little village in Wales, and on Saturday nights it was a big treat to walk round to collect a takeaway from one of the best Indian restaurants in south-west London. They always ground their spices fresh for each weekend and the delicious aromas would waft over our garden wall on Friday mornings. There was no way we could have done that out in the sticks in Llansannor with no pavements and no street lighting.

I had retired from all competitive rugby at the end of the 1981 season but as we lived so close to the St Mary's sports ground, I started playing some rugby again and discovered a completely different side to the game I had loved for so long. Playing for St Mary's B on the flank really opened my eyes to how the other half enjoyed their rugby and, to use a medical term, it was a great antidote to the serious stuff that had gone before. The side would be picked in the pub at Saturday lunchtime or even from those, like me, who just pitched up with their kit on. Our tours to Dublin and France were as much about the bar as the rugby. We were working very hard all week and it was great to get out in the fresh air, run around and then socialise together afterwards.

My work at St Mary's was fascinating. The consultants, George Bonney and Rolfe Birch, were world-renowned experts in the field of brachial plexus and peripheral nerve injuries with referrals from hospitals all over the UK. I soon discovered that I was working in a highly specialised field and operations took many long hours with meticulous attention to dissection. It required patience and great anatomical knowledge and, as the first was not my strong point, I was relieved that I could make up for the shortfall in temperament with my good anatomy skills. I had, after all, been an anatomy demonstrator at that hospital in my early years. My natural impatience was not the only thing I had to contend with. My big hands with their large fingers were about as delicate as a bunch of bananas so it was not long before I received the nickname of 'poor Williams' from Mr Bonney.

I could not have been too awful, though, because George Bonney rewarded my 'try hard' attitude by asking me to help with writing up his life's work in researching cervical neck operations. This was a major honour and I knew that it would be a great help to me in my drive to be a consultant. In a special paper, published in *The Journal of Bone and Joint Surgery*, we described how operations could be performed from the anterior approach, instead of the posterior approach, which needs the patient to be on his front for five hours – an anaesthetic nightmare.

In mid-1983, I returned to Reading for the next part of my senior registrar post. I already had fond memories of the place, having been a casualty officer there in the seventies but, as it turned out, the orthopaedic unit at the Royal Berkshire Hospital was the best that I ever worked in and, in retrospect, I think it probably spoiled me for anything else that came later on in my career. I had a wonderful twelve months; the balance between my work and my social life seemed to be just right, as the team seemed to know how to work hard and play hard. It was never a question of whether you had another life outside the hospital, simply a question of what that other life was – in my case, a busy mixture of rugby, squash and pro-celebrity tennis. One of my bosses, Art Themen, was and still is a highly successful jazz saxophonist and we had some great times on Monday mornings, comparing what we had been up to over the weekend, he at Ronnie Scott's and me at the Albert Hall!

Even when I had to be on duty for the whole weekend, it was not a burden as my family enjoyed coming down to Reading to stay. The girls loved sleeping in the bunk beds in the on-call flat and there was also a thriving doctors' quarters where the medical staff could get meals and drinks and even play squash – I was in heaven. I really liked the set-up at Reading and I think it is a sad reflection on the state of some of our modern NHS hospitals that facilities like these are not routinely provided for the junior staff. No wonder there is such poor morale when the doctors cannot meet up, share experiences and feel just a bit apart from the rest of the staff and the patients. These days consultants mix with patients and nursing staff alike in communal dining rooms. Gone are the days when we were made to feel special and the most important members of the hospital hierarchy. I think it has got something to do with the political correctness that pervades today's society and, in my opinion, it is all wrong.

By this time, I was doing my own lists of joint replacements, arthroscopies and other orthopaedic procedures. It was the best possible training for an aspiring consultant but before I could think about that, I still had one more year of my senior registrar post to complete at the Royal National Orthopaedic Hospital in Stanmore, north London. This specialist hospital took nothing but orthopaedic referrals and there must have been at least thirty consultants, many of whom also worked at the teaching hospitals and were specialists in their own fields. Initially, I worked in the scoliosis unit, treating young adults and children with deformed spines, and then in knee and paediatric surgery. It was always fascinating and rewarding but I knew after working at Stanmore that this was not the path I wanted to take. I had learned enough to know where I should refer any specialist cases but not enough to think I could perform some of those procedures myself.

It was not just that. A lot of the work in Stanmore was in paediatrics and I had never wanted to work with ill children. It was too emotive and sometimes I found it difficult to deal with. Early in my career there had been awful cases of cot death where the parents would rush their baby into hospital and, although the child was obviously dead, they just could not believe it. I did not want to work with any bone cancer, especially in youngsters. The field I worked in was to do with getting people better after car accidents or sports injuries, not about dealing with terminal illness. When I put my surgical drapes on, I preferred to go into theatre knowing that I could put all my energies into improving the patient's life and not dealing in the possibility of death.

The period at Stanmore had been like a finishing school – it put the icing on the cake of my orthopaedic training and told me exactly where I stood in the scheme of things. My specialities were arthroscopy, ACL reconstruction and scoliosis so, when I moved back to inner London to the St Charles Hospital, I felt ready for the coveted consultant position. But where was that going to be? The last year before I found my consultancy was a strange one for us. We were rather in limbo because we had no idea where a suitable position would come up. Whenever we travelled around the UK, for whatever reason, we always classified places by the hospital – who might be retiring and what the nearby villages were like. I suppose it was a kind of defence policy as I really wanted to return to Wales but did not dare to exclude any other possibilities.

Eventually, in 1986, the dream job came up and I became a consultant at the new hospital in Bridgend, my home town. We were all so pleased to be going back to Wales at long last and, when I returned to London after my interview, I found the girls with their fingers still crossed. It was wonderful to tell them that we were going home permanently, instead of just spending every third weekend and the school holidays there. I know that many people thought it a foregone conclusion that I would get the post back in Bridgend but nothing could have been further from the truth. I really had to prove my worth as a medic because there, at home, more than anywhere else in the world, I was JPR the ex-rugby player not Mr Williams the surgeon.

The new Princess of Wales Hospital was the perfect setting, with modern premises, up to date theatre facilities and an enthusiastic staff. We were a close-knit team and my colleague Mike Blayney and I were responsible for running the casualty department and training the junior doctors, so we could control admissions, the follow-up procedures and the staff involved in the treatment. We shared the on-call work between us for ten happy years and the fact that we were very different characters worked well. It meant that Mike could cover on a Saturday afternoon if I wanted to get to a rugby match and I would return the favour in the evenings if he wanted to go to the opera. With a long-range bleeper, I found that I could get to most of the rugby grounds in South Wales.

Eventually, with an increasing workload, things began to change and two new consultants had joined our team by 2000. The problem was that the number of patients that I was seeing stayed about the same, one hundred in the fracture clinic every day, and the wards were constantly full. The idea that two extra consultants would cut our waiting lists was naïve, to say the least, because without extra theatre space, extra nursing staff and extra beds, it was impossible to send for more patients. How the administrators could have thought differently, I cannot imagine.

The seeds of my discontent with the modern NHS had been sown. Changes were deemed necessary at the hospital and, certainly in my mind, they were not always for the good. The casualty department was given its own consultant, which turned into two and then three, so that very soon there was no liaison at all between A&E and us in orthopaedics. In fact, there was a growing animosity between different sections of the hospital. My profession had changed so much in a relatively short space of time and I began to wonder if the new-look NHS was where I really wanted to be.

A date that had been etched in my mind for the previous twelve months was 2 March 2004, my fifty-fifth birthday and my retirement day from the consultant post at the Princess of Wales. I was well aware of the statistics on the medical profession and life expectancy and they did not make for pleasant reading. Doctors who carry on working until the age of sixty-five often live no longer than two more years after their delayed retirement, whereas those who finish before sixty have a much better chance of seeing their seventieth birthday. That convinced me! I had been responsible for the health of other people for the last thirty years on a sort of medical hamster wheel and it was time to get off. Occasionally I teach in specialist areas and act as a consultant but stepping back from day to day involvement in a hospital has given me the opportunity to assess the state of the NHS – and in my opinion it is not in the best of health.

One of the reasons that I decided to retire from the NHS was because administrators had become involved in the medical world and they had no idea what makes people like me tick. All doctors want to do is perform the operations that really matter. Towards the end of my medical career my outpatient clinic would regularly be cancelled to give me time to act more like an auditor than a doctor. That was not what I had been trained for! Sitting through audit sessions to discuss the waiting-list problems was ridiculous when I had actually had to cancel patient appointments so that the meetings could take place. The waiting list was being lengthened by talking about reducing it and it made no sense at all – it was totally the wrong way round.

124

Patients need quality not quantity and in the world of medicine, just like in education, you cannot treat human beings like mere numbers. Doctors are being distanced from the people who have been referred to them for advice and treatment, and at my hospital even the operating lists were under the direct control of the managers instead of the surgeons. Some administrators think that it is more important to perform a number of smaller operations that will get the numbers on the waiting list down rather than to perform two or three really useful joint replacements. In their eyes, the best doctors are those who see the most patients and perform the most operations, regardless of the medical problems the patients are experiencing or the relative complexities of the treatments.

I cannot stress enough how wrong I think all this is. Ill people are what matters, not figures, and it is unfair that someone should have to wait longer for a more complex and time-consuming procedure just because the consultant could fit in two or three less problematic cases in the same amount of time. I also believe that it is only morally right that patients should be operated on within three months of seeing the consultant. If a doctor has a waiting list longer than this then, as a surgeon, you should stop seeing new patients and treat your existing ones. It is an outrage that patients can have waited so long to be seen in Bridgend that they are transferred to the waiting list in Cardiff, only to find that they fall off that list too – they are just being passed around the system.

We need more doctors and nursing staff to be able to combat this, working in well-equipped hospitals. At the moment much of the money being poured into the NHS is being eaten up by pen-pushers and not what I call the real workers. Administrators appoint more administrators and they change their name every six months. Doctors can see the waste better than anybody – A&E departments are busy and half the people do not need to be there. If everybody going into casualty was charged £1 or even 50p it would cut the numbers by half. If a patient is loaned a pair of crutches, they are rarely returned but nobody seems to care.

Uninformed cost-cutting is at the root of what I believe is the biggest issue facing the NHS at the moment, and one that will unfortunately continue to face it for years to come. The plan to save money by contracting cleaning out to external companies has gone horribly wrong and left us with dirty hospitals. The hospital has become a dangerous place to go. A patient can enter with a minor complaint and come out with an MRSA infection. MRSA is pretty prevalent in every hospital now and when you work in that environment you realise how serious it is. I am sure that the situation will only get worse and, within the next five years, we will be witnessing a major event.

Our emergency services in the UK are excellent. If you get knocked down in the street here, you are treated very well but, with the closure of many A&E departments around the country, an ambulance can take much longer to get there. Many hospitals are being shut down in the drive to amalgamate departments and create efficient specialist centres of excellence. I can understand it when local people campaign against closures. They want to be able to reach a hospital quickly when they need one. It makes me sad when I think that three out of the four hospitals that I worked in during my Cardiff surgical training have now closed – the East Glamorgan, the Cardiff Royal Infirmary and the old Orthopaedic Hospital at Rhydlafar. Most of this land has now been devoted to housing estates and, whilst I know people need somewhere to live, they need somewhere to get better as well!

In my later years in the NHS, I got the impression that, most of the time, we were just bolstering up the government's chance of re-election and being used as part of their agenda, whether that government was coloured red or blue. I do not think that any political party will ever own up to the reality that the NHS is a bottomless pit that will swallow up any amount of money thrown into it. I am not stupid – I know that a statement like this would never win votes but the NHS as I see it now is a nightmare.

If our healthcare system is not to descend into terminal decline, the medical world has to do something about it. Having let off some steam about what I think is wrong, it is only fair that I should try to come up with a reasonable solution to these problems. I think that a lot could be improved by making a fundamental change to how patients pay for their NHS treatment. Under a graded income system, we would pay an amount that is in proportion to our earnings to provide much-needed extra funding, reduce abuses of the health system and ensure that those who need treatment get it quickly and effectively. This is democracy at work and I am sure that it would attract people back from the private health sector where they are paying an arm and a leg for their insurance cover. In my mind, this is a much fairer system. It already works in Canada and Australia, and it would work well in the UK too.

Despite these problems in the twilight years of my medical work, I am still able to look back with great fondness and immense pride that I achieved my childhood ambition of becoming a surgeon and, at the same time, was able to play rugby at the highest level. I just hope that, with all the strife and anxiety within the health service at present, the doctors of today manage to find at least some of the enjoyment that I had.

13

FIGHTING MY CORNER

O F all the changes that have occurred in rugby over the last quarter of a century, it is the influence of money that has to be the most profound. Some of the Welsh side who won the Grand Slam in 2005 have signed endorsement contracts worth thousands of pounds, a situation poles apart from the 1970s when maintaining amateur status was everything. I do not begrudge those lads one penny. The modern professional has to earn as much money as possible from a brief rugby career and they would probably think it incredible that I went to so much effort to prove that I was not paid anything!

I am, and have always been, a diehard amateur. At no time did I ever receive a wage from playing. I had my medical career and, besides, if I had wanted to make money from my sporting talent, the opportunity was there as I could easily have switched codes and played rugby league. The essence of that game, with its confrontational straight running and hard tackling, would have suited me very well and I get the impression that league people share that view. On visits to Wigan for medical business, I have always been treated with respect in that rugby league stronghold.

In the seventies, merely speaking to a rugby league scout was tantamount to being professionalised. Nevertheless, in 1977, Hull Rugby League Club approached me and offered a £10,000 signing-on fee with a string of other inducements: a car, a house, a job as a registrar at Hull Infirmary and a £100 a game win bonus. I have to admit that I was tempted. I had no great hankering to play rugby league but there was no getting away from the fact that the offer on the table amounted to serious money in those days and it would have made a significant difference to our lives.

In the end, there was too much to lose if I left union. My father, who was out of the old amateur school, had made it clear that if I ever went to rugby league he would never speak to me again and, because he felt so strongly, it was never going to be a viable option. Fortunately though, I shared Dad's opinion and remaining amateur was a point of principle for me too. Rugby league did not cross my path again, although in the early 1980s I heard on the radio that I had joined a newly formed league team called Kent Invicta, but it was news to me!

It was appalling to be branded a liar in the national newspapers over the publication of *JPR*. To my mind the facts were incontrovertible and it was difficult to understand what else I needed to say to make people believe me. I had decided to forgo a substantial amount of money which in 1979 would have helped to buy a bigger house, a better car and holidays abroad because I wanted to stay true to my amateur principles and I had gone to a considerable amount of trouble to redirect the money to a charitable cause. What more did they want, and why me? It was as if they had made up their minds and nothing would convince them otherwise. It was a horrible time and it made me feel quite paranoid.

After the Welsh authorities pronounced themselves satisfied that I had acted honourably I thought that would be the end of the matter but I was to be disappointed – John Reason, in particular, was determined not to let the issue drop. In the circumstances, it seemed that the only way to clear my name was through the courts, which was why I brought libel actions against the *Daily Telegraph* and the *Sun*.

The *Sun* had printed small articles in the same vein as the *Daily Telegraph* but their lawyers settled fairly quickly once they realised there was no mileage in it for them. I understand that this is quite a common occurrence for a paper like that, with people almost expecting them to err on the side of inaccuracy, due to the nature of the stories that they run. It made sense to me that, having got it wrong, they would withdraw and apologise to me in print.

It was a completely different situation with the *Daily Telegraph* and I was not prepared for the long drawn-out legal battle ahead. Although my threat to sue for libel had not been an empty one – as I know is sometimes true in such cases – I expected that, once the newspaper had looked into the matter, they would realise that I was serious about remaining amateur and back down. What I did not know then was that the *Daily Telegraph* prided themselves on pursuing and winning all their libel cases to preserve their reputation as a trustworthy paper. They had no intention of retracting anything.

My libel case came to the High Court in 1982. Those few days up in London were extremely difficult. It was a completely new world to me and very different from my usual spheres of sport and medicine. Instead of standing as a full-back fielding high balls from the opposition, I found myself tackling questions from a quick-witted QC who had been hired by the *Daily Telegraph* at great expense. The way that words were used and twisted to catch people out and to swing the jury made me furious. It was an extremely stressful experience and, whilst I just about managed to hold myself together, my father, who stayed with me in London, and Scilla, who was coming up from Cardiff each day, found the whole ordeal very distressing. They were both sucking Rennies to calm their ulcers during the sittings and downing gin and tonics afterwards. Back home, my mum was taking it badly as well and the effect that it was having on my family made me even more resentful.

It was most embarrassing to be asked about my bank statements and to have to explain every pay cheque or entry into my account. They even questioned why my mother had loaned us £2,000 towards our house extension. It was worse than I imagined an inquisition from the tax man would be. The barristers acting for the *Daily Telegraph* seemed totally convinced that I had received money from my publishers and laundered this as a gift but they could not locate the funds, and try as they might, they could not catch me out in the witness box. At the end of the fourth day, the judge gave a very sensible and heartening summing up, the jury believed my testimony and found in my favour and against the *Daily Telegraph*. I was awarded costs and damages of £20,000.

When we emerged from the High Court, the media were not gathered on the steps outside as they would be today and we went straight across the road to the Wig and Pen to celebrate our win. The family was delighted and relieved, but we were foolish to think that this would be the end of it. We soon heard that the *Daily Telegraph* had been given leave to appeal because the judge had swayed the jury too much in his summing up. It was a massive blow.

I was fast learning how different law was from medicine. One thing was the length of time that everything hung over us and it was almost another two years before the case came before the Court of Appeal in 1983. By this stage we were living in Teddington and I am sure that this was a good thing. The majority of our friends in that part of the world had no idea what it was all about and did not care if I was amateur or professional anyway. It was very different in Wales, however, where the newspapers had been full of the story, especially a fortnight before the appeal.

At the same time, the so-called 'boot money' saga was also making big headlines in the papers. In his autobiography, Mike Burton, the England prop turned agent, had described how, for some years, adidas had been supplying top rugby players with boots and rewarding them for using the company's products. Very little money was ever involved, possibly a maximum of £50, which was just about enough to cover expenses for a weekend of international rugby as we always bought our own drinks at the bar at the Angel

Hotel. There was also the matter of the time not spent at work. As amateurs, we were not supposed to get anything in lieu of missed time from our jobs – that was the reason why rugby league had started in the first place. In my case, I would often use the money to pay for tickets for the doctors who covered for me during squad training sessions or London Welsh matches. In the case of the players who were steelworkers, their boot money barely covered the cost of their lost shift.

The bottom line was that none of us thought the money was a big deal, it seemed such a small sum. Semi-professionalism had been rife for some time in the southern hemisphere and we knew that players there were being paid and breaking all the rules. We wanted none of that, but despite quite generous travel expenses, we were almost always out of pocket. The boot money arrangement was kept fairly quiet, not because we were trying to avoid detection, but because some players did not receive anything. We did not want any inequality to become an issue within the Welsh squad, so the players who did get money regularly agreed to share it out of a central pool. What was absolutely certain was that none of us considered that our relationship with adidas meant that we were being paid to play.

Boot money was something that had been around for a number of years but, suddenly, it seemed to have been blown up into a major issue. The problems arose when the adidas agent, Arthur Young, was worked on to tell his story. It was a pity. We had come to treat Arthur as a friend but he could only tell his side of it, after all. Immediately, it was a major news story and everyone wanted to know about it. I can never be sure whether the *Daily Telegraph* had anything to do with the timing of the coverage but the headlines were dramatic and certainly damaging for me in the Court of Appeal.

Of course, boot money had nothing at all to do with writing a book and then keeping the proceeds but the *Daily Telegraph* barristers saw it quite differently. They made the most of the chance to use the story against me and, in court, I was asked many times which other players had been wearing adidas boots and possibly receiving payments. I am proud to say that I kept everyone else out of it. It was not for me to implicate others just to help myself and I saw my stance as a sign of the solidarity of the Welsh team.

Some of the boys who had travelled up from Wales to support me for the first case in the High Court found the whole thing absolutely ridiculous. Steve Fenwick and Tommy David had become professional in the interim by playing for the Cardiff Dragons rugby league side. They knew at first hand the real difference between amateur and professional rugby and, in their experienced eyes, I was certainly not a professional. I was also grateful for the support that I received around that time from other players outside Wales. For example, when I had played in the 1980 WRU Centenary game as part of the England and Wales combined team, Peter Wheeler, the English hooker, turned to me and said that he was sorry to hear about all the trouble I was having with the book. That kind of comment meant a lot to me. I only wish that Peter's old international front-row colleague, Mike Burton, had not written what he had but, as he was already on the road to becoming a top agent, I can understand why he did not think twice.

The Court of Appeal was very different from the High Court. Although I had found the first hearing difficult, I had at least risen to the presence of the jury. In the Court of Appeal, we were in a smaller room and the witnesses gave evidence directly to the judge. It was much more clinical and, without the humanising effect of the jury watching and listening, there was nothing to temper the barristers' aggression as they used even more complicated arguments to get their points across. In the end, the Court of Appeal ruled against the previous judgement that I had not professionalised myself and I lost the £20,000 damages that I had been awarded in the High Court.

I was furious at the outcome because I had been judged on factors other than the point of principle that I had not taken any money from the book. Now I was being made out to be a liar and trying to get away with something. I wanted to take it further, to the European Court, but I was talked out of it by my parents, particularly my dad, and by Scilla. They were much more sensitive than I was to the publicity and just wanted an end to it all. They argued that there were more important things for us to turn our attention to, such as getting my surgery qualifications finished and thinking about moving the family back to Wales. They were right, of course, but it was very hard to walk away.

The lingering pettiness of some people did not make the disappointment any easier to live with. The RFU tried to investigate my appearances for the St Mary's B team, acting like fifty-seven old farts long before Will Carling gave them that infamous tag. Thankfully, the Bs were having none of it and were definitely not going to wait until the next RFU committee meeting before they could play me. Despite a suspicious phone call from English rugby's governing body, I appeared as a back-row forward under the name of J Williams – dropping the P and the R!

I had a great afternoon playing with my old name in my new favourite position in the back row and coming up against someone who had been involved in a match with me when I was at medical school back in the 1960s. Here he was, still turning out for the Old Paulines, whilst I had gone on to the Lions and the Welsh Grand Slam sides. Now we were opponents and old friends again, enjoying our rugby just as much as we did way back. I thought, this is what it's all about, having a bath in those old tubs at the St Mary's ground and a few beers afterwards, nothing grand, just rugby mates together. How on earth could the RFU ever think that I had turned professional?

The question of my 'professionalism' continued to hang over me, even when I returned to Wales and started to play for Tondu in

1987. Whilst it was apparently acceptable for me to play for the run-around fun team, the Thirds, it was not the same thing when I wanted to appear for the Firsts when Tondu got to the final of the Silver Ball competition. As it was, I respected the opposition's possible objection to me moving up a few teams and contented myself with a place on the bench. I was delighted when Tondu won; not just for the boys but also because I felt that we had struck a blow for the amateur ethos that I still treasured.

The slurs never went away completely but, by the 1990s, it seemed that most people had forgotten about my struggle in the courts. It was a time of rapid change and the general move towards professionalism meant that many rugby players in Wales were earning a reasonable amount of money from the sport before it officially went professional. There was a sort of tacit acceptance that this was the way the sport had now gone and the allegations surrounding me paled into insignificance. But, for Scilla and me, it was not until 1994 that we finally felt that the stigma was totally removed. That was when the Sports Injury Clinic finally opened with financial help from the Mid-Glamorgan Health authority. It was wonderful to see it up and running and, at last, we felt the bitterness recede and were able to close what had been a very unsettling chapter.

Looking back, I think I was a scapegoat for those who had tried to claim they were amateur when they were not but I am not a man to harbour resentment and I realise that I was around at just the wrong time. Rugby was changing and society was changing as well, becoming more suspicious and less well disposed to those in the public domain. What was so upsetting about the court case, though, was the way that many people assumed that I was guilty until proved innocent, rather than the other way around. My advice for anyone tempted to bring a libel action is to think carefully and to think twice about what your lawyers say. Remember, they are the only ones who are certain to make money out of it.

Inevitably, I have wondered whether writing the book and then going to court were worth it but I have concluded that it was the right thing to do on both counts. The book was something to be proud of and I was a strong enough character to stand up for my principles and stick out the legal row. Then there are all the people who have benefited from the clinic, none of whom would have been helped had I taken a different path. I am also extremely proud that I never earned money from my sport. I am a very stubborn person and I know that I was right to see it through as one of the last of the Corinthians.

14

TONDU AND BRIDGEND

I N 1987, after I had moved back to Bridgend as a consultant, I was invited to watch Tondu, one of Bridgend's feeder clubs, play Llanelli in the Welsh Cup. Tondu is four miles up the valley from Bridgend and was once a thriving iron foundry village. Horace Brown, a colleague of mine in the operating theatre, was chairman of the club and his son Gareth played in the First XV. There was nothing particularly grand about Tondu RFC, in fact they lost quite heavily that day, but I had a great afternoon and suddenly realised why I had not felt comfortable watching behind the posts at Bridgend – I missed playing rugby and knew there was no prospect of it for me at the Brewery Field.

I decided to get back in training with Tondu and, after a while, put my name forward for the Third XV and was selected as a sub. That was the club's policy – everybody had to be a replacement for the Thirds before playing in that XV. It suited me just fine. At Tondu, no one stood on ceremony, and I knew that, had I not been the type to muck in, they would not have wanted to know me.

This is not to say that my presence did not cause a bit of a stir in my first game at Bedwas. Our First XV was playing too and there was quite a big crowd watching them but they all came over to our pitch to see the Third XV when we ran out. It was a marvellous feeling to be back out there. This was what had been lacking from my life and, at Tondu, the rugby was at a level I could easily play without too many problems as long as my body was still up to it. Plenty of people simply could not understand how I could bear to

137

operate at such a different level but I was just happy to be back on the field doing what I knew best – putting in big tackles, getting filthy and having a beer afterwards with the lads.

The back row was my new playing department. Some would say that the more abrasive aspects of my game meant that I had been a frustrated forward for many years anyway, and they would not be far wrong. I was not a total novice, as I had played flanker for Wales in 1978 when injury struck on the tour of Australia, and then more regularly for the St Mary's B side. For Tondu, I would stay in the middle of the field waiting for somebody to come along to tackle and soon realised that I did not have to get to every breakdown – I was loitering with intent! I moved from number seven to eight to six, trying out all three positions, although I preferred it on the blindside flank because it was easier to hide there. But I was happy to play anywhere just to get a game. The Tondu Thirds regular back row became known as the Three Ds – the doctor, the dentist and the dustman – myself, Patrick Daly and David Evans.

I became totally immersed in the club and in 1991 was First XV manager when Tondu went all the way to the quarter-finals of the Welsh Cup. I was immensely proud of the achievement of our players as they went past two senior clubs, Glamorgan Wanderers and Ebbw Vale, to earn the honour of meeting Swansea in the last eight. We missed out on promotion that season because of the distractions of our Cup run, although we were voted Junior Club of the Year. By the time the team came to the play-offs, they were mentally and physically knackered. There were some really excellent players at the club and in 1992 I believe we had the best front row in Wales. Our props, Wayne Terry and Mike Stonehouse, were highly talented but extremely underrated and never received the credit they deserved. Neil and Ian Boobyer, who later won caps with Wales, were also part of that side, together with their brother Roddy.

The highlight of my Tondu playing days came in 1996. We won the Bridgend and District Third XV Cup on a day when our back row numbered more than 130 years between us and I was voted Third Team Player of the Year. I was even presented with the Cup and was as emotional about receiving it as I was when I got my fiftieth cap, much to the surprise of my great mate Gareth Edwards, who was making the presentations that night. In all, I played for sixteen wonderful, unexpected years at Tondu until I was fifty-four, just one year before I retired from my work in medicine. I had nearly had to call it a day after my knee gave up in a veterans' match against England but a cartilage operation in the early 1990s kept me going until, in March 2003, I realised that the game was finally up. I had scored a try for the Second XV against Wick and could hardly get up off the floor – by now my hips were starting to go too!

That would have been my last appearance on a rugby field but for a special match in May 2003 that Tondu very generously put on against another local side, Cowbridge. They had gone to so much effort, I thought it would be churlish not to play, especially as the game took place on the pitch at my children's old school. In the end, I was pleased to get it over with as my body was really cracking up. I do remember making one extraordinary tackle – a big guy ran at me and, when I absolutely flattened him, every player on the field just stopped and clapped, whilst I roared with laughter. It was almost the perfect end for me, as I always had preferred the tackle to the try!

Tondu won comfortably and afterwards in the Cowbridge Rugby Club bar, I was presented with a Tondu RFC shirt with my name and the number seven on the back. I still wear that shirt. The badge and the number remind me how special my times at the club were and how different the rugby was compared to what had gone before. My children tease me for wanting to wear a shirt with JPR on it, saying, 'I think people know who you are, Dad!' Winning with the Tondu Third XV might not have been as vital as it was when I was playing for Wales but it was still better than losing. The other Ds in the back row, plus Gareth Greenslade, Dai Staples, Mark Thomas, Martin Dingle, John Thomas and all the others, might not have ranked alongside the greatest names to have played rugby in Wales but they were loyal team-mates and I am honoured to have been on a rugby field with them.

Joining Tondu was another of those life-changing moments for me. It reassured me that my unease at Bridgend had been nothing to do with failing support for the club but everything to do with the need to keep on playing. I was accused by some of being disloyal to Bridgend but, of course, this was not the case. All the time I played for Tondu, I supported Bridgend in the big games and often visited two clubhouses on a Saturday night, the club that I played for and, just two miles along the Tondu Road, the club that I had always followed.

Tondu Rugby Club is a world apart from the professional game and it was a haven for me during the turbulent years when my sport struggled to come to terms with the earth-shattering events of 1995. In that year, the late Vernon Pugh, then chairman of the International Rugby Board, announced that, for the first time, players could be paid to play rugby union. Of course, for some countries this was welcome news and certainly the big three from the southern hemisphere, New Zealand, Australia and South Africa, were well placed to deal with the change. Rugby was virtually professional there already and there had been immense pressure for the game to lose its 'shamateur' status for some time.

It was a very different story in the northern hemisphere. The news sent shockwaves through Wales, where, like the other Home Nations, the game was still basically amateur. What was required was a twelve-month warning period to allow the game here to get its act together. We were totally unprepared for professional rugby and the overnight revolution led to serious financial difficulties.

Suddenly it was a players' market with a new maxim that you simply played for the club who could pay you the most. All over Wales, leading players, and some not so leading players, decided that large amounts of money should be on offer and were demanding overpriced contracts from amateur administrators.

With all this going on, training at Tondu on Monday nights with the youngsters and their enthusiasm was like a breath of fresh air for me. Although the club was on its way up, those boys knew that they could not demand wages for playing, but for the more established big names of Welsh rugby, professionalism was the beginning of a slow death for the club system as we knew it. Throughout the 1970s and 1980s the Welsh club game had been the envy of the other Home Nations. There was no official championship and not all clubs were guaranteed to play each other home and away over the season but the matches were compelling spectacles built on local rivalries and this gave them an almost unique intensity.

Bridgend's fortunes began to slip almost immediately after professionalism arrived. Internationals Mike Hall and Rob Howley were lured to Cardiff, and trying to keep up with the bigger sides with more money led to major financial problems. It was not only the stars who left, we were unable to retain some of our excellent youngsters whom we had coached and nurtured for years. Bridgend would win the DC Thomas Cup, the Under-11 competition, more times than Cardiff, Swansea or Llanelli, but then our young talent would leave to play elsewhere when they grew older. I know that the odds were stacked against a relatively small outfit such as Bridgend but, frankly, the club was not professional enough in its approach. As our support dwindled and the club spiralled downwards, I watched with dismay and feared the complete demise of rugby in the town as I had known it.

I felt so angry and frustrated with the situation that I decided to try to help bale out the sinking ship and I agreed to offer advice on rugby matters, whilst refusing to get involved in the financial side.

We decided that our first move should be to behave more as they did in the southern hemisphere and, with this in mind, we appointed a New Zealander, John Phillips, as coach in 1997. The selection was conducted via the internet because, in the circumstances, we thought that this would be the best and most modern way to gather the information we needed about him. We really believed we had done our homework but the appointment of Phillips was a disaster for Bridgend. I hold my hands up here. I was wrong to suggest appointing somebody without talking to them face to face and looking them in the eyes. It is a big regret of mine that I was part of this mistake, although I am not sure how much difference it really made in the long run.

Instead of conferring professionalism on the side, John Phillips was exposed as a coach. When he resigned, we were left realising that that our knowledge of contract law was flimsy at best and, despite the club's lack of money, we had to find a hefty pay-off for him. In truth, however, this was only a part of our financial problems. Bridgend's chairman, Derrick King, seemed to be rather naïve when it came to dealing with the players' demands and appeared to be paying them exactly what they wanted. By the end of the 1998–99 season, I think that we owed the taxman £100,000 and, staggeringly, the players' wage bill was in the region of £850,000.

I had agreed to become rugby manager and, looking back, I think probably took my role a little too seriously because I was so desperate for the club to do well. I would be there early on match day and got involved with the preparation as much as if I was playing myself. I suppose it filled a gap in my life because, due to my involvement at Bridgend, my rugby playing at Tondu had naturally taken a back seat. I wonder, though, whether the team found my presence too overbearing. I was honest with the players, who sometimes did not like being told the truth. If they were not playing well, I would tell them straight and I felt it would have helped if some of them had taken their roles rather more seriously. I was also amazed at the disorganisation of some of the players. They seemed to have no concept of how to act in the professional world. That said, if I were ever to manage a rugby team again, I would try harder to accommodate the needs of all the different types of players. I would still call a situation as I saw it, however; if in doing so, I happened to tread on some toes, then so be it. I would also make sure that I was paid for my troubles. In my days at Bridgend, my work was voluntary and I never wanted nor received a penny.

There was one brief highlight in 1997 when the team played Grenoble in the European Challenge Cup and our victory made us the first Welsh side ever to win on French soil in the new European competitions. Aside from this, things were generally sliding downhill. Although our love of rugby could not be questioned, we were a gang of amateurs and we could not transfer our passion for Bridgend into the practicalities of running a club in the professional era. The problems seemed so insurmountable that, when we travelled to Pau the following season, we fully expected the club to go into receivership in our absence. We were in for a welcome surprise on our return from France. Unknown to us, businessman Leighton Samuel had agreed to inject £1 million into the club to buy it and cover all ongoing debts.

The news generated a lot of excitement in the town and many people thought that we had found our messiah. Samuel's involvement came as a big surprise to me. He had not been seen at Bridgend games and, although he was successful locally, I had never met him and he was not terribly well known in the area. I suppose that made me suspicious of him at first but, as we had thought that the club was about to close, we were happy to take anybody's money. We were certainly not in a position to say no. We also thought it preferable to being in debt to the WRU, as Neath were, but, as it turned out, the clubs who were baled out had their debts absorbed. In purely financial terms, it would have been better for Bridgend to have gone bust.

Since I have got to know Leighton better, I have always got on very well with him and he has been very kind to me. He does not flash his wealth around and that, for somebody in his position, is laudable. Any reservations that I had about him back then were purely based on the fact that he was not a 'rugby man'. On a visit to Biarritz for another European tie, he went to bed at ten o'clock on the night of the game. He just could not understand it when I told him that that kind of thing did not happen on rugby trips.

There is no doubt that Bridgend's fortunes improved on and off the field with Samuel at the helm. Brian Powell was appointed coach and I worked well with him. I respected his methods and he certainly improved the squad's fitness and instilled some team spirit in the side. But coaches continued to come and go quite frequently: Dennis John took over from Brian, and Allan Lewis from Dennis. We went through four coaches in just six years but, despite all the chopping and changing, Bridgend won the last Welsh professional club championship in the 2002–03 season, a massive achievement for us and a great credit to Leighton Samuel.

Many may disagree with me but, without him, we would not have had those extra years of relative success. Samuel not only kept the club afloat and developed our players amidst the financial fragility, he transformed the Brewery Field into one of the best venues for rugby spectators in Wales. It is a lovely stadium now and it is a waste that it is not used for more high-profile games although, ironically, it has now become the home of Welsh rugby league with the Celtic Crusaders starting up there. I think that for Samuel, being in control of the union club may have been an ego thing but he gave an awful lot, which should never be forgotten.

The biggest tragedy of all was that the town of Bridgend could not match the financial input of the owner with their support. Some people would come from outside the town to watch but the local community in Bridgend seemed to lose its loyalty. The diehard supporter base dwindled to about 1,500 and, frighteningly, about half of those were folk who used to watch me in action – it was an ageing audience that was shrinking in number. I think that the loss of interest in rugby was one result of the changes that were taking place in Bridgend. The building of new estates such as the Brackla and Broadland developments altered the old community life forever. People moved into Bridgend because housing was cheaper than elsewhere but they did not have the same affinity for the area. It is now a very different town from the one I grew up in.

The contrast between Bridgend and Tondu, where today the whole village still turns out to support the rugby team when they have a good Cup run, could not be greater. It is like the old days that I cherish so much. I remember talking about it in 1993 when I met up with the consultant I had worked with in California. I was describing my days training, playing and acting as manager for Tondu and how all the grannies in the village would knit scarves, people would make rosettes and whole families would kit themselves out in red and blue and travel down to Swansea for a match. His response surprised me at the time: 'I'm so envious of that part of your life. We live here behind security gates in expensive houses, no one knows their neighbours and there is absolutely no community spirit.' I am afraid that I am no longer surprised – that is exactly what seems to have happened with the new housing estates in Bridgend.

By the time Bridgend won the 2002–03 title, our first for over twenty years, I had become president of the club, following in my father's footsteps. Our coaching team, Allan Lewis and Richard Webster, were fantastic and complemented each other greatly – Allan the tactician and Webby the motivator. Huw Bevan, the fitness coach, was also brilliant with the players; he could beat most of them in training, particularly up the hills of Merthyr Mawr, in the sand dunes near Bridgend! The team was excellently led by

Gareth Thomas, backed up by two unsung heroes in openside flanker Cory Harris and prop Chris Horsman. These two did the hard work that often goes unnoticed by spectators and media alike. At last, we had professionals acting as such with the right attitude for the modern era. Sadly, it was a last hurrah for the club. Set against the euphoria of winning the title was the knowledge that the following season Bridgend RFC as we knew it would not exist.

In 2003 David Moffett, the chief executive of the Welsh Rugby Union, had decided that Wales could no longer finance teams in the club championship format. In place of the traditional structure he wanted four regional teams that would represent Wales in both the Heineken European Cup and the newly formed Celtic League. There was a great deal of heated debate but the clubs finally agreed to form five new regional teams, manufactured by merging old local rivals together into new entities. It was a move that completely changed the face of rugby in our country forever.

I dare say that it was done with the best of intentions – to rejuvenate Wales' national sport and to help us compete on the world stage – but in my view it had very mixed results. The majority of the regional clubs now have a serious identity crisis, with at least three of the original five teams acting more as 'super-clubs' than regions – the Cardiff Blues, the Llanelli Scarlets and the Newport Gwent Dragons. Smaller teams, such as Pontypool and Ebbw Vale, that once played against them so proudly have been swallowed up and I wonder in years to come whether anyone will remember that they once competed on an equal footing.

Any sporting club's greatest rival is usually its closest neighbour and there is always an extra edge to derby matches. So combining clubs from the same locality has resulted in some very uneasy bedfellows in the regional sides. The Gwent region is in turmoil because people from up the valley in Ebbw Vale and Pontypool will never follow a side playing at Rodney Parade in Newport – that is simple fact. A great sadness for me is that Cardiff, once the most famous rugby club in the world, has had its history diluted by joining with its previous rivals.

Thankfully, the Ospreys, the regional club created by amalgamating Neath and Swansea, have fared better, although I think this is a major accomplishment considering the bitter rivalry that used to exist between the two sides. As for Llanelli, less troubled by the need to link arms with local foes, they have gone to North Wales in search of new support, but to my mind this is fanciful.

Bridgend was to join with Pontypridd to form the fifth regional team, the Celtic Warriors. Over the years we had been friendly rivals, so at least it seemed that we were more suited than other teams. At the outset, I disagreed strongly with the whole concept of regional rugby but, once it had been introduced, I felt I had to get behind it out of loyalty to my club and because I am at heart a pragmatist. It was important for people like me to try to move with the times but, in reality, I had no choice – my loyalties to Bridgend were stronger than my disillusionment.

Allan Lewis of Bridgend and Lyn Howells of Pontypridd were appointed as the Warriors' main coaches and our first season got off to a reasonable start, although there was still a clear problem with low crowd numbers. Bridgend fans were thin on the ground so attendances were never going to be good at the Brewery Field and only a few games were ever played at Sardis Road in Pontypridd because Leighton Samuel felt that the facilities there were not up to scratch. This upset the Ponty fans, who were already reluctant to travel to support the new side. There was no great animosity towards us in Bridgend, it was just that they did not want to lose the special club that they already had.

There was also a different atmosphere at the Brewery Field under the new regime. I remember the first match there when a security guard stopped me as I was going up the stairs to the president's room. I pointed to my photograph on the wall and said, 'But I am the president!' The reply came, 'Sorry, sir, but I have my instructions from the chief executive of the Celtic Warriors.' They were difficult times for everyone connected with the new team and matches were played against a constant backdrop of stories about how little money was in the pot and how job losses were inevitably around the corner. Yet the Warriors determinedly made the most of their talent and provided their fans with some memorable moments, like the day in January 2004 when they beat England's champion side, London Wasps, in the European Cup.

It was one of my proudest days as a supporter, even though it was a regional side. I must admit that deep down I thought that the Warriors had no chance and when we arrived in High Wycombe, Wasps seemed to be supremely confident. My daughter Fran was with me and we talked to the Wasps captain Lawrence Dallaglio before the game. He said that they did not expect much of a contest! I at least thought that we would give them a game and I was proved right. Our players stood up magnificently in very wet conditions to become the only team to beat Wasps in Europe that season.

For the return game the Brewery Field was jam-packed with our biggest crowd since the day I captained the club against the All Blacks back in 1978. It was amazing. The kick-off had to be delayed because so many spectators were outside queuing to get into the ground. Even the famous ceremonial goat from the Welsh Regiment, which is paraded on international days at the Millennium Stadium, was there. For a few special hours, it was like the old times had returned and I was starting to believe that regional rugby had a chance.

It was just a shame that we could not be as successful at home as we had been in the away match. The Warriors lost by just 5 points, although I think that the result could have gone our way had our main kicker, Neil Jenkins, been on from the start. In the end, Wasps headed our European Cup pool and Dallaglio's men went on to triumph over Toulouse in that memorable Twickenham final. The irony was that a former Bridgend boy, Robert Howley, scored the dramatic last-minute try by snatching the ball out of Clement Poitrenaud's hands. Howley had moved away because Bridgend could not embrace professionalism and who could blame him?

In the first season of the new regional system, the Celtic Warriors had the best winning record of the Welsh regions across the Celtic League and the Heineken Cup. If we could just have beaten Wasps, who knows what might have happened? At the very least, it would have been much more difficult to get rid of us. But the new team was doomed. I think that David Moffett actually never wanted us to progress in Europe that season because it suited his grand plan of four and not five regions. Even the newspapers did not make much of our efforts and it was as if they were accepting the situation that we would not be around for much longer. At least the players, on the strength of their performances, were able to hold their professional heads up high.

In the summer of 2004 the WRU made the unilateral decision to disband the Celtic Warriors for financial reasons. We knew that the patient had been ill but no matter how well prepared you think you are, the moment of death still comes as a tremendous shock. Two hotbeds of rugby that had produced hundreds of international players over the years were left to wither away and, suddenly, the whole of the Bridgend and Pontypridd areas had no professional club to support. What a ridiculous state of affairs. Pontypridd used to have the strongest fan base in Wales but now their team is just a feeder club for the Blues. These people have been told to go and support Cardiff if they want to see some first-class rugby – something that will never happen. Likewise, Bridgend's supporters will never truly follow the Neath-Swansea Ospreys. Be it right or wrong, these are the facts and David Moffett chose to ignore them. Anyone with any real knowledge of the Welsh game could expect it.

Moffett got his own way after all and ended up with his preferred option. I do not think that he ever realised the full extent of the damage he did to the future of rugby in Wales. He never understood rugby here and thought he could bring his regional rugby model from New Zealand and impose it on us. If I am going to be totally fair, David Moffett did a good job in making much-needed financial changes at the WRU, the main part of his brief. He reduced the bloated administration of Welsh rugby and dramatically cut the costs that it was incurring, but he will always be remembered for creating the Welsh regional teams and, because of that, my lasting memory of him will not be a good one. Although I actually got on with him quite well, I think he was totally wrong in what he did and, in the end, I think that he was relieved to get out of Wales, although he arrived with a reputation of being a quick-fixer, never staying in a job for too long. When he left his post in 2005, I said good riddance.

So what next for the regions in Wales? Regional rugby is still in its infancy but it remains to be seen whether it will improve our overall position as a rugby nation. Ironically, our national side has been resurgent since the game went regional but I think that this had more to do with the appointment of a Welsh coach than anything else. As a fan, I have to live with the situation and make the best of it. I tried that first with the Celtic Warriors and then faced disappointment. What was hard for me was being totally powerless to do anything about the problems, and this caused huge frustration and sadness. Now, on Saturdays, I find myself back watching grass-roots, old-fashioned rugby again at Pontyclun, Bridgend or Tondu, or joining the ranks of so many teamless Welsh people watching rugby on television. It is a whole different culture.

I do go to see the Neath-Swansea Ospreys when I can and I applaud what they are achieving there at the superb new Liberty Stadium. Perhaps a new ground is the key to a successful merger in that it creates neutral territory for previous rivals to come together. Perhaps Cardiff should leave the Arms Park and join up with the football club, should that new ground ever be built. There is also a perfectly good stadium in Cwmbran, not too far from Newport, that is currently used for athletics. I think that the Dragons would be well advised to go there if they can survive their financial difficulties. The Llanelli Scarlets are moving to a new site in the town, which will undoubtedly help their cause.

All this still leaves one major problem unresolved however – the competitive rugby that Welsh teams are actually playing. I think the Celtic League competition is a waste of space. Everybody in all three of the competing countries knows that it ranks a poor second to the Heineken Cup, whereas in England the Guinness Premiership title has great value. The Powergen Cup is an attempt to fill the Anglo-Welsh gaps in the calendar but that too lacks competitive bite and direction. If the Welsh regions could join in with an English or even a European league this would help greatly and I would certainly be an active supporter. What I would really like to see is a set of Welsh leagues, consisting of Welsh clubs, with promotion and relegation, for all real Welsh rugby fans. Somehow, I know it will never happen.

15

THE FALL AND RISE OF WELSH RUGBY

B Y the early 1980s it was indisputable that the glorious days of the seventies were behind us in Wales, but what I did not appreciate was how far in the past they would be before another Grand Slam came along. In between there were very few moments to reignite the fire in our national game and some huge disappointments too.

It gives me immense pleasure when people talk about my playing days with such enthusiasm but no one is more delighted than I am when a contemporary Welsh team does well. I think that former international players have a duty to support their national side in the most positive and constructive way possible. That, however, has sometimes been easier said than done over the last few decades.

For a generation we have been searching for the best way to recapture the spirit of Welsh rugby. In doing so, I think it is beneficial to try to pinpoint why those teams of the 1970s were so successful and why our national side then disintegrated so badly in the years that followed. We should identify mistakes that need not be repeated and strengths that we should incorporate into our future plans. A fundamental point is that, like so many things, the rise and fall of rugby in Wales was down to a combination of factors, both on and off the pitch. Likewise, success in the future will depend very much on achieving the right blend and capturing the essence of Welsh rugby – understanding what makes us tick.

Of course, any team in any sport is only as good as its players. If I had to pick my strongest Welsh XV from the 1970s, it would be the pack from 1976–78 and the backs from 1971 – but, in my view, getting on for half the Welsh team in my international playing days, whatever the year, could have been described as world class. Those players were blessed with natural talent in abundance and, as they excelled at a number of different sports, they were able to adapt their minds and bodies to the many different situations thrown up by top-flight rugby and to mould themselves into winners.

But players alone do not make teams of the calibre of those sides of the seventies. We were fortunate in Wales to have thoughtful, forward-thinking coaches to guide us at the time. When Ray Williams introduced national squad training in the late 1960s, it was seen as revolutionary and even frowned upon by other countries that deemed it to be far too professional. Needless to say, the detractors soon followed suit when they saw the success it brought but we stayed ahead in the coaching game. Critically, our coaches knew when to let the players take control and, like all great sides, we felt that it was never enough for us to win, we had to win with flair and thought of ourselves as entertainers. Yes, we would listen to the team talk from the coach but then we would look at each other and say, 'Oh, let's just enjoy it!' To play with a smile was central to our success and, crucially, that is exactly how the coaches wanted it too.

Behind the scenes, the Welsh selectors also helped us grow together by giving us continuity and a degree of security. Right until that very last game of my career at Murrayfield, I never felt that one bad game would be taken out of all proportion. This is not to say that we were not worried about losing our places but there is a subtle difference between healthy competition and inconsistent shuffling for the sake of it. It may not have seemed this way outside Wales but then we had strength in depth in nearly all positions and many fine players went through those years without a single cap.

We only dared to drop out of the international side if an injury made it absolutely necessary because we were constantly afraid that our replacement would come in and take our spot for good.

On match days, we played in front of the most inspirational crowd in the world. When the Celtic fervour was unleashed in Cardiff it made us feel as if the gods were on our side and the tensions of the occasion were channelled into an almost musical form. Even the New Zealanders cannot express their love for their team in quite the same way as the Welsh. When I went away on tour, I soon realised that our supporters gave us a certain something that no other nation possessed and that, whatever it was, played a very significant role.

That passion for rugby in Wales has never died but in the 1980s and 1990s it seemed virtually impossible for the national team to harness it. Errors were made by those in charge of the sport but, to be fair, a number of factors were beyond their control: the demise of the grammar schools, the loss of the heavy industries and the defection of many of the top players to rugby league all played their part in the downturn.

The school system had been key to the development of future players as, rightly or wrongly, rugby was the number one sport in Welsh grammar schools. If you were seen with a football during my school days, it would be confiscated. This guaranteed introduction to the game was slowly eroded by changes in education policy and, with fewer school teams, the clubs had to take the brunt of teaching rugby to Welsh children.

For years the coal and steelworkers had a natural fitness and strength that they carried onto the rugby field but, during the recession of the 1980s, many lost their jobs and their self-respect. It was a traumatic experience that tore communities apart and the depression that followed hung over the whole of Wales. In that environment it was difficult for sport to occupy its former position as a positive release from the hard-working daily grind.

In addition to these all-embracing social and economic problems, rugby union's traditionally strong power base in Wales
was starting to be eroded by the public's widening interest in other
sports. In the 1980s, I remember marathon running was attracting
vast numbers of new followers, just as cycling did in the 1990s. It
was a complete contrast to when I was growing up; then all my
friends would have given all they had to play rugby for Wales but
suddenly this was not necessarily the case. The situation worsened
when many of the country's best players left to seek their fortunes
in rugby league and it quickly became a vicious circle for union.
With nobody left at home to look up to, people associated Welsh
rugby union with failure and the stars of the future were turning
away from the game.

It is impossible to deny that these factors had a profoundly
negative impact on rugby in Wales and I am also sure that the
achievements of the teams of the 1970s weighed heavily on the
shoulders of those who were destined to follow us. It was always
going to be a tall order to replace such an array of talent so quickly
after our glory years but, to my mind, the severity of the decline in
Welsh rugby was undoubtedly hastened by infuriating off-field
politics, highly questionable coaching appointments and some
stunning selection gaffes. There also seemed to be a mystifying
loss of pride in the jersey from the players who did pull it on – and
that is what hurt me the most.

In 1982 the writing was on the wall when Scotland won in
Cardiff, their first victory there for twenty years and Wales' first
Championship loss at home since 1968. The Arms Park aura had
vanished and we were annihilated with the Scots scoring five tries.
If that was not bad enough, there was worse to come a year later
when Wales were beaten by Romania! Although I watched these
events with consternation, I tried to be constructive in my comments, as I hate it when ex-players go straight into print to voice a
negative opinion as soon as they retire. My problem was that the

management, coaches and players did not seem to care less what was happening and seemed to take it for granted that the conveyor belt of talent that had fed the successes of the 1970s would just keep on rolling. It was inexcusable and the WRU should have acted but, when things are wrong at the top, it always filters down to the playing field. There seemed to be hundreds of international players in the early 1980s who were not worth their place in a Welsh team – we called them 'confetti' caps.

By the middle of that decade, the image of Welsh rugby had plummeted to an all-time low, but with a new coach, Tony Gray, and a new selector, Derek Quinnell, there was a glimmer of hope. Despite the fact that our best players such as Terry Holmes and Robert Ackerman were still heading off to rugby league at an alarming rate, some pride was restored with third place at the first-ever World Cup in 1987 and a Triple Crown the following year. Sadly, this was not enough to keep Gray and Quinnell in their posts and they paid the price for heavy drubbings on the tour to New Zealand in 1988. It was an unnecessary and ill-timed change. The All Blacks were world champions and one of the greatest ever teams but this seemed to be conveniently forgotten by the WRU.

Perhaps the ignominy of a second defeat by Romania later that year, this time in Cardiff, led our big hope, Jonathan Davies, to become his country's most high-profile recruit to rugby league. He was brilliant during the Triple Crown success and was just the sort of fly-half that Welsh supporters love to watch because he played it off the cuff. In my mind, Davies can be placed in the same bracket as Barry John and Phil Bennett. He was one of the best outside-halves that I have seen since my playing days finished – right up there with Australia's Michael Lynagh.

I think that the relentless decline throughout the 1980s was best summed up right at the end of that decade when Bridgend played a Welsh XV as a warm-up for the international against the touring All Blacks. Bridgend actually won and I could not have been more dejected. I did not want to take anything away from my former club but they should never have beaten the national side. If this was a litmus test on the state of Welsh rugby, then it looked like there was still worse to come in the nineties.

By now Wales were making some really odd coaching appointments. After the sacking of John Ryan, Ron Waldron of Neath was brought in and I thought his training method of endless runs around the pitch before the players ever got near a rugby ball to be mindless in the extreme. The Neath approach of not appreciating individual skills squashed any initiative dead and the wooden spoon in the 1990 Five Nations after a clean sweep of defeats was no more than Waldron's Wales deserved.

Many dark days followed and the home World Cup defeat by Western Samoa in 1991 told the Welsh people exactly where their team stood. Then, out of the blue, the new coach, Alan Davies, and team manager, Bob Norster, visited me at home to ask if I wanted to put something back into the national side as a selector. I accepted without hesitation and, along with old international team-mate Elgan Rees, the plan was to guide Wales through to the 1995 World Cup.

Getting more closely involved actually made me more depressed about the apathy that was endemic to Welsh rugby at the time. It sometimes seemed to me that mere inclusion in the squad and a free weekend away for the girlfriend were more important to some players than being picked or even winning. I definitely knew it was not the sort of rugby I subscribed to when we were all at the bar in the Copthorne Hotel after beating the Japanese in Cardiff in 1993. The coach ordered champagne and the management team were acting as if we had beaten England! I could not wait to get back to training at Tondu on a Monday night after such weekends. I needed real rugby with people with real lives and real jobs, not just jumped up football wannabes.

The defeat by Canada a few weeks later was my lowest ever point at the old Arms Park. I felt complete shock and no one could find anything good to say in the team debrief after the game. But eventually there was some light at the end of the tunnel when, the next year, Wales lifted the Five Nations Championship trophy – we had been going for the Grand Slam at Twickenham but just failed. It appeared that things might be on the turn but, for me, it went badly wrong again in 1995, the year of the World Cup in South Africa.

Before the game against Ireland in the Five Nations, there was a long selection meeting but we eventually reached agreement on the fifteen and I went home to mull over our choice. It was not necessarily the team that I would have picked yet I was aware that, in situations like these, compromises have to be made. The next day, however, I found out from the press that Alan Davies had changed the side without any consultation. It was totally embarrassing and I decided to resign there and then. What was the point of wasting my time if the agreed view was going to be ignored? Nowadays, if I was to be involved in selection again, I would simply write down my twenty-two, give that piece of paper to the coach and leave him to decide.

Aside from this, I thought Alan was a good coach, although there were far too many flip charts for my liking and, at times, he made matters unnecessarily complicated for the players. But I accepted that he was modern in his methods and we did need updating on new training aids, such as video analysis. Defeat in that Irish game ended Alan's tenure and Wales were once again plunged into managerial turmoil. Needless to say, we did not impress in the World Cup and the new coach, Alex Evans, brought me back as a selector for the one-off international against South Africa in Johannesburg, the match billed as the first professional rugby Test. It was actually Gareth Thomas's full debut and I am proud to say that I played a small part in setting 'Alfie' on the international road.

The job of Welsh coach is a poisoned chalice and, I believe, the most demanding role in world rugby because of the pressure the nation puts on the top man. Kevin Bowring, a man with a fine technical knowledge of the game, was next to have a go. I always felt that his middle-class image never really sat well in Wales where the sport is relatively classless; Welsh people like a coach with plenty of *hwyl* (spirit) and Kevin did not seem able to give that. The embarrassments kept on coming. I could almost live with the 96-point thrashing at the hands of South Africa in 1998 because we had in effect sent our third team out on tour that summer but France's 51–0 win at Wembley earlier in the year and the 60 points we conceded at Twickenham stuck in my throat.

These failures were not all down to the coaches, though, and the players have to take their share of the blame. In Wales, we had lacked the levels of fitness required for international rugby for some time but this came to a head once the sport went professional. Our top players seemed to believe that their work was done on the training ground and that their spare time, of which there was now much more, belonged exclusively to them. There was a lack of personal responsibility and the drinking culture that existed in places such as Swansea was the perfect illustration of profession-alism not being taken seriously. With members of the national team setting that kind of example, it was bound to filter through to all levels of the game.

In view of this, I totally understood the decision to appoint New Zealander Graham Henry as the new coach at the end of the 1990s. Henry came with a reputation for straight-talking and innovation. He certainly instilled off-field discipline into our players and the training sessions had much more of a southern hemisphere flavour, concentrating on power and skill development. Of course, what I could never stomach was that he was not Welsh. Nor did I like the amount of money that he made out of Wales – it seemed excessive and I could not help making the comparison with the top surgeons in the hospitals where I had worked over the years. They were in the business of saving lives and were paid nowhere near £250,000 a year but then if we were stupid enough to offer so much, it was not Graham Henry's fault for taking it.

When Henry first arrived, he invited me, along with a number of other ex-players, to watch a day of trials in Swansea. There was a sense that he was trying to get a few of the big names of Welsh rugby on-side but equally, it showed a willingness to listen and learn about the intricacies of the country he was now operating in. I was to pay particular attention to the full-backs and I ranked the six candidates in my order of preference: New Zealand-born Shane Howarth was my number one, followed by Matt Cardey and a young Rhys Williams. Graham seemed to agree with my choices because, during the season, he worked through my list when injury struck, but little did I know then that Howarth was not actually qualified to play for Wales. The ensuing 'Grannygate' scandal was the most embarrassing legacy of the Henry years and, as a nation, we were made to look like fools.

I do accept, however, that Graham Henry did a lot of good for Welsh rugby. We had some famous and much-needed wins, which began to lift us back towards the top. After an incredible victory in Paris, we beat England at Wembley in 1999 to deny them the Grand Slam. I had the perfect view of Scott Gibbs' charge to the line and watched as if it was in slow-motion, my smile gradually getting wider and wider as Scott powered over. To see the old football ground turn into a sea of Welsh red will live with me forever.

Henry's Wales also recorded our country's first-ever win over South Africa in the match that marked the official opening of the new Millennium Stadium. This ground has now become a symbol of a much more positive phase in Welsh rugby and victories like that certainly helped the feeling grow. As a playing surface, I admit that it has never set the standard but, as a place for the fans to visit and enjoy unhindered views close to the action, it is the best around. I will never change my view that the atmosphere of the

I was often required to attend to injuries on the field. This time an Australian player is in need of help.

Phil Bennett leads out the Lions in 1977. Barry John was the hardest act to follow in British rugby but 'Benny' proved to be great in his own right.

I delivered a few rousing words in my time as captain of Wales.

Receiving the MBE at Buckingham Palace in 1977 alongside footballer Tommy Smith (*centre*) and my old tennis opponent, Roger Taylor (*right*).

Socialising with Willie-John McBride and Gerald Davies.

Above: My last appearance against England in a full international came in Cardiff in 1981 – another victory over the old enemy.

Right: I can't hide a smile of satisfaction as I lift the Welsh Cup in 1979 on one of Bridgend's greatest days.

The Welsh Grand Slam team of 1971.

Among the former international players who gathered at the Parc des Princes in 1997, Gareth Edwards and I represented Wales. We were there for the last match to be staged at the ground, where I used to love to play.

Sir Clive Woodward and his controversial aide Alastair Campbell make notes during the Lions tour to New Zealand in 2005.

Martin Johnson and his team celebrate England's World Cup win in 2003, a triumph that won the respect of the world game.

The Millennium Stadium – a national stadium of which to be proud.

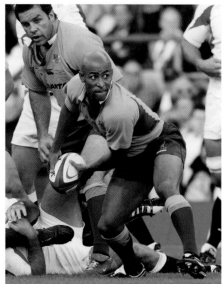

New Zealand's Richie McCaw is the only current player in my Greatest Ever Team.

George Gregan of Australia is the world's most capped player. I also played international rugby for twelve years but won half the number of caps, proving how many Tests there are these days.

Gavin Henson and his girlfriend Charlotte Church represent the glamorous world of the modern-day rugby star.

The latest Lions captain, Brian O'Driscoll, is capable of turning any game.

Escorting Prince Charles at a WRU Cup final.

'Built more like a carthorse than a marathon runner,' said television commentator David Coleman during the first London Marathon in 1981. He had a point!

Rugby and medicine come together as I take a look at Willie-John's knee in the physiotherapy department in Belfast in 1994. Syd Millar (*far right*) looks on, all of twenty years after plotting the downfall of South Africa with Willie-John.

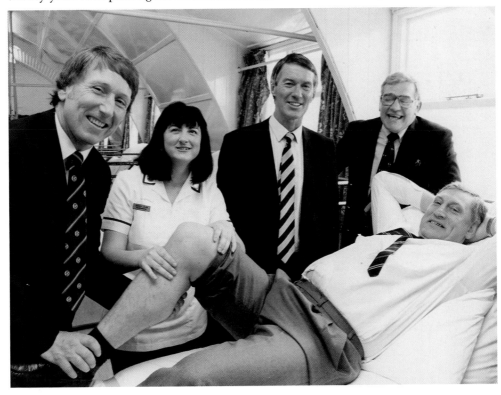

Lauren's wedding in 2002 – a proud Dad with his girls and young son.

Arms Park could not be bettered because, when people stand on terracing, they make more noise – a roof on that old ground would have been blown off! But the Millennium Stadium, albeit built on a wing and a prayer, is exactly what a modern facility should be and the Welsh nation is right to be immensely proud of it.

When Graham Henry returned home to New Zealand, he left his deputy and countryman, Steve Hansen, in charge of Wales. Before the 2003 World Cup in Australia, the team worked really hard on their fitness and their minds appeared to be on the job – even their apartments in Sydney were suitably less glamorous than they might have been. But, as we stumbled through our early group games, I was struggling to see any logic to Steve Hansen's selections. Then came that famous meeting with New Zealand when, out of no-where, Wales conjured up the kind of rugby that we had not seen them play for years. The moment when winger Shane Williams opted to run and jink at the All Blacks was the moment when Welsh rugby rediscovered its heart and soul. I talked to Shane afterwards and asked if any of it had been scripted. You can imagine what the answer was; the players had spontaneously decided that this was the way to go and it reminded me of how Barry John and Gareth Edwards would listen to Clive Rowlands planning a set game plan and then go out to play in their own impromptu style. Wales had not only challenged but genuinely frightened the All Blacks and it was wonderful to see the respect from the opposition spectators and the relief that they tried to disguise when New Zealand finally ran in the extra tries that sealed the win.

Looking back, I think that scintillating performance was a com-plete fluke on Steve Hansen's part. When it came to the crunch, he had done no more than chuck what he thought were the no-hopers into the big game, saving others for the encounters still to come. Now the squad had shown their coach the way, England were next to get a scare in the quarter-final in Brisbane. Had the World Champions-elect not brought on their utility back, Mike Catt, I believe Wales would have made the last four. Despite our exit, the style in which we played suggested that there would be much more to come from this team. We had glimpsed the future and seen the past at the same time – Wales were set to play the Welsh way again.

Off the pitch, however, it was the same old story of incompetence. The manner in which the WRU appointed Steve Hansen's successor threatened to undermine all that had been achieved at the World Cup. It was a shambles and served as another reminder of how the governing body had let Wales down during the previous twenty years or so. Gareth Jenkins of the Llanelli Scarlets and Mark Evans from Harlequins in England were shortlisted for the post but the next thing we heard was that Mike Ruddock had been chosen. Mike had not even applied because he had been told by the WRU that he had the job when Graham Henry was appointed, only to be shabbily overlooked. Now it was Gareth Jenkins' turn to be treated badly. Some people tried to defend what had happened to Gareth by saying that this was 'the way things happen in business' but I can tell you, it never happened in my business like that. Again we were the laughing stock of world rugby.

I believe, however, that Mike Ruddock was the right man, regardless of how he came into the job. His cv was perfect; he had plenty of top-class coaching experience in Wales and Ireland but, above all, he had shown himself to be honourable. I had admired the way he stayed at Ebbw Vale when others tried to entice him elsewhere. Mike had committed to a club and was determined to see it through and make those average players into a good team. It soon became clear that he also had the right vision for the national side so, after the rather self-contained and stereotyped style of rugby adopted by Steve Hansen, it must have come as a huge relief to the Welsh players that Ruddock would allow the flair to flow. Mike, as a Welshman, understood our inherent need to side-step and swerve away from contact.

After a promising autumn, the 2005 Six Nations Championship

came along and a rejuvenated Wales were ready to seize every possible advantage as they took on an English team who seemed burdened by their endless World Cup-winning publicity. Most people in Wales will always remember where they were on the day of that match in Cardiff. Beforehand, I really thought that we would do it if we played to our strengths and ran the ball but, ironically, our victory was not pretty. Yet, in winning this way, Wales proved that they could triumph when not playing at their best and, having performed well against other big guns and just lost, it was a great relief to secure a major win. Gavin Henson's massive hits on the England players lifted the crowd out of their seats and then his famous long-range penalty won the match. Those 3 points from Gavin's boot proved to be the turning point of the tournament but what really mattered to me was that Wales were on England's line when the final whistle went – we were trying to score points and not merely defend our lead.

Six tries against Italy followed and great potential was unfolding before our eyes. The heroes were different with each game and it seemed that everyone was contributing to the side's progression. I was understandably reluctant to draw comparisons too soon but could this young Welsh team possibly be about to rekindle the golden days? I knew from personal experience how tough the next match in Paris would be but what I did not know was what an amazing game was about to be played. During the first half, Wales were not in it; they were insecure on their own ball and missing tackles all over the place but then, vitally, a Stephen Jones penalty just before half-time made the score a much more comfortable 15–6 to France. Whatever Mike Ruddock said at the interval, it worked! The Welsh came out a totally different team and the brilliant Martyn Williams scored twice within five unbelievable minutes. We were in the lead and the conclusion was incredibly tense as France kept coming back at us, as we knew they would, but the boys showed tremendous character in one of the greatest Welsh wins of all time – up there alongside any victory that I was involved in for Wales.

Scotland are renowned as Grand Slam spoilers and the game at Murrayfield was a banana skin in the path of our hopes, but after eighteen minutes the match was over as far as I was concerned with 24 points already on the board for Wales. It was the worst Scottish display I had ever seen in that first half but Wales were now unleashing all their attacking intent. The back three of Kevin Morgan, Shane and Rhys Williams scored breathtaking tries and the handling of the forwards was fantastic – at times it was more like watching basketball. As bad as Scotland were, I cannot remember seeing a Welsh side play so well for a whole forty minutes and, again, that includes our team.

And so the ghosts of the 1970s were finally laid to rest on a beautifully sunny day in March when Ireland came to Cardiff. The fans were bustling in the streets, red and green jerseys jostling good-naturedly with each other and history was in the air. The thousands without tickets settled down before a big screen on 'Henson Hill' – not surprisingly, the singing far outmatched that of 'Henman Hill' at Wimbledon. As we walked to the match, the anticipation was overwhelming and, once inside the stadium, I have never heard the anthem sung so passionately – and that was from Mr Ordinary in the crowd, not just Charlotte Church and Katherine Jenkins!

I sat at the end where prop Gethin Jenkins charged down Ireland fly-half Ronan O'Gara's kick. I could see the concentration on Gethin's face as he controlled the ball and carefully touched down, saying to himself, 'I mustn't knock on . . . I must keep my cool.' Wales held well until half-time and then came my moment of the match – the angle taken by Tom Shanklin, my man of the match, to give Kevin Morgan a straight run to the line. We gasped at the sheer beauty and simplicity of it and needed the replay on the big screen to believe it had really happened. The Irish looked old and tired, whereas the Welsh boys, many of them not even born when we last won the Grand Slam, remained full of energy. Best of all, we never stopped trying to play in the true Welsh tradition of adventurous rugby. I thought that the late, great Carwyn James would have been looking down with an approving twinkle in his eye.

We stood and soaked it in as the players came round for their lap of honour. Then the journey to the ex-players room under the stand was unforgettable. Going against the general flow of the crowd, I was walking with Lauren on my left and Scilla on my right, with our arms linked like a front row, but we could not get very far as people kept coming up to congratulate me! I told them that I had nothing to do with it but this made no difference. It was as if the supporters were grateful for what had been before, and what had happened that day had finally put an end to the years of hurt. They recognised that the Grand Slam winners of the past could now hand over the responsibility to these young players and, like me, they felt not only pure joy but also huge relief. They could tell how happy I was because I could not stop hugging my wife and daughter.

Mike Ruddock and his staff had done a great job. The specialist coaches, Scott Johnson, Andrew Hoare and Clive Griffiths, proved to be a fine mix, even though I tease Clive about his defensive skills because, when he came on for me in 1979 against England, he was hailed as adding more attacking presence to the side – well, he was certainly not noted for his defensive game at the time! But as defensive coach Clive knows his stuff. The emphasis in 2005, though, had been on attack, and skills coach Scott Johnson deserved a lot of credit for his input. Together, they had all played a major part in what Wales had achieved. They had also managed to create the spirit that was there when I played for Wales, the special bond that makes you feel like a club side. Instead of a collection of individuals, here was a real team that instinctively knew where the other players were on the pitch, what they would do and how they could rely on each other. It gave them the confidence to take risks and play exciting rugby.

History shows, however, that it is not only hard to win a Grand Slam, it is even harder to retain it. I was not surprised then when we started the 2006 Championship with a loss to England at Twickenham. Furthermore, our injury situation going into that match meant that resources were stretched to the limit and I acknowledge that if you play the high-risk game, sometimes you come unstuck. The victory over Scotland a week later calmed my fears that all the good work of the previous Championship season and the autumn win over Australia was going to unravel, but then came the most unexpected piece of rugby news that I have ever heard.

I was listening to the car radio on the way back from choir practice on the night of 14 February 2006 when it came over that Mike Ruddock had resigned from the position of Welsh coach, right in the middle of our Six Nations Championship defence. I, like the rest of the nation, was absolutely shell-shocked. There had been rumours that some of the senior players in the Welsh team preferred Scott Johnson to Mike – after all, Scott's style is to be one of the lads – but I was not unduly worried by it as this situation often emerges in teams because the head man, the hirer and firer, cannot afford to get too close to his players. I had also heard that Mike Ruddock was trying to implement a more structured and conservative style of play that the players did not necessarily agree with. Now that did concern me a little and I would understand the players' perspective on this because their expressive rugby had served them so well. Mike had always been a forward coach at heart and perhaps he was looking to tighten up this area but, regardless of that, he had still gone into the Championship talking about his commitment to 'sexy rugby'. I concluded that the differences of opinion between Mike and his players could not have been so great as to cause this kind of dramatic reaction.

After family reasons were cited for Ruddock's resignation by the WRU, this inevitably signalled a period of gossip and rumour that even the small and insular world of Welsh rugby had never previously witnessed. My feeling was that, if he did want to go at the end of the season because of the looming World Cup, we should respect his commitment to his family. But, to my mind, Mike had been sacked – I was pretty sure that he would not leave Wales in the lurch mid-season.

We needed some answers from the WRU and their chief executive, Steve Lewis. I am ashamed to say that, in my opinion, the WRU has consistently been the worst run governing body in the world of rugby. There are some good people in the organisation but they have not been well led. Our wonderful supporters deserve more; they do not have a lot of money but they travel all over the world backing their national team and the way that the Ruddock affair was handled was yet another kick in the teeth for them. Is there something in the Welsh genes that makes us continually shoot ourselves in the foot? I think so. The personnel change but we just keep doing it, as if we cannot handle success.

The players robustly denied the accusation that player power had been at the root of Mike Ruddock's removal. Their captain, Gareth Thomas, normally a happy-go-lucky and positive guy, collapsed as he watched his television interview on the row go out. Since then, the diagnosis of a damaged artery and mini-stroke threatened to end Gareth's career. I feel it emphasised just how stressful the situation was for the captain and I must say that I saw some parallels with what happened to me at the end of my career when, as Welsh captain, my good name and amateur status were publicly questioned.

Gareth's immediate absence and a loss to Ireland were severe blows for Australian Scott Johnson when he took over in a caretaker capacity for the rest of the Championship. Scott is a talented coach and a genial, laid-back man. I can easily understand why he is so popular. I admit I was never a fan of his antics on the field, playing the cheerleader role with the crowd in those shorts, but that is modern sport and I accept that times have changed. I would say, though, that he is much more of a number two than a head coach. There is a big difference between the two roles and some people are undoubtedly more suited to being an assistant, so Johnson's decision at the end of the 2006 Championship to return to Australia as part of John Connolly's coaching team is, I feel, the right one for Scott and for Wales.

In the last two games of the Six Nations, Wales, rather alarmingly, drew with Italy but then put in a much more heartening performance against France. The positive attitude of the Grand Slam year seemed to return, even though the day ended in defeat. The new coach, on this evidence, will still have plenty to work with.

Gareth Jenkins' appointment came as a great relief to me and there was no doubt that, having missed out before, he was the firm choice of the people. I have known Gareth for a long time and we used to have some great battles against each other when he played for Llanelli and I was with London Welsh. He is the kind of man who understands Wales' attacking style and his teams have always played in a very progressive way. As coach at Llanelli over a long period of time Gareth has done everything that he could but, crucially, he has also proved himself outside of that club environment. He was part of the Welsh Championship success in 1994 as assistant coach to Alan Davies and, even more importantly, he was by all accounts a very popular and clearly successful mid-week coach on the last Lions tour. The only other realistic candidate for the Welsh job was Phil Davies, another ex-Scarlet, who had been out of Wales for ten years working with Leeds. I am sure that one day Phil will also coach Wales but Gareth was the right choice at this time. One thing that I am convinced about is that the turn-around in viewpoint from the WRU as far as Gareth Jenkins is concerned was motivated by the desire of the decision-makers to preserve their own positions! Now I just hope that the Welsh public give Gareth the time to develop the team by using all the internationals prior to the next World Cup to help Wales towards perhaps a semi-final place in France. I feel that this should not be beyond them.

So, apart from the obvious need to continue to rebuild the squad's confidence, how well prepared for the World Cup are we? A major issue over the months ahead will be finding the back-up that is essential to mount an assault in 2007 because it is a country's second string that determines how strong that challenge will be. The biggest loss to Wales in the 2006 Championship was our midfield supremo, not Gavin Henson but Tom Shanklin. I think Shanklin is an even better player than Steve Fenwick was in my day and that is saying something. Without Tom and Gavin, our resources in midfield look thin. The second row is another problem area and we just do not seem to have the depth of numbers in that department either.

On the positive side, we must not forget that these Welshmen are still young and we should delight in the new crop of performers – scrum-half Dwayne Peel for instance. Wales may not possess the sheer numbers of world-class players that it did in the seventies but the current team has managed to throw off the heavy burden that was imposed on so many Welsh teams by the success of my generation. They deserve immense credit for doing so and I sincerely hope that they go on to achieve even more – how much only time will tell.

16

LIONS WITHOUT CLAWS

I PLAYED during what was probably the greatest period in the history of the British and Irish Lions, although we did not know it at the time. The back to back series wins over New Zealand and South Africa seem incredible feats, given the relative lack of success that the Lions have had since, but it happened simply because both squads were made up of top-class players who were managed in a way that maximised their potential.

Comparisons between the 1971 and the 1974 Lions teams are inevitably difficult but picking my strongest combined team is far more straightforward. My answer is always the same: the '71 backs and the '74 pack. But, do not forget, dream teams may not work in practice as well as they do on paper; for instance, would we play as well in the backs if we were dominating the ball so much? Sometimes, it is more difficult when you have the ball all the time because the opposition know they might as well stand up in defence and stop you playing. In 1971, with less forward power, we always had the element of surprise when we got the ball. As a pure three-quarter, I loved our running style in New Zealand but the beautiful weather in South Africa made handling and back play a pleasure there too – it was like rugby heaven.

Since I last played as a Lion, there have been eight Lions tours to the southern hemisphere and, regardless of where I have followed them, at home or away, my interest has been all-consuming. 'Once a Lion, always a Lion.' I think it is nearly impossible to have been a

Lion and not have the strongest and most heartfelt opinions on all subsequent tours.

I was so tempted to go back to New Zealand in 1977 to defend our 1971 victory but, by then, my life had moved on and I needed to concentrate on my medical career in Cardiff. It was the right thing to do but it was far from easy just watching the games on television. By the end of the tour, however, my impression was that it had been a good one to miss. The Lions lost the Test series 3–1 and that winter in New Zealand the rain did not seem to stop falling. I winced as I watched Scotland's excellent full-back, Andy Irvine, dealing with high ball after high ball as they dropped out of the dark clouds in the face of a howling gale. Irvine was one of the finest runners with the ball of his era but, on this trip, his chances to show his prowess were few and far between. The Lions generally lacked a cutting edge behind the scrum and it was frustrating to see the pack winning so much ball but losing because the backs could not do anything with it.

I could have toured again in 1980 on another controversial trip to South Africa. There were so many injuries at full-back that the Lions tour manager, Syd Millar, phoned me to see if I would come out of international retirement and join them as a replacement. It was very flattering but, even more than in 1977, I knew that my working life had to take precedence over rugby tours, even for the Lions. With Bill Beaumont's men losing that series to the Springboks 3–1, both New Zealand and South Africa had regained the ground that we had taken so comprehensively in the early 1970s. The Lions' invincibility was definitely a thing of the past and, in 1983, they failed to win even one Test against the All Blacks. The captain on that tour was the Irish hooker, Ciaran Fitzgerald, a disastrous appointment because he was not worth his place in the Test side. In my opinion, the Lions captain has to be chosen from players who are certain to play in the Tests and the selection process should not attempt to share the places and power between the four Home Unions.

In 1989 there was a chance for a fresh start against some different opposition, the Australians. To me, this winning tour was particularly memorable as Ian McGeechan's first as Lions coach. I would say that, alongside Carwyn James, Geech has been one of the two greatest Lions coaches of all time and, because of his longevity, some would say that he is the best. He may not agree because he is too modest! McGeechan is an excellent rugby strategist and, like all good coaches, operates to the strengths of his players and never tries to adopt a gameplan that they are not capable of playing.

The Lions captaincy on the 1993 tour to New Zealand was again a big talking point, with selection on merit and inter-union politics becoming issues as they had done in 1983. Gavin Hastings was chosen as a leader who could gel the team together and give them spirit. He undoubtedly achieved what he was asked to do and certainly fared better than England's Will Carling would have done – his captaincy would have been more divisive. That said, I feel that the bad press Carling has received over the years about his attitude has often been unfair and it has certainly obscured the fact that he was a good, often underrated, player whose bravery meant that he never let his side down.

On Ian McGeechan's third consecutive tour, he coached the 1997 Lions to a memorable series victory against the Springboks. All Lions fans were gripped by the recapturing of the spirit of the '71 and '74 sides and, in games such as the mid-week victory over Free State in Bloemfontein, the Lions showed the watching world what their brand of rugby was all about. Ironically, they did not carry this attractive style into the Test matches but they knew how to win the big games and, to my mind, that was what mattered. My abiding memory of the whole tour is that tackle by the Welsh centre, Scott Gibbs, on the giant Springbok prop, Os du Randt in the Second Test in Durban. It typified the determination of the Lions to win.

In a massive break with tradition, Ian McGeechan's successor for the 2001 Australian tour was a foreign coach, the New Zealander

Graham Henry. Henry had proved himself with Auckland and Wales but, if I had been uncomfortable with him as Welsh coach, I was just as uneasy about putting him in charge of the Lions. A Lions tour is about taking British and Irish rugby to the other side of the world and, to my mind, this necessitates a home-grown coach. Under Henry, however, the Lions lit up the rugby world and in their stunning First Test win in Brisbane played the best rugby of any side that year. Had it not been for some bad luck in the Second Test, Henry would have won the series but this did not prevent him being pilloried by the media after the tour. It was as if people had been waiting for him to fail because of his nationality. I was not one of them. He is a fine coach and I felt that it would be wrong to do him down purely because of where he was born.

Ironically, Graham Henry occupies a unique position in the history of the British and Irish Lions – the only man to coach both for and against them. In 2005, he was back in his homeland, now in charge of the All Blacks and lying in wait for Sir Clive Woodward's team. There has been no other tour since my playing days to stir my emotions quite like this one. It was a sporting disaster and I believe that it is imperative that the reasons behind the failure are identified and important lessons learnt.

It was my first visit to New Zealand since 1971 and, during the tour, I wrote a column for the *Sunday News*. It really made me analyse why things were going so badly wrong. I realised that some of my views would not have been going down too well with certain members of the Lions party but, equally, I felt that I wanted to get across how a lot of us were feeling. I have since spoken to a number of the players and they have agreed with what I said. I never wanted it to become personal and I hope that Clive Woodward never took it that way. I think it is important to express a view honestly and openly but to restrict your opinions to rugby matters only.

Of course, I desperately wanted these Lions to become the first to win in New Zealand since my day and I genuinely felt after the 2005

173

Six Nations that they had a reasonable chance. I was positive about the appointment of Sir Clive Woodward too as, although he was not the most liked man in United Kingdom and Ireland rugby circles, he was certainly not stupid and had been very successful. The reality was that he had led England to the World Cup in 2003 and that had to be respected.

Sadly, my pre-tour optimism rapidly turned sour and I wondered whether the trip was doomed from the start. The composition of the Lions squad was a huge disappointment. Where were all the Welsh players? Wales' Grand Slam seemed to count for nothing in Woodward's eyes and it hurt me to the core that so many of my fellow countrymen were seen as being surplus to requirements. Ryan Jones and Brent Cockbain were perfect examples of those who should have definitely been included on form alone. There were also glaring omissions from the other nations, for instance, England's Mark Cueto and Ireland's Simon Easterby. The fact that three of these four players made a significant contribution after they joined the tour as replacements underlined how wrong their initial omission had been. Surely there had to be room for these players, given the sheer size of the tour party? Woodward's justification for taking so many with him was that he would need cover for injuries, but three matches in and already three replacements had been sent out, totally contradicting his initial safety first selection policy.

That policy was also undermined by the half a dozen players who were carrying injuries when they went out to New Zealand. Why this was ever considered a sensible move, I cannot imagine. It is my view that, on a relatively short tour to a country where the rugby is as physically hard as anywhere in the world, a player is unlikely to get fit enough to compete if he is already on the sick list when he boards the plane. The reaction in New Zealand to the huge squad was one of amazement. When you factor in the vast entourage of back-up staff, it gave the Lions the image of a travelling circus. How many coaches does it take to confuse a squad of players? I feared that we were setting oursleves up for a big fall.

The tour began at home with the terrible warm-up game against Argentina at the Millennium Stadium, when the Lions managed to get away with a draw only because of a penalty from Jonny Wilkinson in the ninth minute of injury time. I think that the players underperformed because they were terrified of getting injured and not making it on to the plane, just like we were in Eastbourne all those years ago. Ultimately, the game served little useful purpose other than as a means of generating much-needed money to help cover the astronomical costs of the tour. I firmly believe that the Lions should never play at home – the touring ethos should be sacrosanct in order to preserve its magic and mystery.

When in New Zealand, the Lions were written off by what seemed like the whole of the nation. Players from my day, such as Laurie Mains, right through to the modern-day greats, such as Sean Fitzpatrick and Zinzan Brooke, were predicting a 3–0 'blackwash'. I was keen to see them eat a large slice of humble pie but the disjointed way in which the Lions played in their opening matches troubled me.

We were always going to know much more about the 2005 Lions after their meeting with the New Zealand Maori in the unofficial Fourth Test, one week into the tour. I was alarmed when the Welsh fly-half Stephen Jones was thrown straight into this tough fixture, whereas England's Jonny Wilkinson was given more time to ready himself for his away debut, the smoother ride against Wellington a few days later. I feared that Jones was not getting a fair crack of the whip. I did not have a problem with Jones playing against a tough team; I just thought that he needed an easier game first to reach a peak of performance. Jones's confidence was eroded by this early baptism of fire and it was also unfair to ask him to play outside Matt Dawson of England instead of his Welsh team-mate Dwayne Peel, who looked destined to be the Test scrum-half.

The loss to the New Zealand Maori was when I knew that the Lions were destined to go home with nothing. Despite only 6 points separating the two sides, it had been a comprehensive defeat and especially concerning was the way in which the Lions had been outplayed at the contact area. This was becoming a recurrent theme and I felt sorry for the Six Nations Player of the Season, Welshman Martyn Williams, who seemed to arrive at the rucks with no support at all. The coaches never managed to sort this out.

The Lions' problems were not confined to forward play, however. In the Wellington match they struggled to find any cohesion behind the scrum, with Jonny Wilkinson and Gavin Henson looking like complete strangers in midfield. At the root of this was the management's apparent desire to try to give everybody a game and, although I could understand the coaches wanting to keep things close to their chests, it did not seem there was a Plan A, let alone B, C or D.

It was becoming clear to me that the team for the First Test in Christchurch would be stacked with Englishmen, the men that Woodward trusted to deliver him a second massive prize on the world stage. When the team was announced, it seemed to me that Woodward had largely decided on the make-up of the side before the Lions had left London. It was a shambles of a selection. The impressive Josh Lewsey had been shunted onto the wing to allow out-of-form Jason Robinson to play at full-back. Stephen Jones was in but so too was Jonny Wilkinson, giving the Lions two regular fly-halves with no recognised inside centre. It was madness. Worse still, Jones, Wilkinson and Brian O'Driscoll had played together as a midfield unit for only twenty minutes and that was never going to be enough game time to take on the mighty All Blacks.

In the pack there was more bad news with England's second row, Ben Kay, and flanker, Neil Back, going into the biggest rugby match of the year woefully short of their best form. Even the English supporters that I spoke to could not see the sense in it. In my view,

Woodward's failure to select the side for the First Test on form had undermined the whole concept of a Lions tour and had effectively created two teams – the players he knew and felt comfortable with, who were dominated by the English contingent, and 'the rest of them'. You could have written a book on why the New Zealanders deserved their billing as clear favourites. The only thing I and the rest of the Lions supporters had to cling on to was the X factor of the Lions jersey and all that it meant to the players.

The First Test defeat was inevitable as the Lions were dreadful but the score-line of 21–3 would have been so much worse were it not for the truly awful conditions. The All Blacks failed to finish off several attacking moves because of the greasy ball and biting wind – on another day, it would have been 50 points. In my old position, Jason Robinson had one of the worst games I have ever seen from a full-back at this level.

Of course, the Lions cruelly lost their captain, Brian O'Driscoll, in the opening seconds of the match. The so-called 'spear tackle' from the All Blacks skipper, Tana Umaga, and hooker, Keven Mealamu, ended O'Driscoll's tour there and then. Had the captain stayed on, I am convinced that it would not have made any difference to the outcome of that match or, indeed, the series. Up until then, he had been too quiet during his games, both vocally in his role as leader and as a runner with the ball but, at his best, O'Driscoll can be a match-turning player and I concede that his injury was a devastating blow to the Lions. I cannot believe that it was a premeditated attack but both New Zealanders should have been cited because it was an illegal challenge and a danger-ous one too. At the very least, Brian deserved an apology; it took me back to the incident at Bridgend in 1978 when I was caught in the face by the boot of the All Black John Ashworth – all I wanted was a 'sorry' but it never came then either.

Gavin Henson was O'Driscoll's replacement in a much-changed team for the Second Test in Wellington. His fellow Welshman,

Gareth Thomas, was the new skipper and I was certain that, with 'Alfie' in charge, we would see fire and brimstone! Sure enough, the captain scored a fine early try and I was delighted for this popular son of the Welsh game. Thomas is a Bridgend boy and I have known him for a long time but even Gareth's spirit was never going to be enough that day because I doubt that I have ever seen such superlative rugby from any team as I witnessed from New Zealand. A 48–18 win is a drubbing in anyone's language – English, Irish, Scottish or Welsh! The All Black fly-half Dan Carter showed us all what a magnificent talent he has become and, quite frankly, he made Jonny Wilkinson look very ordinary. I felt sorry for Wilkinson but he should never have gone on that Lions tour; he should have had the summer off to get fit for the following season.

Having gone 2–0 down, the Lions proved that you cannot play catch-up rugby against the All Blacks. They lost the Third and final Test 38–19 and their humiliation was complete. It had been the most expensive tour in the history of the Lions, yet they left New Zealand with absolutely nothing to show for it. Ultimately though, I am not prepared to lay the blame for this on the players. It is my view that the management should take the brunt of the criticism and, therefore, their leader, Sir Clive Woodward, was the most culpable. He simply did not create the right environment for the players to shine. I was so disappointed for them because that tour should have been the highlight of their rugby careers.

Even Woodward's media manager Alastair Campbell, the former aide to Tony Blair, could not spin the tour result. I did not relish the sight of Campbell wearing the Lions tracksuit and felt that this kind of heavy-hitting approach to the media had no place in rugby. My old mate Bill Beaumont was the tour manager but what did he do on the tour? The answer – exactly what Alastair Campbell told him to and, with all Bill's rugby experience, that was not good for the Lions.

It would be wrong to say that my experience in New Zealand was totally negative. In fact, I have some very happy memories of the tour, many of them concerning the conduct of the Lions supporters. They followed their team through thick and thin – well, actually nearly all thin. The fans never let their spirits or good humour drop but it must have been hard at times. Some of my friends at the squash club in Cardiff actually cancelled their trip out for the Tests; they were so disgruntled about what they had seen on their television screens that they were prepared to lose their deposit. But the many who did spend so much money to go on tour were a credit to themselves, their countries and the sport in general.

I wondered if the New Zealanders might learn from our ability to be good losers as well as winners. Yet I concluded that those rather mean thoughts on the Kiwis harked back to another age. I have mellowed over the years since 1971 and now I think that I understand the New Zealand people more. I used to feel that they were a dour bunch but I have come to realise that they are very hospitable and it is just their passion for rugby that makes them a little too intense at times – and as a Welshman, I can empathise with that!

So what should be the lasting impact of this ill-fated tour and what lessons should be learnt? In my opinion, the biggest change that must be made is to align the Lions with other commitments on the professional rugby calendar. As it is, the schedule is too long to fit in well with other competitions. In 1971 I was able to go away as a Lion for over three months but, in 2005, even the six-week trip was not really feasible. It is unrealistic to expect the Lions to dominate in this way. I would suggest that the Lions play one or two warm-up games as a prelude to a three-match Test series. The Tests themselves should never be watered down but a truncated trip would relieve so much of the pressure on the players and management. It would also drastically reduce the expense – the next tour simply cannot cost as much as the 2005 version. I do not think the southern hemisphere countries will ever allow the Lions to die because of the revenue it brings to them but all sides should surely see the value of a shortened tour.

Whatever the duration of a Lions tour, it will always remain one of the greatest sporting experiences for players, coaches and supporters alike. One of my most vivid memories in 2005 was after the First Test in Christchurch. We were freezing cold, had fielded the wrong team against the All Blacks, had underestimated them and lost. To top it all, we were marooned at our hotel and could not even get into town for a drink! It was looking like a dreadful night, but then, out of nowhere, came one of those unforgettable Lions evenings when both sides join together. A New Zealander, stripped down to his singlet, belted out a superb rendition of the 'Sheep-Shearers Song' and the party kicked off. A Welshman in his Lions kit prowled up to the microphone and was the next best thing to Tom Jones as he launched into 'What's New Pussy Cat?' The sounds filled the hotel bar, lobby and probably many of the rooms as well. We were all mates together and we drank long into the night.

The next day, it dawned on me – the beauty of that night was that it had not been planned or orchestrated. I realised that Sir Clive Woodward's coaching style was like karaoke; but no amount of money or technology, with a script already written, can replace a spontaneous performance. That, to me, is the fundamental message to be heeded before the Lions tour South Africa in 2009.

17

THE PUBLIC FACE

FAME is a fickle beast. Take the current Welsh team. They have experienced the rapid succession of pleasure and pain that comes from being in the media glare. In today's society the knives can come out very quickly if it starts to go wrong for a professional player even if, only five minutes earlier, they were the hero of the hour. So I have some sympathy for modern sportsmen, particularly the youngsters. As amateurs, it was unusual for us to be criticised because we were giving up our free time to play the game and we certainly never had to face the intrusion that constantly hangs over the big stars of today. On the whole, we were able to lead relatively normal, albeit very busy, lives – we were in the spotlight but rarely under the microscope.

Not only were we left alone to a much greater extent, the volume of our media involvement was far smaller. I was expected to give interviews as part of the honour of playing or being captain but I certainly never had to work my way along a long line of television cameras, being quizzed by one crew after another. Importantly, nobody could demand that we had to do it, there was no contractual or financial hold over us and the fact that there was no monetary benefit was almost reassuring; you did not feel obliged to chase the deals to supplement your income. Playing for your national team was deemed to be sufficient reward for your commitment and it suited me fine.

This is not to say that there were no superstars in the seventies – rugby's first celebrity was Barry John. On the Lions tour of 1971, the

New Zealand public awarded him the nickname 'King John' and the world seemed at his feet but, even then, he did not have a hard time with the press. I think Barry's decision to retire early in 1972 was mainly financial; it was not just because the attention was getting to him although it undoubtedly was. Barry had taken advice from his then father-in-law that he should cash in on his fame and he became a male model, appeared in advertising campaigns and so on, making a fair bit of money. His self-confidence on the field was not reflected in his commercial dealings off it, however, and although Barry would appear to be lapping it up, he sometimes found it hard going because, deep down, his character was not made to be always on show. He was great friends with the late George Best and, in many ways, they were kindred spirits.

One thing that really helped me in the days when my fame could have been a problem was that I lived in London and, if I wanted, I could be totally anonymous, the unknown Welshman. It would have been very different and quite claustrophobic in Wales so, in that respect, I believe I was much luckier than Barry and the other members of that team. As soon as I was recognised on Oxford Street, I remember thinking it's time to get out. I knew that I was hopping out of the frying pan and into the fire by returning to Wales but I felt that there was no disadvantage in going home if I was getting the same sort of attention in such a big city as London.

Perhaps my inherently shy character also equipped me better for the Welsh limelight. When we went out, Scilla would spot the spotters and we would try to avoid certain situations like restaurants where everybody would know you and want to come up and chat. Of course, I never refused to sign an autograph but there were always one or two people who would go over the top. If that happened, I would just walk away and say to myself, 'Stuff you, I'm going home.' It led some people to brand me as arrogant but it was my way of managing the situation.

All players find it hard when they retire because the adrenalin rush suddenly disappears and I think Barry John would be the first to say that he stopped doing what he was best at too soon. I played all the way up to the top and back down again, whereas he retired at the top, full stop. Also, having my medical career to fall back on had always been a great means of escaping but it became invaluable when I eventually retired from international rugby. I did not have time to dwell on the past because my job soon filled the vacuum left by the absence of top-flight sport. I was a busy surgeon then and, remember, we call it an operating 'theatre' because you have to perform in an incredibly demanding environment.

I am sure that I have been helped by the fact that public interest in what we achieved as a side has never seemed to wane. For us, it was certainly not a case of being famous one minute and then largely forgotten the next. This has had its drawbacks, however, and we have had to handle the pressure of waiting for a Welsh team to replace us. But, as I have got older, it is very nice to be recognised; it shows that people remember and appreciate what we achieved and as time goes on I, like anybody, have become better placed to deal with the effects of being well known.

Back in the 1970s I was very conscious of my image. It was fashionable to be different and I went for a look with long hair, sideboards and socks rolled down to the ankles, which was pretty unconventional in rugby at the time but I enjoyed not being one of the crowd. Anyway, the look evolved naturally, as a reflection of my personality, I did not cultivate it. Believe me, I would have looked the same had I not played international rugby. My reputation on the field was fairly unconventional too – a new breed of totally uncompromising full-back with an eye for the attack. Now this part of my image I did play on, as I sensed some of my opponents were almost in awe of me and that gives you a good start in any game, in any sport.

Gavin Henson would probably be the first person to come to mind as a modern Welsh player with a distinctive image. Granted,

Gavin's look seems to be more manufactured than mine was but, when I met him to conduct an interview for the *Observer* in 2005, he struck me as a very ordinary and likeable lad who loves playing rugby. I could not care less about his hair. How could I after my long locks? The leg-shaving and fake tan I am a little less sure about, but does it really matter? All I want to know is how Gavin is playing his rugby. The same goes for his relationship with the singer Charlotte Church – they are two young people enjoying themselves and what is wrong with that?

What I will say is that Gavin does need to get the off-field stuff under control and to learn not to bring trouble on himself. He was wrong to talk about his team-mates in the way that he did in his controversial book. To break ranks and make public the dressing-room talk like that would hurt any close-knit group and I am sure that our side in the 1970s would have reacted in exactly the same way as the current Welsh team did. We were well aware that the superstars in the backs could not have been stars had our forwards not won the ball. I do not think Gavin realised what sort of uproar he was going to cause and, unfortunately, he has made more enemies than friends over that book. He should put it down to experience and get back to concentrating fully on his rugby because, if he does, he has every chance of being a world-class inside centre as he is crammed full of talent that is genuine and not just for show.

Gavin Henson's story takes me back to the plight of the modern player and the way in which their lives are analysed and scrutinised. In my day, everything was much tamer. More often than not people were well disposed to you and sympathetic and, when anything did happen that was newsworthy, the initial approach was generally positive. Take the 1974 Lions tour for example. It was a long trip so Scilla had arranged an overseas posting in Durban with the intention that we would stay out in South Africa after the tour had finished. Even though her life was quite independent of ours, I kept her presence in South Africa a secret from the Lions captain and management. I did not want them to know when we met up at various points in case it looked like I was going 'off-tour' and this might have had an adverse effect on the squad.

When we finally reached Natal towards the end of the trip, Scilla arranged for us to have dinner and carefully selected a venue where we would not be recognised – she even wore a wig to make absolutely certain! We could not believe our eyes when we saw Willie-John McBride and Syd Millar sitting at the adjacent table. I introduced her to Willie-John as my wife and he looked at me a little oddly. He must have thought that I was out with a bit of stuff on the side! When he realised that I was telling the truth, he made it clear that he did not mind. Despite my fears, there was no pressure to act in a certain way, either from within the squad or, for that matter, from outside. My private life was exactly that, private.

I am astonished at the modern trend for intrusive radio phone-ins that discuss whether wives and girlfriends should be anywhere near to a touring sports team or if a sports star should return home to be present at the birth of a child. It is nobody else's business! When our first child, Lauren, was born in 1977, there was a cartoon by Gren in the *South Wales Echo* which showed a nurse throwing a baby bottle into a packed maternity ward, with newborn Lauren the baby about to catch it. The caption read: 'Don't worry – it's JPR's nipper.' That was about the extent of the press intrusion into my private life and, anyway, I saw a Gren cartoon as a sort of honour.

Times have certainly changed. Take the instance of when I borrowed an old Morris 1000 from a friend who had temporarily lost his licence and let the tax disc on his car expire. As it was not my vehicle and I was only using it for a short time, I tried not to worry about the lapsed tax disc but, one night, I looked in the rear view mirror and saw blue flashing lights. I admit that I was worried; I was a sports star with a big name and was there to be shot at, metaphorically of course! When the policeman came to the car window, he said that he had stopped me because my back light was not working and then asked me to produce my driver's licence and to sign my name on a piece of paper. 'Thanks JPR,' he said before getting back into his police car and driving off. There was nothing wrong with the back light; he had just wanted my autograph!

Another time, I was on my way to the Welsh Trial when my car was crashed into by an oil tanker on one of the narrow lanes near Llansannor. The front of my Capri caved in completely and I was lucky that it had a long bonnet as otherwise I really would have been in trouble. I was a little shaken up at the time but my main thought was that I should not be late. I managed to ring Scilla who picked me up and took me to the match. I thought nothing odd about going to play a game after the accident. After all, I had received fewer bruises than I normally did on a Saturday. When Gareth Edwards heard the news that the tanker and my car had both come off decidedly worse than I had, he was heard to say, 'Bloody typical!'

My car had been stationary at the time of the accident and I had not been drinking the night before – indeed the police were not even called – but imagine what the reaction would be now to such a potentially serious crash and how stories would fly around about a rugby player being involved in an act of alleged dangerous or drunken driving. Back then, the response was the complete opposite, with the Welsh poet, Tom Bellion, penning some flattering lines on my apparent indestructibility: '*JPR collides with tanker – the tanker has spent a comfortable night and is expected to make a full recovery.*'

Indeed, being famous could really be quite good fun. How else would I have been able to visit Tom Jones at his house in Hollywood? I really enjoyed that! My 'fame' also led to appearances on hit television programmes of the time including *Superstars* and *This is Your Life*. In *Superstars*, I rubbed shoulders with fellow sportsmen at the top of their sports and it was fascinating to see how they prepared and coped with the different disciplines in the competition. The boxers were surprisingly poor whilst the motor racing drivers were unexpectedly good. Of course, the full-time athletes excelled at almost everything but, from rugby, Gareth Edwards more than held his own and qualified for the world final. I finished in mid-table in my heat. Of course, I chose tennis as one of my events and beat the world squash champion Jonah Barrington in the final. I was let down by my poor swimming and, in the rifle shooting, I was never going to do well as it was the first time I had ever picked up a gun.

Appearing on *This is Your Life* was very special. I was tricked into going up to the Thames Television studios in London, supposedly for an interview with my old pal John Taylor, who had gone into broadcasting after his retirement from rugby. Instead, I remember how shocked I was when my rugby team-mates and Eamonn Andrews ambushed me wearing doctors' white coats. There were people present from all walks and periods of my life: Illtyd Williams, my early rugby coach; David Lloyd and Dan Maskell from tennis; and even the unsung heroes who worked with me on the wards. It was an unforgettable experience.

In 1977, the Silver Jubilee year, Scilla and I were invited onto *Britannia* when the Queen visited South Wales as part of her celebrations. I had to pinch myself afterwards – I had been talking to Her Majesty and sipping champagne on the famous royal yacht! Later that year, whilst on duty at the Cardiff Royal Infirmary, my bleeper went off and the switchboard operator informed me that I had been awarded the MBE for services to rugby in the Queen's Honours List. Believe me, there were some envious consultants on the ward round the following morning. With hard work, I would eventually achieve the same medical letters after my name as they had, but very few of them stood any chance of getting the letters that had now been bestowed upon me. The trip to Buckingham Palace in December for my investiture marked the end of a truly remarkable year, and who should be there receiving the same award but my old tennis contemporary Roger Taylor, twice a Wimbledon semi-finalist.

Twenty-seven years later, in 2004, I had another royal experience, which brought home to me how much my life had moved on. For a start, my retirement was just beginning but there was no time to think I don't have to go into the hospital. It was St David's Day and I had been invited to a service at the Holy Cross Church in Cowbridge to celebrate 750 years of the charter being granted to the town. Prince Charles was attending and everywhere was bedecked with flags and daffodils, and school children were cheering and waving on the streets. As we sat down in the church, I was intrigued to discover that the group of six people to whom I was chatting had all been guests at the Prince of Wales' Investiture at Caernavon Castle back in 1969. I had been there to represent Glamorgan Youth. Looking at the heir to the throne forty-five years on I was moved to reflect on the fact that I had just retired from thirty years working for the NHS and had actually completed two careers, if you consider my rugby as the other one, whereas Prince Charles was still waiting for his main career to begin. I have always felt a parallel tracking of our lives and have great respect for him, and the difficult situation he has been thrust into.

After the ceremony, we were on a tight schedule to get to the Glee Club at Cardiff Bay for another St David's Day event. This was something completely different and there was none of the formality of Cowbridge or the sycophantic behaviour towards Prince Charles that we had witnessed earlier in the day. Instead, we were celebrating the contributions made by all the other 'Princes' of Wales over the centuries – a salute to the 'Heroes of Wales'. The live radio broadcast was the culmination of weeks of online voting to find the top one hundred nominations for the title of 'Welsh Hero'.

I was delighted to have been invited and even more chuffed to see a painting of me up alongside Richard Burton, Dylan Thomas and my old mate, Gareth Edwards. The achievements of all sorts of

Welsh people were being recognised and sitting listening to the impact that these famous Welsh men and women had made on people the whole world over was very humbling. I was honoured to be ranked amongst people whom I considered to be great, such as Tanni Grey-Thompson and Simon Weston. Rugby made it into the top ten thanks to Gareth and I was amazed to learn that I had come in as high as twenty-fourth.

There was one more twist for me, however. At the time when I was leaving the NHS, Wales' number one hero was none other than Aneurin Bevan, the instigator of the NHS. It was not a night to dwell on negative thoughts, but I could not help reflecting that Bevan would be turning in his grave if he could see the state of his great organisation now: the suffering of those waiting for joint replacements whilst consultants happily put others on their private lists; the wastage of prescriptions; and the money frittered away on complaints and litigation . . .

We rounded the day off with a walk back into the centre of Cardiff; one minute I was so famous, I was a 'Hero of Wales', and the next I could not even find a taxi. For old time's sake, Scilla had booked us into the Angel Hotel where I had spent my nights before international duty at the Arms Park. She had even managed to get Room 303, which I had shared so often with Gerald Davies, but somehow it was not the same. The room had been altered and I could not even find which door was the bathroom. It was a fitting reminder that times really had moved on since the glory days of the 1970s.

Rugby has given me some marvellous moments, on and off the field, but I count myself fortunate to have had my time in the limelight when I did. I am not sure that I would enjoy it as much in today's high pressure, celebrity-driven environment. Perhaps one reason for the goodwill towards rugby players in the seventies was that, whilst we had the 'fame', we certainly had none of the 'fortune'.

18
THE GAME TODAY

I N 1995 I would not have had to worry about the repercussions of writing my book, selling comments to a newspaper, speaking at dinners or even being given a house by the club signing me on; the age of rugby players being officially paid for their services had finally arrived. Although the passing of the amateur days saddened me, I was realistic. The sport had been living a lie for some time and the southern hemisphere countries were beginning to run the show. My attitude was that if we were to beat them, we would have to join them.

The rising stakes now, right across the board, at international, regional and club level, have heaped pressure on the individual players. I tasted what life as a professional must be like on the Lions tours and loved being able to live and breathe rugby, but that was only for a few months, not six or sixteen years. I wonder how the modern player copes after losing yet again and waking up – to what? Another session at the gym, more training, another chance to get injured and then more worry about the contract for next year? No, thank you, it is not a lifestyle that appeals to me.

It seems that some of the fun has gone out of playing but that frequently happens when a much-loved hobby turns into a means of paying the mortgage. I was lucky to play rugby for sheer enjoyment, right from when I first appeared with London Welsh as a young medical student, pitting my wits against the steelworkers and miners of the Welsh valleys, to my final years as a forward at Tondu when I made sure that the young speedsters knew why amateur rugby meant so much to the old lags like me. In between, I played with a host of world-class players who were of like mind and just wanted to express themselves on the pitch and excite the crowds. All this was worth far more than any amount of money that I could have been offered as a professional.

To an amateur, an integral part of the sport was the fellowship that was created by socialising with the opposition players after a match. Understandably, this too seems to be on the decline in today's professional world – it was always going to be the case when the game became a job. Players have moaned about after-match functions since rugby began but, once you have sat through a few boring speeches, you realise that spending time with the men whom you have battled against all afternoon is important. The best way of dealing with any bad feeling and antipathy that may have grown during a game is for the two parties to chat the issue through over a drink.

What would also irk me if I was a modern-day professional would be the over-reliance on coaches. Worse still, in my opinion, many of them are holding the game back. Too much coaching and too many coaches create a confused situation where the player tries to satisfy all his masters and simply has too much to think about on the field. We are creating automatons. A strong head coach provides a coherent structure for the players to operate in but also trusts them to think for themselves. Involving his men does not undermine the coach's standing in the team, it enhances it. The 2006 Six Nations Championship illustrated this only too well. The tournament was excitingly unpredictable but the standards attained were low, especially from those who should be setting their sights high. England, with all their resources, and even the title winners, France, played gloomily predictable rugby, characterised by a lack of invention. The brightest moments were provided by a rejuvenated Scotland and Italy, who won many plaudits for their style.

The fitness coach has been charged with making the players bigger, stronger and faster. Many do their job well but whilst our players are undeniably fitter, I believe that their core skills have been neglected. Bulking up in the gym has frequently been at the expense of working on basics such as passing and kicking. Too many modern coaches have forgotten that you can beat eighteen-stone brutes by using pace and guile.

Another breed of specialist that is an increasingly dominant force is the defence coach, many of whom have been imported from rugby league. A disproportionate amount of time is spent on defence and some sides seem to have lost the art of creating scoring opportunities. As a full-back, I know the value of a strong defence and that this can win matches but, as my fellow number fifteen, Andy Irvine, used to say, 'I don't care if I give away two tries as long as I help to score three.' It is generally the case that if a rugby team scores more tries than the opposition, they win. The team at the top in the world game as I write is New Zealand and the All Black management have found the perfect balance between attack and defence. It is a model that other teams, whatever their level, would do well to follow.

One coach I just cannot see the point of is the modern motivational coach. If a professional player needs extra motivation, he should not be in the job. Staying at the Angel Hotel in Cardiff provided all the incentive we needed for internationals as the team rubbed shoulders with the supporters on the morning of the game, tapping into their anticipation and excitement. Admittedly, this had its downside after a defeat because the last thing we wanted then was to talk about it but, in retrospect, perhaps having the thought hanging over our heads gave us an extra incentive to win. Sadly, teams are now incarcerated in hotels for what feels like weeks before internationals. I have seen no evidence that this schedule prepares a player better than meeting up on the Thursday before the game as we used to; in fact, it cannot be good for a player to be locked away for so long. I remember Dafydd James walking out of the Welsh team hotel and going back to his home a few miles away in an attempt to relieve the boredom – and he got dropped for it. Where was the sense in that?

Yes, I have some problems with the professional game but I would hate to give the impression that I do not enjoy modern rugby – far from it. There is a lot to admire and I get a tremendous buzz from watching the top players in action. The pace is fantastic and there are some spectacular matches full of intelligent, running rugby. Whilst I do not like the overemphasis on defence, the standard of the actual tackling is very high. As a player, I was unusual in that I made my name by tackling but now these sorts of challenges are expected from everybody in the team. Other skills have also improved beyond recognition from my day. Look at the standard of goal-kicking now.

I love being able to see matches from all over the world in the comfort of my armchair. My current favourite is the Super 14 series between the regional teams in Australia, South Africa and New Zealand. Competitive rugby of this calibre, together with that played in the northern hemisphere competitions such as the European Cup, cannot fail to attract supporters to our sport. As well as raising the profile of rugby, the increased television coverage, both in terms of the number of games televised and the number of cameras present to film each game, has reduced the incidence of violent play. An awful lot can go on behind the referee's back and if a player thinks that he may be caught on camera and then receive a lengthy ban, he is far less likely to act illegally in the first place. The vast majority of players act within the laws of the game. Indeed, it is considered unprofessional to lose your discipline to the extent that your side is penalised.

Refereeing today's fast-moving game is one of the most difficult officiating jobs in sport. I have tried my hand at refereeing at junior level and even with my background, the parents on the sideline still give me a hard time. So imagine what it must be like to have thousands of fans bellowing out their instructions. The video referee has been an excellent move to help the officials and something that I believe should be expanded beyond try-scoring moments. There is nothing to stop communication between the video referee and the match referee on, say, forward passes; if the technology is there, there should be no half measures. However, even the video referee can get it wrong sometimes.

Of the current laws, there are definitely some that I would like to see changed and, right at the top of my shortlist, is the absurd substitution law. How can a player get an international cap for coming onto the field for one minute and, in some cases, earn more money for doing so? It makes a mockery of the prestige of playing. An old friend of mine, Roy 'Shunto' Thomas, the old Swansea and Llanelli hooker, was on the subs bench twenty-eight times for Wales and never won a cap! Tactical substitutions should not be permitted in the last twenty minutes, particularly in the front row. The modern trend to swap the whole front row in the second half is ludicrous. It is one thing for a substitute to come on if a prop is injured or sent off as, for the safety of the players, he must be replaced by someone with the right expertise, but quite another for a substitute to come on merely as a pair of fresh legs. Even I, as a full-back, realise that it takes about an hour for a prop to get the better of his opponent; it must be galling to have finally won that battle, only to have your foe replaced with an energetic deputy.

The off-side line needs attention as well. Players are constantly cheating and, if they are not off-side, then they are almost off-side every time the ball is released from the breakdown. As a consequence, no one can operate with any freedom and I would suggest that both sides are moved back the ten metres to allow more initial space and encourage inventive play. On that subject, the law governing the penalty kick to touch should also be changed. If a team has a penalty and elects to kick the ball out, they should not maintain possession by throwing into the resultant line-out – the point of rugby is to promote attack by keeping the ball in play. Why not encourage the tap penalty if the kick at goal is rejected or not a feasible option?

I am proud that Wales have been one of the teams to prove that adventurous rugby can be both entertaining and successful in the modern age. But, as the paying public, we must be wary; too many games are dominated by negative attitudes and constant stoppages for inquiries to the referee or a slow movement towards the set piece. Stopping the clock for 'time-out' is a great step forward but there is too much wastage of time. Frequently, we fork out for an expensive ticket and end up with much less than the eighty minutes of play that we have paid for, although this is being rectified with the match clock. Alongside this, paying just £5 to listen to the Bridgend Tabernacle Choir's performance of Karl Jenkins' *Dewi Sant* seems like a bargain. I know this is not everybody's idea of a night out but we sang, the orchestra played and the conductor 'batoned' for eighty minutes, with not a water bottle in sight. Even better, nobody disturbed their neighbours in the audience by leaving the 'action' to get another pint of beer.

Rugby players have a lot to be proud of and the way in which they generally conduct themselves, on and off the pitch, is applauded by the public. I believe that they deserve huge praise for this, especially when you compare them to the footballers whose exploits are splashed across our screens and newspapers on a regular basis. Footballers are overpaid and spoilt – rugby players are not and they deserve all the money that comes their way. Today's player is constantly required to risk serious injury and face an awful lot of physical trauma and stress. We should never forget this.

19

INJURY TIME

I HAVE the greatest admiration for modern rugby players but, as a medic, I also have the greatest concern for them. Rugby is a dangerous sport – it always has been and always will be – but since professionalism there has been an alarming surge in the number of injuries. The power in rugby has increased and the forces being applied to the players' bodies are growing with every passing year. More than ever, scientific and medical opinion has a fundamental role in ensuring that rugby players receive the best treatment when injuries occur.

As a medical student and then a doctor, I would often be asked to examine injuries in training and I took it for granted that this would be the case. In matches, however, I felt less comfortable. If I had to help a member of the opposition, it could put me in rather a difficult position – how was I supposed to give an unbiased view on their star player? Of course, I did so honestly and without question but, with all the other pressures on a professional today, I am sure that this simply could not happen. I would be left open to all kinds of accusations and, anyway, it would break my concentration on the field and that would surely be deemed unprofessional.

I was lucky to have such easy access to medical treatment and physiotherapy and this was a great help to my rugby career. Most of the top-class rugby clubs had a doctor available during games but the clubs lower down the divisions were not so fortunate and their players could find themselves waiting for hours in casualty departments around Wales on a Saturday evening. This discrepancy still exists between the higher levels of the game and the junior club sides. The new regional teams in Wales have incredible medical back-up: they might have two doctors, two physios, sports massage therapists, psychologists and nutritionists, not to mention the crack fitness coach, all waiting to assist the players. Meanwhile those taking part in, say, Crynant versus Porthcawl have scant support. Financially, I do not see any way around this, as doctors cannot be posted at all matches, but it is a real problem, especially as a situation could easily be envisaged where the home club could be culpable if they do not have a qualified medic on site when a serious injury occurs. American football matches cannot take place without a doctor present and the rugby authorities should distribute as many resources as possible to ameliorate the situation for the junior clubs.

Physiotherapists are the most important medical presence in a rugby squad, providing assessment on the field and rehabilitation off it. Gerry Lewis was the physiotherapist for most of my time with Wales and it is a great credit to the WRU that they respected his experience on a range of matters instead of turning to others with lots of letters after their names. Gerry was a great guy and the players loved having him around – he had the job of giving out jerseys in the dressing room, a task he always performed with immense pride. But, above all, we trusted his judgement. He was not just a physio, he was also a great psychologist, and I would think nothing of driving down to Newport after a day's work to let Gerry treat a hamstring or a shoulder injury if he could convince me that I would be fit for Saturday.

Gerry's work would be very different today because, without the MRI scan, he had to rely on clinical findings that were based on his prior knowledge of how the player had responded to previous injuries. To a large extent the players had to use their instinct as well to help determine when they could start back playing. There was undoubtedly a lot of guesswork involved but it seemed to work.

Gerry was also expected to be a one-man band. He was the first stop for the whole team and would refer us to other specialists only if absolutely necessary. In today's world he would save a team two or three other salaries. I firmly believe that the current-day physiotherapist's role should be expanded because part of their training is to deal with matters such as psychology, fitness and nutrition.

Nutritionists were unheard of when I played at international level and it was not uncommon for the Pontypool front row to eat a huge meal of steak and chips on the morning before a match. As I was in a position to access medical advice, I managed to persuade the 'Pooler' boys and the rest of the Welsh squad to increase their carbohydrate intake and cut down on the unwanted extras. Whilst I am sure that it was beneficial to us, I am not wholly convinced that 'carbo-loading' is as useful in rugby as some think it is. Most of the evidence on this matter comes from studies on long distance, purely aerobic sports, such as cross-country skiing; in fact, I published a paper on this back in 1970. In comparison, rugby is a mixture of aerobic and anaerobic exercise, played over eighty minutes, and that means quite a difference in nutritional terms. Even so, it cannot do any harm to consume the pre-match 'carbs' and that is why most players do it.

Hydration is also very important in sport but frequently the players go about it in the wrong way. Water bottles are perpetually being brought onto the field when they should not be. Players have a small sip and throw the bottle back over the touchline and this achieves very little, apart from annoying the crowd. Instead, players should come over to the side of the pitch and have a proper drink if they are thirsty because, by that time, it is too late and dehydration will have set in. Again, the need for the athlete to keep fluids up by taking on lots of water before the kick-off was something that I stressed to the lads back in the seventies.

Naturally, I have always been interested in sports injuries as well. Way back in 1978, I researched neck injuries in rugby and compiled a register of all the injuries that had occurred over the previous ten years. The results were published as a short paper in *The British Medical Journal* under the guidance of Professor Brian McKibbon of the Cardiff Royal Infirmary and my research seemed to have great impact, leading directly to a change in the scrummaging laws at junior level to restrict driving at the scrum to no more than one metre. As time has gone on there have been further changes to increase safety at the very top level and, with scrum engagement now synchronised, there is much less collapsing. Shortly after I completed my paper, Scilla conducted a two-year research programme on rugby injuries in Wales for the International Board to determine whether there had been any increase in neck problems during this period. Irritatingly, they mislaid her work but we would like to feel that, between us, we helped to start the ball rolling in this area and encouraged the authorities to protect players in cases where there was an irrefutable medical argument for change.

One of the main protective measures at rugby's disposal is the law book and one law that requires immediate attention from the International Board relates to lifting at the line-out. This addition to the modern game is, in my professional opinion, a dangerous activity and it is only a matter of time before there is a high-profile spinal injury. It almost happened in the opening match of the 2003 World Cup when the Australian lock David Giffin fell awkwardly on his neck during the match against Argentina. He was very lucky that no serious damage resulted but it could so easily have been different.

Thankfully, when spinal injuries do now occur on the field, the standard of treatment is much better. Thinking the worst is crucial with these problems and, even though it can take a long time to get the injured player away from the action, it is imperative that no further damage is done during this vital period. The stretcher carts that are used in the southern hemisphere should be available at all leading matches world-wide as they would greatly improve the treatment offered. I am very pleased that the WRU has announced the introduction of pitch ambulances at the Millennium Stadium.

There has been a disturbing increase in the incidence of head injuries in recent years and I am worried that we could be sitting on a time-bomb here, with players who are getting repeatedly hurt having problems in later life just as boxers do. But at least head injuries are now addressed in a far more professional way compared to the old days when a player would often stay on the pitch to avoid the statutory three-week rest period. Concussion is a very subjective diagnosis and the time out of the game after a blow to the head is now scientifically assessed. Any investigation that makes the situation clearer is both safer and fairer on the player.

I see this as progress and the sensible application of medical knowledge in sport but we have to be careful that our attempts at accident prevention do not backfire. The wider use of head guards is a contentious area and, in my view, they can actually lead to an increased likelihood of neck and head injuries. The issue has been around in American football for some time where the helmets that are designed to protect the head have been used as a weapon in the game. The resultant force is deflected into the neck, leading to some tragic disabilities. In rugby, the softer head guard is not like a hard helmet but it can give a player a false sense of security and I do not think that we should be encouraging the use of the head as the point of a battering ram. Head guards give confidence after injury and protect recent cuts but I would not recommend their use for any other reason.

The blood bin, frequently the first stop for a player with an injured head, has been a highly beneficial addition to the game (and I cannot help thinking that I might have merited my own special place there – a sort of private ward!) Other players must be protected from blood-borne infections and, off the pitch, the wounded man can be treated properly to avoid infection from contaminants, unlike my experience with the Arms Park mud in my calf wound in 1979.

My initial cut was due to a boot stud, as were several of my other injuries as a player, and I am relieved that great strides have been made to combat this hazard since I retired. Those old aluminium studs led to some horrific head wounds and, after some early hesitation, the International Board has got there in the end. Unbelievably, there are still horror stories of players who, having had their studs checked by the referee before the match, then change their boots to something more dangerous. This is, however, one problem that has to be eradicated through peer pressure; the appropriate regulations are in place and the referee cannot keep halting the game to re-check. Players have to take responsibility and that means abiding by the safety rules and identifying anyone who is wearing dangerous studs. They are fools to themselves if they do not.

With pay cheques and future contracts at stake, there is huge pressure on coaches to pull players off the pitch to avoid the possibility of any further injury and to protect them for future games. One of the things that worries me most about the modern approach to rugby injuries is the massive increase in 'defensive' medical diagnoses. In my specialist area of orthopaedics, knee injuries are extremely common in rugby players and the most serious is a tear to the anterior cruciate ligament (ACL), the ligament responsible for the stability of the knee joint. These injuries were hardly recognised at all thirty years ago but most professional rugby players suffering with a torn ACL will now have reconstructive surgery. I believe that this is not always necessary. The Welsh half-backs in the early 1980s, Gareth Davies and Terry Holmes, both had ACL tears. Clinically, their knees were unstable but they did not undergo surgery and had successful careers with knees that were technically injured.

One reason why there is so much surgery is that, since professionalism, it seems that an MRI scan is carried out on any kind of injury before a decision on treatment is made. On the one hand, this is understandable, given the pressures on all concerned, but as MRI is a very sensitive procedure, all sorts of minor abnormalities are picked up that do not necessarily need operating on and might well not have been detected anyway. The problem is that, once they are reported, they have to be discussed and acted on. From the days when, at least some of the time, ignorance was bliss, most players now end up with an operation even though many injuries would clear up on their own if given time. Pressure from rugby management and insurance companies, and the fear of legal re-percussions, is forcing surgeons into operating, despite the fact that many players could be back playing earlier if they had adequate non-operative rehabilitation.

Notwithstanding this, injuries have increased dramatically during the professional era but, interestingly, more and more occur in training and not just in matches. I have always thought that the emphasis on gym work not only prevents skill development but does not prepare the player for the three dimensional aspect of rugby – pushing, jumping and tackling. The weights, the running machine and the exercise bike can in no way compare with the real thing of playing with a ball and absorbing impact. Of course, being out there on the pitch requires fitness but a player's reflexes and co-ordination need fine-tuning if he is to make the breaks and the tackles. Playing matches is the best training method available and, then, if the proper rest is permitted, the players could drastically reduce the time they spend on the training field.

In summary, I am of the opinion that the increasing incidence of injuries is not because there are too many games for the players per se; it is due to overtraining and the season itself being too long and poorly structured. Weekly match-play should be achievable, even with the heavy-hitting modern game, but the intensity of competitions should be allowed to grow gradually for the benefit of the players' bodies. In the southern hemisphere, they have got it right. Look at New Zealand, where the Super 14 builds to a climax and is then followed by the international in-coming tours that gather momentum towards the Tri-Nations. Those not involved in the international squad take part in the National Provincial Competition, along with any of the international players who need more game time. The season is rounded off with an overseas tour and an adequate rest period for everyone.

The result of the northern hemisphere's inability to settle on a suitable structure for our season will be the shortening of the playing lifespan of our professional rugby players. There are some older players still around but others have bodies that simply cannot take the combination of sustained training and tough competitive matches. Think of Britain's most famous rugby player of recent times, Jonny Wilkinson. He is the perfect example of a man whose body has been pushed too far. He has so much commitment and I sincerely hope that he can successfully continue his career, but will his body allow him to reach the high standards that he once achieved? Wilkinson has made enough money to set him up for life but I detect that he cares little for that, compared to playing the sport that he loves. I can empathise with his love of rugby but Wilkinson's case makes me wonder whether the modern game is medically sustainable at current levels of playing and training.

For the record, these are the major injuries that I received during my career:

1964 Fracture of right clavicle and a/c joint – school match
1964 Fracture of left scapula – school match
1968 Dislocation (compound) of right index finger – Bridgend v Cardiff
1969 Facial laceration – St Mary's Hospital v Bridgend
1971 Fracture (depressed) of right zygoma – Wales v England

1972 Fracture of maxilla – Wales v Scotland
1974 Torn posterior cruciate ligament in right knee – London Welsh v London Scottish
1976 Facial laceration – Wales v England
1978 Facial laceration (severe) – Bridgend v New Zealand
1979 Laceration of right calf – Wales v England
1981 Hyphaema (blood inside the eye) – Bridgend v Cardiff

This eye injury was my final first-class rugby injury. Someone's finger poked me whilst I was taking a high ball and I was completely blind in that eye. It was very frightening and I was advised to rest for forty-eight hours. When I telephoned my orthopaedic consultant the following day and told him that I had a hyphaema, he thought I meant a 'high femur fracture' and told me to come in and get it fixed on his list! Even injuries can have their funny side sometimes.

20

MARATHONS
AND MOUNTAINS

I THINK it is safe to say that I am a man who likes a challenge. I
also like to be active; retiring to a beach is not my style as I can
only read a book in the sun for an hour before I am up and about
again. Having been so used to one contest after another throughout
my life, perhaps I will always need an objective to work towards.
This was certainly the case when my international rugby career
came to an end and I desperately wanted to be part of another
major sporting event, no matter how different.

1981 was the year of the first London Marathon, the brainchild
of Chris Brasher, a co-athlete at Oxford University with Sir Roger
Bannister, and although I had never been known as a runner, the
concept caught my imagination and I decided to enter. The race
took place in March and, as I had been dropped by Wales, there
were no international rugby commitments but there was a big club
game coming up three days later. Most of the Bridgend committee
and my team-mates were decidedly unhappy about my risking
injury but I was adamant. I really felt the need to prove my fitness
after my reverse with Wales.

John Taylor and his agent were supposed to be running with me
but they both had to pull out and I was left to take it on alone. I had
sometimes used running as a way of keeping fit after missing
training sessions but, until that marathon, I had never run farther
than eight miles in one go, and that was only a fortnight before the

London race. Despite this, I was pretty confident. With my attitude, I convinced myself, I could do anything once I had put my mind to it.

Looking back, many other aspects of my preparation for the run were rather naïve, to say the least. I did not even have any proper trainers and ended up wearing Astroturf shoes with pimples on the soles because they seemed slightly more useful than my tennis shoes or even my rugby boots! I also pitched up at Greenwich wearing my favourite but highly inappropriate tracksuit, a bright blue one sent over from France by Jean-Pierre Rives as a swap for a number fifteen jersey of mine. Many of my fellow runners were more sensibly attired in plastic bin-bags and, although I had planned to hand the tracksuit to Scilla at the six-mile mark, when I judged that I would be working up a bit of a sweat, the arrangement went horribly wrong and she missed me at the staging post. As the last stragglers brought up the rear, she began to panic – she thought I had not even made it that far! Luckily, I caught sight of my brother Mike, who was still a medical student in London at the time, and put the Rives tracksuit in his safe keeping. Not only that, he then felt duty bound to link up with me throughout the race and keep me company, and how grateful I was for his support.

I hit the famous marathon runner's wall as I was going around the Isle of Dogs and I was only able to carry on to the finish because of Mike's vocal encouragement. Later, on the television replay, I heard the BBC commentator David Coleman say, 'And here comes JPR, built more like a carthorse than a marathon runner!' I could see what he meant as I galloped in a rather ungainly fashion over the finishing line after more than four gruelling hours. I felt extremely proud, though, to have taken part in and finished the first London Marathon. Perhaps it was a stupid thing to have done with an important game only three days later but, luckily, the Bridgend committee forgave me, I played at Pontypool Park and we won the match.

That day I really had found something to replace my thoughts of getting back into the Welsh side and I went on to run the next five London Marathons and the second Cardiff Marathon. After that first struggle, I prepared properly for the next one and, over the years, the races got progressively easier. Determination is at the heart of marathon running so the sport suited my character very well but recently something came along really to test my strength of mind and put my marathons into the shade, the biggest and most punishing challenge that I have ever faced.

It all began in the autumn of 2005 when David Pickering, the WRU chairman, mentioned to me that he and his wife were trying to raise money for the NSPCC's 'Full Stop' campaign by climbing Mount Kilimanjaro, at 5896 metres the highest mountain in Africa. Would I like to join them? I had no doubt – the idea appealed immediately – but Scilla sensibly insisted that my daughter Annie join the climb to look after me!

Sixteen of us were to make the trip in January 2006, a mixed bag of people from the worlds of business and sport, with an age profile ranging from twenty-six-year-old Annie through to sixty-two years – so at least I was not quite the oldest. What we did have in common was complete inexperience in mountaineering and the slightly uneasy knowledge that there was a significant degree of risk attached to the trip. Climbing Kilimanjaro was going to be a serious test for us. There is a pretty high mortality rate on the mountain and there are no rescue facilities, no helicopters, no oxygen packs, no nothing. If you get into trouble on Kilimanjaro and cannot go any farther, then you have to sort it out by yourself.

The organisation and leadership of the party was in the capable hands of army men, Major Mike Laing and his long-time climbing partner and paramedic, Captain Ian Blackwood. They made sure that we were as well prepared as possible, with two climbing weekends before Christmas in Snowdonia and the Brecon Beacons. It was essential training, but it made us even more realistic about what we were taking on. Mount Snowdon had been tough but Kilimanjaro is six times higher and, on our approach into Moshi on the final leg of our journey from Nairobi, we saw just how high. We were travelling at 17,000 feet and, when we looked out of the aeroplane window, there was Mount Kilimanjaro above us. We glanced at each other as if to say, how the hell are we going to get up there?

On arrival in Tanzania, our feelings turned from trepidation to impatience and we just wanted to get on our way. Heavy rain threatened to delay the start but we decided to begin the climb one day ahead of schedule and after lunch on Thursday, 12 January all our planning became reality and we left camp. We were to follow the Umbwe route up the mountain, the most difficult and, there-fore, least popular of the seven major tracks.

That first day was hard. The rainforest, whilst undoubtedly a thing of beauty, was the one place where I questioned whether I would be able to complete the course, and we had barely started. It was stiflingly hot and we had more than twelve kilometres to climb along a track that was muddy, slippery and very steep. As we climbed over the rocks and through the trees, less and less light was getting through and, when darkness fell, the rain and clouds kept the full moon hidden. I really felt that serious injury was only a second away and knew already that this was one the toughest things that I had ever done in my life. At 2580 metres, we arrived at Umbwe Cave camp, tired and ravenous, but in reasonably good spirits to have put the heat of the forest behind us.

Day 2 brought sunshine and our mood remained positive. After travelling through a less dense area of forest, we emerged out of the low clouds and felt as if we were getting somewhere. Perhaps it was a good thing that the higher cloud hanging over the top of the mountain was disguising the enormity of what still lay in front of us. We had seen only two other climbers up to this point and, unfortunately, both had reported how they had had to abandon their climbs because of bad weather conditions and the snow and the ice that lay ahead. After scrambling over some knife-edged rocks, we made it to Barranco Hut at 3950 metres, still ahead of schedule and in relatively good shape. The altitude was beginning to give some mild headaches but the atmosphere in the team was still upbeat.

We woke the next day to bad news: our original route via the Western Breach had been closed because of a serious rockfall that had killed a climber a few days earlier so, instead of continuing upwards, we would have to traverse around the mountain towards Karanga Hut. Much of Day 3 was spent trudging up and down, and knowing all the time that we would only gain a paltry fifty metres of height at the end of it. It was very dispiriting and, to make matters worse, Dai Pickering had picked up a bug that was clearly weakening him. The humour of our three local guides, especially the constantly smiling Munna, was essential to keep us going. We were 'tagging' two other teams along this southern circuit around the base of the mountain, some Scandinavians and a rather loud group of Americans – we were determined not to let Wales down.

In the morning on Day 4, we could actually see the summit of Kilimanjaro above us for the first time and below were the flat plains of Africa and Moshi, the town from where we had started out. It was daunting to see what we still had to achieve but Dai was feeling better and this boosted the whole party. The downside was that we were really beginning to feel the effects of the high altitude in a much more significant way. Even bending down to put my boots on was agony, as my breathing was erratic and the gasps for air were making me wonder where the next burst of oxygen was coming from. Going out to have a pee in the night was a real effort because of having to put my shoes on, so I must admit that, on medical grounds, I succumbed to the use of the plastic bottle!

We knew that if the oxygen saturation level in our blood fell to below 80 per cent, then we would have to turn back. Altitude sickness is not an illness to be taken lightly and, in an effort to conserve energy, we started to climb slowly upwards to Barafu Camp, our springboard for the bid to reach the summit. On this final ascent, at midnight on Day 5, it was snowing quite heavily and, after a last briefing from our guides that was much sterner in tone than the previous ones, we gathered our kit to set off with the moon and stars lighting our way. There were to be stops only every one and half hours on this leg and, although it was physically tough, I was finding that the mental side was harder as the climb was now so monotonous.

There was no choice, though; I simply had to make it but, all the time, the effects of the altitude were kicking in very dramatically. A pounding headache and nausea are the first signs and I was becoming worried about Annie. She had put on too many layers at the outset and had suffered from overheating but, ten minutes into the latest climb, she was overheating again, despite the fact that the temperature was minus 15 degrees Celsius. Some tablets seemed to cool her down and I trusted that her inherent fitness from the Iron Man competitions would see her through. It was unsettling. If someone as fit as Annie was struggling, then it would only be a matter of time before I started to encounter problems and she was meant to be looking after me!

Two hours later and another member of our party, Simon, was in big trouble with vomiting and diarrhoea. He was suffering from acute mountain sickness (AMS), a potentially fatal illness, and, although we knew that it was likely that somebody was going to experience this condition, it was not pleasant to see one of the team struggling in this way. Simon could not stand up as he lost his balance easily and he started to remonstrate angrily with the team leader – irrational behaviour is another of the main symptoms of AMS. In such circumstances there is only one treatment, to go down the mountain or risk cerebral or pulmonary oedema. At a lower altitude, the body recovers almost straightaway so it was vital for Simon to head off downhill for Barafu Camp immediately. The group was left upset and deflated and, inevitably, we wondered who would be next.

So many times we thought we could see Stella Point, the top of the mountain, but they were false dawns. Kilimanjaro's summit was much farther away than we could have imagined, even at that stage, but then the sun came out and, there it was, in all of its glistening glory at 7 a.m. on a wonderful morning of clear blue skies. Inspired, we pushed on up a gentler incline to the top and, in the last two hours, passed the Decken Glacier and the Southern Icefield. At 9 a.m., we were finally there – on Uhuru Peak at 5896 metres, looking down on the world. We hugged each other in triumph before unfurling the NSPCC banner to remind us of why we were there. Annie, feeling much better by now, even went for a run on the top – what a place for a jog! We had been warned, however, not to linger up there for more than half an hour because the altitude that we had now reached would soon start to play havoc with our oxygen saturation. I must confess that, although I was ecstatic to have climbed the mountain, my joy was tempered by the thought of the dreaded descent ahead. My knees were starting to hurt badly and I suspected that years of rugby injuries were about to take their toll.

I was right, going downhill was an ordeal as I jarred my knees agonisingly into the ground with every step. After four painful hours we met up with Simon at Barafu Camp and it was wonderful to find that he had totally recovered. But we could not hang about there either and, after an hour's rest, we slogged on for four more hours. It seemed never-ending, the aching in my joints simply would not stop and I actually had to be carried into one of the camps after a search party was sent to find Simon and me. After his misfortune, Simon was helping me in my difficulty; he was proving to be a rock and I think that the assistance he was able to offer me helped him to come to terms with not reaching the summit and gave him a sense of purpose within the group. I will certainly never forget his generosity and we will be lifelong friends after the experience.

On Day 6 we walked for four more hours to the exit gate at Mweka through some pleasant and almost familiar moorland – it was rather like being back in Wales. Then, after passing through the rainforest again, it was suddenly over. Sensing that we needed to come slowly down from our high, Dai Pickering suggested that we book into a five-star hotel in Mombassa before returning home. Sitting on a bar stool in the warm pool, sipping a G & T and feeling the old bones relax was about as good as it gets.

It was amazing that so many of us made it up and down the mountain. The businessmen in particular did magnificently well because they had never been in such a physically demanding situation before, unlike myself, Annie, Dai, Kate Morgan, who had over one hundred caps for Wales at hockey, or Jeremy Pugh, another former Welsh rugby international.

Apparently, our guides had said amongst themselves on the first day that they thought less than half of us would make it to the top and, indeed, this had been the case with the American and Scandinavian teams ahead of us as AMS had taken a heavy toll on their numbers. Fifteen out of sixteen Welsh men and women was a highly respectable success rate and the fact that we had raised over £200,000 for the NSPCC campaign meant that it had been a complete and utter success. Despite his cold hands, Andrew Howell even managed to keep an excellent diary to help us recall the emotion of each step for years to come.

It is strange but, after all that climbing, I found reaching the summit of Kilimanjaro an anticlimax, rather like when I crossed the finish line in a marathon and did not quite know what to do with myself. For me, the unforgettable moments were the camaraderie, the team-work, the togetherness and the fact that we are all now friends for life, no questions asked. As with all the best challenges, it perfectly illustrated the spirit of man. If I had known how hard it was going to be, perhaps I would never have gone, but making it at my age with my joints is something that definitely ranks alongside any of my other sporting achievements.

On my return to Wales, it was satisfying to be known for something else other than rugby again, just as used to be the case with my tennis and medicine. When I visited Bridgend Rugby Club for the first time since the climb, more people came up to say, 'Well done,' than when I used to return to the club after winning for Wales. The average person can really identify with taking on a mountain peak and winning.

I do not know what my next challenge will be, but I do know that I will need one. I will keep up my running, on the beach with our new dog, Frodo, and there is always cycling, which I find much easier on the joints than Kilimanjaro. The Ogmore Valley Wheelers can expect to get a few more visits from me. Then there may be grandchildren and what a challenge they will be. Despite all the achievements in my life, my family has always meant far more to me than anything else.

On our way up Kilimanjaro, we were asked to give a talk about our lives to the rest of the group. I finished mine at 1979, the year when my last book was published, cheekily saying to everyone that they could read about the rest in my new book. I sincerely hope that my companions from the climb have enjoyed my story and you have too.

CONCLUSION

My Greatest Ever Team – JPR's XV

In choosing my greatest ever team, I have restricted myself to those players whom I have played with or against, or watched as a spectator. To the greats who were around before my day, I apologise, but I did not feel that I could select on hearsay. In truth, however, any great player from any era would be a great player in any other era. There has been a natural tendency for me to pick from my playing days but I suppose that this is understandable as sharing a rugby field with someone does provide the greatest opportunity to appreciate their skills. I count myself fortunate to have played with or against these men. I wish that I had been able to do so with those of my selections who came after me.

I have been careful to assemble a team that would work well together, with complementary units within the side. I know that, over the course of a pint or two, people may try to argue for changes but, whilst I respect their views, I have made my decisions and stand by them.

Full-back – Pierre Villepreux (France)
When I was growing up, Pierre made a major impression on me and I think that I subconsciously tried to model myself on him. A full-back's primary function is to be his side's final line of defence; Pierre could certainly defend but he was also outstanding in attack. This extra element to full-back play is what the French really like to

see and, for that reason, if I had to play for any other nation than Wales then it would have to be France. When Pierre went on to become an outstanding coach, he coached like he had played, with flair and superb vision.

Right winger – Gerald Davies (Wales)
This position had to be reserved for my room-mate, TGR Davies. I played with Gerald for a decade and can never remember him dying with the ball – he either scored or passed it back inside. He had an ability to beat men like no other and I will never forget the four incredible tries that he scored against Hawkes Bay for the Lions in 1971. He also scored four tries for Cardiff against Pontypool in a Cup match, having only had possession of the ball four times in the match.

Outside centre – Philippe Sella (France)
Philippe played over one hundred times for France during the days when caps were not as cheap as they are today. He was a silky runner but also very strong and powerful. He was made for the outside centre role because he had the eye to see the gap, the body to get him through it and the speed to go on the outside of the defender if required. Without doubt, Philippe was the complete player in his position.

Inside centre – Mike Gibson (Ireland)
An extremely gifted player, Mike could step off either foot and could kick with both feet as well. He was not a big man but he was a tremendous tackler and would deal with people twice his size. His strongest suit, however, was his great feel for back play and he could always see what was feasible and what was not. Remember that he appeared in a series of relatively mediocre Irish sides but never stopped scoring tries. On the 1971 Lions tour, when he was surrounded by other great players, he was one of the stars.

Left winger – David Campese (Australia)

People either love David or hate him but, whatever they think of his character, they have to agree that he was one hell of a player. I actually like the way he used to stir people up off the field. Campo is one of those men who, when you meet him, is even better in real life and almost larger than life itself. He scored so many unorthodox tries for Australia – yes, he might have been difficult to play with on occasion because his team-mates would not be sure what he was going to do, but that made him great to watch.

Fly-half – Barry John (Wales)

There could be no other fly-half in my team. Barry had the most fantastic self-confidence that I have ever known in a player; it rubbed off on everyone who played with him whilst unnerving the opposition. He played the game at his pace and, like all great number tens, left no one in any doubt that he was in command. The only flaw to his game was his tackling, or the lack of it, as he never much cared for getting stuck in. I can live with this, however, because it made me as a player – after all, I had to do his tackling for him!

Scrum-half – Gareth Edwards (Wales)

Even today with the strong back rows, Gareth would still score every time from five metres out. He had such a low centre of gravity that he could get under any tackle. Gareth's kicking was of the highest standard too and nobody has box-kicked better than he did in the history of the game. His service to his fly-half was near perfect and his speed of thought was matched by his speed over the ground. There simply was not a weakness to his game and, as an athlete, he set the standards then and would probably do so now. In my view, Gareth is simply the best of all time.

Loose-head prop – Ken Gray (New Zealand)

Ken was so impressive on my first trip to New Zealand in 1969. He was a tall man for a prop, certainly in those days, and he was awesomely strong, killing our forwards all by himself on that tour. His technique at the scrum was first-rate and this is my priority when selecting props. It helps if they are mobile, but win the battle at the scrum conclusively and then the game is more often than not yours. Ken would see to that.

Hooker – Sean Fitzpatrick (New Zealand) Captain

This was another simple selection: Sean could do everything a hooker should be able to do and more. His throwing was unerringly accurate and he had all the necessary power at the scrum, plus excellent skills in the loose. He was a master of the referee and, in my XV, it would be a competition between him and Gareth to see who could get control of the official first. Sean was also a winner and that is why he would not only be my hooker but my captain as well.

Tight-head prop – Fran Cotton (England)

Like Ken, Fran was not the most mobile prop but he was the strongest man that I ever went up against in the scrum. Yes, you read that right, I used to do that kind of thing at Lions training just to calm me down a bit! Fran played for an England side that was constantly being changed by selectors who seemed not to know their own minds but, when he was with the Lions, you could appreciate that he was a world-class prop forward.

Lock – Colin Meads (New Zealand)

By today's standards, Colin would be far too short to be a second-row. On second thoughts, perhaps with lifting allowed in the line-out, he would be amazing as, after all, he was so good when he had to do the jumping on his own. He had massive natural strength and was another man with great leadership qualities, a player that you would follow into battle and probably to the end of the earth as well.

Lock – Frik du Preez (South Africa)
Frik's may be the name in my team least known to a wider audience but, believe me, he was an exceptional player. Like Colin, he was not the tallest lock but he was an athletic jumper. He was devastating around the field and you only have to recall the try he scored for South Africa against the Lions in 1968 to see that. He came out of the line-out and ran from the halfway line like a born sprinter. Poor Tom Kiernan was left for dead. Frik was another player who made a significant impact on me in my youth.

Blindside flanker – Michael Jones (New Zealand)
The sheer magnitude of Michael's talent is best demonstrated by a brief look at his career history: after he suffered a serious knee injury when he was the best number seven in the world, he moved to a position that required marginally less pace and became the best number six the game has ever produced. Need I say more?

Openside flanker – Richie McCaw (New Zealand)
Richie is the best number seven that I have ever seen and the only current player in my selection. I love watching him play: to me, he is an ideal openside, contesting every breakdown, it seems, and usually winning the ball. He is a real pain in the neck for the opposition but a wonderful asset to his side. He is the perfect size for his position – not too big and not too small – and this ensures that, whilst he is not driven off the ball, he can get down low enough to win it.

Number eight – Mervyn Davies (Wales)
If I did not pick Mervyn in this team then I would never hear the last of it! But Merv is not only one of my best mates, he was also a

wonderful player. His engine would never stop running during a game and, when he was on the ball, he showed off his considerable skills. On the floor, he would contest everything. I have lost count of the number of times that he won turnover ball for us. The way the game was then, it was not such a big deal but now, with that kind of possession being like gold dust, Merv would be worth his weight in gold.

My Greatest Ever Match –
27 January 1973, Cardiff

Barbarians 23 New Zealand 11
This match has such a prominent place in the history of our sport because it was not only a great spectacle, it effectively launched rugby as a world-wide game. Everyone's eyes were on us that day – it was billed as the 1971 Lions versus the 1973 All Blacks – and millions of people were watching a rugby match on television for the first time. They had been drawn in by the pre-match publicity and, with the end-to-end excitement and extraordinary skill levels on display, it was the best advertisement for a sport anyone could ask for.

Although there were inevitably one or two changes from the team that had toured New Zealand eighteen months earlier, the Barbarians side was essentially the British and Irish Lions of 1971. Our famous victories on the other side of the world had led to a huge amount of public expectation and Cardiff was buzzing on the morning of the game. For a Barbarians team we were unusually nervous; normally, as Baa-Baas, the mood was relaxed because we felt that there was nothing to lose but, this time, we felt we had everything to lose.

In accordance with the tradition of the Barbarians as the ultimate amateurs, we had no coach but our captain, John Dawes, who had come out of retirement for this match, had invited Carwyn James to visit us in the dressing room before the game. Just as he had done so successfully as Lions coach in New Zealand, Carwyn was able to put us in the right frame of mind for the Cardiff match with a few well-chosen words. I remember his advice to Phil Bennett, who was in for the now retired Barry John and was fretting about stepping into such distinguished shoes. He said, 'Phil, just imagine you are at Stradey Park.'

Three minutes into the match, Phil's scarlet Llanelli socks famously danced away from the would-be All Black tacklers as if he was indeed playing at home to initiate the most well-known try in rugby history. Cliff Morgan in the commentary box uttered his epic words: 'This is great stuff . . . Phil Bennett covering, chased by Alistair Scowen . . . brilliant . . . Oh, that's brilliant! John Williams, Brian Williams . . . Pullin, John Dawes . . . great dummy! . . . David, Tom David . . . the halfway line . . . Brilliant by Quinnell! This is Gareth Edwards! A dramatic start! . . . What a score . . . Oh, that fellow Edwards!'

Of course, I was John Williams in those days and, after Phil's magical side-steps, I recall taking a high tackle from my namesake Brian Williams and then watching as the try unfolded in front of my eyes. Gareth was behind me when it all started but he soon sped past like a train whistling through a station. If Derek Quinnell had given the ball to John Bevan on the wing, then we would not have scored because we needed Gareth's momentum. As I saw him hurtle towards the corner, I began to think it was on but I was not sure until the very last second when he put it down – it was that close. The atmosphere at the Arms Park, which was already sensational, was transported to an even higher level by that score. It was certainly a good try and we were pleased with it at the time, but we had no idea how we would all dine out on it for years afterwards!

Welsh crowds love the Barbarians because of their style and, continuing to play with attack firmly fixed in our minds, we took our chances to lead 17–0 at half-time. It was certainly not a one-sided game however. The All Blacks had been territorially dominant in the first half and soon started to score points. At the end, we found ourselves needing one last try to seal the victory and I was fortunate enough to be the man who scored it. Once again, a New Zealand winger, this time Grant Batty, tried to take my head off after I had just avoided Joe Karam's tackle and I fell over the line completely exhausted, physically and mentally.

Recently I watched a re-run of the game and noticed that there were a fair number of errors. I am sure that the technical experts would say there were far too many turnovers and dropped passes but, on that special day, both sides wanted to play an expansive game and, overall, the skill levels certainly stand the test of time. It was a southern hemisphere Super 14 type of game with everybody offloading the ball before the tackle. The kicking from hand was also good with Phil Bennett, in particular, punting the ball a long way up the touchline by using the old-fashioned torpedo or screw kick and, remember, that was with a much heavier ball.

It was fascinating to see how much the game has changed over the years. In 1973, there was much less power in the scrum and some of the props had almost spindly legs in comparison to modern front rows. In general, all the players on the field were smaller than today's professionals. With no lifting, the line-out was much more 50:50 and it was more compressed than a modern line-out, both in terms of length and width, allowing for far more space in midfield. People may be surprised now to see the New Zealand wingers throwing into the line-out using a bowling action but this happened regularly then and, for the Barbarians, it was very useful – it meant that they were already a back down when the game restarted.

These changes are undoubtedly interesting but what struck me most about this game was how the players obviously relished being there. They were playing rugby in the way that they wanted to and, despite there being a great deal of honour and pride at stake, this did not have any negative impact on the style of play. I have found it to be true throughout my career that if the players enjoy a match, it usually means that the spectators will too and this was certainly the case on that remarkable, entertaining day. I do not think that I have ever enjoyed a game more.

As I listened to Cliff Morgan's evocative commentary, one line seemed to encapsulate my approach to all the contrasting elements of my busy life: 'John Williams, that fellow never ever shirks not only a tackle but any situation at all.' I would like to think that just about says it all for John and JPR!

JPR'S TEST CAREER FOR THE BRITISH AND IRISH LIONS

- Williams, JPR (London Welsh and Wales) 1971 NZ 1,2,3,4, 1974 SA 1,2,3,4
- Eight Tests, five wins, two draws and one defeat.
- Played in winning series in New Zealand and South Africa
- Points – three (one dropped goal)
- Record-holder for most appearances as a full-back for the Lions in Tests

TEST 1 26 June 1971, Carisbrook, Dunedin

New Zealand 3 (1PG) British/Irish Lions 9 (2PG 1T)

NEW ZEALAND: W F McCormick; B A Hunter, B G Williams, W D Cottrell, K R Carrington; R E Burgess, S M Going; R A Guy, R W Norton, B L Muller, C E Meads (captain), P J Whiting, A M McNaughton, A R Sutherland, I A Kirkpatrick
Scorer *Penalty Goal*: McCormick

BRITISH/IRISH LIONS: J P R Williams; T G R Davies, S J Dawes (captain), C M H Gibson, J C Bevan; B John, G O Edwards; J McLauchlan, J V Pullin, J F Lynch, W D Thomas, W J McBride, P J Dixon, T M Davies, J Taylor
Replacement R Hopkins for Edwards (7 mins)
Scorers *Try*: McLauchlan *Penalty Goals*: John (2)

Referee J P G Pring (New Zealand)

TEST 2 10 July 1971, Lancaster Park, Christchurch

New Zealand 22 (2G 1PG 3T) British/Irish Lions 12 (1PG 1DG 2T)

NEW ZEALAND: L W Mains; B A Hunter, H T Joseph, W D Cottrell,

B G Williams; R E Burgess, S M Going; R A Guy, R W Norton, B L Muller,
C E Meads (captain), P J Whiting, A M McNaughton, A J Wyllie, I A Kirkpatrick
Scorers *Tries*: Burgess (2), Going, Kirkpatrick, Williams (pen try) *Conversions*:
Mains (2) *Penalty Goal*: Mains

BRITISH/IRISH LIONS: J P R Williams; T G R Davies, S J Dawes (captain),
C M H Gibson, D J Duckham; B John, G O Edwards; J McLauchlan, J V Pullin,
J F Lynch, W D Thomas, W J McBride, P J Dixon, T M Davies, J Taylor
Scorers *Tries*: T G R Davies (2) *Penalty Goal*: John *Dropped Goal*: John

Referee J P G Pring (New Zealand)

TEST 3 31 July 1971, Athletic Park, Wellington

New Zealand 3 (1T) British/Irish Lions 13 (2G 1DG)

NEW ZEALAND: L W Mains; B A Hunter, H T Joseph, W D Cottrell,
K R Carrington; R E Burgess, S M Going; R A Guy, R W Norton, B L Muller,
C E Meads (captain), B J Lochore, A M McNaughton, A J Wyllie, I A Kirkpatrick
Replacement M G Duncan for Burgess (67 mins)
Scorer *Try*: Mains

BRITISH/IRISH LIONS: J P R Williams; T G R Davies, S J Dawes (captain),
C M H Gibson, D J Duckham; B John, G O Edwards; J McLauchlan, J V Pullin,
J F Lynch, G L Brown, W J McBride, D L Quinnell, T M Davies, J Taylor
Scorers *Tries*: T G R Davies, John *Conversions*: John (2) *Dropped Goal*: John

Referee J P G Pring (New Zealand)

TEST 4 14 August 1971, Eden Park, Auckland

New Zealand 14 (1G 2PG 1T) British/Irish Lions 14 (1G 2PG 1DG)

NEW ZEALAND: L W Mains; K R Carrington, M G Duncan, P C Gard,
B G Williams; W D Cottrell, S M Going; R A Guy, R W Norton, B L Muller,
C E Meads (captain), P J Whiting, T N Lister, A J Wyllie, I A Kirkpatrick
Scorer *Tries*: Cottrell, Lister *Conversion*: Mains *Penalty Goals*: Mains (2)

BRITISH/IRISH LIONS: J P R Williams; T G R Davies, S J Dawes (captain),
C M H Gibson, D J Duckham; B John, G O Edwards; J McLauchlan, J V Pullin,
J F Lynch, G L Brown, W J McBride, P J Dixon, T M Davies, J Taylor
Replacement W D Thomas for Brown (61 mins)
Scorers *Try*: Dixon *Conversion*: John *Penalty Goals*: John (2)
Dropped Goal: J P R Williams

Referee J P G Pring (New Zealand)

TEST 5 8 June 1974, Newlands, Cape Town

South Africa 3 (1DG) British/Irish Lions 12 (3PG 1DG)

SOUTH AFRICA: I D McCallum; C F Pope, J J Oosthuizen, P J M Whipp, G H Muller; D S L Snyman, R J McCallum; J T Sauerman, J F B van Wyk, J F K Marais (captain), K B H de Klerk, J G Williams, J H H Coetzee, M du Plessis, J H Ellis
Scorer *Dropped Goal*: Snyman

BRITISH/IRISH LIONS: J P R Williams; W C C Steele, I R McGeechan, R A Milliken, J J Williams; P Bennett, G O Edwards; J McLauchlan, R W Windsor, F E Cotton, W J McBride (captain), G L Brown, R M Uttley, T M Davies, J F Slattery
Scorers *Penalty Goals*: Bennett (3) *Dropped Goal*: Edwards

Referee M Baise (South Africa)

TEST 6 22 June 1974, Loftus Versfeld, Pretoria

South Africa 9 (2PG 1DG) British/Irish Lions 28 (1G 1PG 1DG 4T)

SOUTH AFRICA: I D McCallum; C F Pope, J C P Snyman, P J M Whipp, J S Germishuys; G R Bosch, P C R Bayvel; N S E Bezuidenhout, C A Fredrickson, J F K Marais (captain), K B H de Klerk, J G Williams, M du Plessis, D A Macdonald, J H Ellis

Replacements D S L Snyman for McCallum (69 mins); M L Vogel for D S L Snyman (76 mins)
Scorer *Penalty Goals*: Bosch (2) *Dropped Goal*: Bosch

BRITISH/IRISH LIONS: J P R Williams; W C C Steele, I R McGeechan, R A Milliken, J J Williams; P Bennett, G O Edwards; J McLauchlan, R W Windsor, F E Cotton, W J McBride (captain), G L Brown, R M Uttley, T M Davies, J F Slattery
Scorers *Tries*: J J Williams (2), Milliken, Bennett, Brown *Conversion*: Bennett *Penalty Goal*: Bennett *Dropped Goal*: McGeechan

Referee C J de Bruyn (South Africa)

TEST 7 13 July 1974, Boet Erasmus Stadium, Port Elizabeth

South Africa 9 (3PG) British/Irish Lions 26 (1G 2PG 2DG 2T)

SOUTH AFRICA: O A Roux; C F Pope, P A Cronje, J J J Schlebusch, G H Muller; J C P Snyman, G H H Sonnekus; N S E Bezuidenhout, J F B van Wyk, J F K Marais (captain), J L van Heerden, J de Bruyn, T T Fourie, J L Kritzinger, J H Ellis

Replacement K B H de Klerk for Van Heerden (67 mins)
Scorer *Penalty Goals*: Snyman (3)

BRITISH/IRISH LIONS: J P R Williams; A R Irvine, I R McGeechan, R A Milliken, J J Williams; P Bennett, G O Edwards; J McLauchlan, R W Windsor, F E Cotton, W J McBride (captain), G L Brown, R M Uttley, T M Davies, J F Slattery
Scorers *Tries*: J J Williams (2), Brown *Conversion*: Irvine *Penalty Goals*: Irvine (2) *Dropped Goals*: Bennett (2)

Referee C J de Bruyn (South Africa)

TEST 8 27 July 1974, Ellis Park, Johannesburg

South Africa 13 (3PG 1T) British/Irish Lions 13 (1G 1PG 1T)

SOUTH AFRICA: O A Roux; C F Pope, P A Cronje, J J J Schlebusch, G H Muller; J C P Snyman, P C R Bayvel; N S E Bezuidenhout, J F B van Wyk, J F K Marais (captain), J L van Heerden, J G Williams, J L Kritzinger, C J Grobler, J H Ellis
Replacement J C J Stander for Bezuidenhout (57 mins)
Scorers *Try*: Cronje *Penalty Goals*: Snyman (3)

BRITISH/IRISH LIONS: J P R Williams; A R Irvine, I R McGeechan, R A Milliken, J J Williams; P Bennett, G O Edwards; J McLauchlan, R W Windsor, F E Cotton, W J McBride (captain), C W Ralston, R M Uttley, T M Davies, J F Slattery
Scorers *Tries*: Irvine, Uttley *Conversion*: Bennett *Penalty Goal*: Irvine

Referee M Baise (South Africa)

JPR'S CAP CAREER
FOR WALES

- Williams, JPR (London Welsh, Bridgend) 1969 S, I, F, E, NZ 1,2, A, 1970 SA, S, E, I, F, 1971 E, S, I, F, 1972 E, S, F, NZ, 1973 E, S, I, F, A, 1974 S, I, F, 1975 F, E, S, I, A, 1976 E, S, I, F, 1977 I, F, E, S, 1978 E, S, I, F, A 1,2, NZ, 1979 S, I, F, E, 1980 NZ, 1981 E, S
- Fifty-five caps, thirty-seven wins, four draws and fourteen defeats.
- Played in Grand Slams in 1971, 1976 and 1978
- Played in Triple Crown sides in 1969, 1971, 1976, 1977, 1978 and 1979.
- Points – thirty-six (five four-point tries and one three-point try; three penalty goals and two conversions).
- Captained Wales five times (1978–79 – Championship and Triple Crown season).
- Record-holder for most appearances as a full-back for Wales in Tests.

CAP 1 1 February 1969, Murrayfield

Scotland 3 (1PG) Wales 17 (1G 2PG 2T)

SCOTLAND: C F Blaikie; A J W Hinshelwood, J N M Frame, C W W Rea, W D Jackson; C M Telfer, I G McCrae; N Suddon, F A L Laidlaw, A B Carmichael, P K Stagg, A F McHarg, T G Elliott, J W Telfer (captain), R J Arneil
Scorer *Penalty Goal*: Blaikie

WALES: J P R Williams; S J Watkins, K S Jarrett, T G R Davies, M C R Richards; B John, G O Edwards; D J Lloyd, J Young, D Williams, B Price (captain), B Thomas, W D Morris, T M Davies, J Taylor
Scorers *Tries*: John, Edwards, Richards *Conversion*: Jarrett *Penalty Goals*: Jarrett (2)

Referee K D Kelleher (Ireland)

CAP 2 8 March 1969, Cardiff Arms Park

Wales 24 (3G 1PG 1DG 1T) Ireland 11 (1G 2PG)

WALES: J P R Williams; S J Watkins, K S Jarrett, T G R Davies, M C R Richards;
B John, G O Edwards; D J Lloyd, J Young, D Williams, B Price (captain),
B Thomas, W D Morris, T M Davies, J Taylor
Scorers *Tries*: Watkins, D Williams, Morris, Taylor *Conversions*: Jarrett (3)
Penalty Goal: Jarrett *Dropped Goal*: John

IRELAND: T J Kiernan (captain); A T A Duggan, F P K Bresnihan,
C M H Gibson, J C M Moroney; B J McGann, R M Young; S Millar,
K W Kennedy, P O'Callaghan, W J McBride, M G Molloy, J C Davidson,
M L Hipwell, N A A Murphy
Scorers *Try*: Gibson *Conversion*: Kiernan *Penalty Goals*: Kiernan (2)

Referee D C J McMahon (Scotland)

CAP 3 22 March 1969, Stade Colombes, Paris

France 8 (1G 1PG) Wales 8 (1G 1T)

FRANCE: P Villepreux; B Moraitis, C Dourthe, J Trillo, A Campaes; J Maso,
G Sutra; J Iracabal, R Benesis, J-L Azarete, E Cester, A Plantefol, G Viard,
W Spanghero (captain), P Biemouret
Scorers *Try*: Campaes *Conversion*: Villepreux *Penalty Goal*: Villepreux

WALES: J P R Williams; S J Watkins, K S Jarrett, T G R Davies, M C R Richards;
B John, G O Edwards; D J Lloyd, J Young, D Williams, B Price (captain),
B Thomas, W D Morris, T M Davies, J Taylor
Replacement P Bennett for T G R Davies (77 mins)
Scorers *Tries*: Edwards, Richards *Conversion*: Jarrett

Referee R P Burrell (Scotland)

CAP 4 12 April 1969, Cardiff Arms Park

Wales 30 (3G 2PG 1DG 2T) England 9 (3PG)

WALES: J P R Williams; S J Watkins, K S Jarrett, S J Dawes, M C R Richards;
B John, G O Edwards (captain); D J Lloyd, J Young, D Williams, W D Thomas,
B Thomas, W D Morris, T M Davies, J Taylor
Scorers *Tries*: Richards (4), John *Conversions*: Jarrett (3) *Penalty Goals*: Jarrett (2)
Dropped Goal: John

ENGLAND: R Hiller; K C Plummer, J S Spencer, D J Duckham, R E Webb;
J F Finlan, T C Wintle; D L Powell, J V Pullin, K E Fairbrother, N E Horton,
P J Larter, R B Taylor, D M Rollitt, D P Rogers (captain)
Scorer *Penalty Goals*: Hiller (3)

Referee D P d'Arcy (Ireland)

CAP 5 31 May 1969, Lancaster Park, Christchurch

New Zealand 19 (2G 1PG 2T) Wales 0

NEW ZEALAND: W F McCormick; M J Dick, W L Davis, I R MacRae,
G S Thorne; E W Kirton, S M Going; K F Gray, B E McLeod, B L Muller,
C E Meads, A E Smith, T N Lister, B J Lochore (captain), I A Kirkpatrick
Scorers *Tries*: Dick, McLeod, Lochore, Gray *Conversions*: McCormick (2)
Penalty Goal: McCormick

WALES: J P R Williams; S J Watkins, K S Jarrett, T G R Davies, M C R Richards;
B John, G O Edwards; D J Lloyd, J Young, D Williams, B Price (captain),
B Thomas, W D Morris, T M Davies, J Taylor
Replacement N R Gale for Young (71 mins)

Referee J P Murphy (New Zealand)

CAP 6 14 June 1969, Eden Park, Auckland

New Zealand 33 (3G 5PG 1DG) Wales 12 (2PG 2T)

NEW ZEALAND: W F McCormick; M J Dick, W L Davis, I R MacRae,
G R Skudder; E W Kirton, S M Going; A E Hopkinson, B E McLeod, K F Gray,
C E Meads, A E Smith, T N Lister, B J Lochore (captain), I A Kirkpatrick
Scorers *Tries*: Skudder, MacRae, Kirkpatrick *Conversions*: McCormick (3)
Penalty Goals: McCormick (5) *Dropped Goal*: McCormick

WALES: J P R Williams; T G R Davies, K S Jarrett, S J Dawes, M C R Richards;
B John, G O Edwards; D Williams, N R Gale, B Thomas, B Price (captain),
W D Thomas, W D Morris, T M Davies, D Hughes
Scorers *Tries*: Richards, Jarrett *Penalty Goals*: Jarrett (2)

Referee J P Murphy (New Zealand)

CAP 7 21 June 1969, Sydney Cricket Ground

Australia 16 (2G 2PG) Wales 19 (2G 2PG 1T)

AUSTRALIA: A N McGill; J W Cole, P V Smith, G A Shaw, T R Forman;
J P Ballesty, J N B Hipwell; J R Roxburgh, P Darveniza, R B Prosser, N P Reilly,
A M F Abrahams, H A Rose, A J Skinner, G V Davis (captain)
Scorers *Tries*: McGill, Smith *Conversions*: McGill (2) *Penalty Goals*: McGill (2)

WALES: J P R Williams; T G R Davies, K S Jarrett, S J Dawes, M C R Richards;
B John, G O Edwards; D J Lloyd, N R Gale, D Williams, B Price (captain),
W D Thomas, W D Morris, T M Davies, J Taylor
Scorers *Tries*: Morris, Davies, Taylor *Conversions*: Jarrett (2) *Penalty Goals*: Jarrett (2)

Referee C F Ferguson (Australia)

CAP 8 24 January 1970, Cardiff Arms Park

Wales 6 (1PG 1T) South Africa 6 (1PG 1T)

WALES: J P R Williams; P Bennett, S J Dawes, W H Raybould, I Hall; B John,
G O Edwards (captain); D B Llewelyn, V C Perrins, D Williams, W D Thomas,
T G Evans, W D Morris, T M Davies, D Hughes
Scorer *Try*: Edwards *Penalty Goal*: Edwards

SOUTH AFRICA: H O de Villiers; S H Nomis, O A Roux, J P van der Merwe,
G H Muller; M J Lawless, D J de Villiers (captain); J L Myburgh, C H Cockrell,
J F K Marais, F C H du Preez, I J de Klerk, P J F Greyling, T P Bedford, J H Ellis
Scorers *Try*: Nomis *Penalty Goal*: H O de Villiers

Referee G C Lamb (England)

CAP 9 7 February 1970, Cardiff Arms Park

Wales 18 (3G 1T) Scotland 9 (1DG 1PG 1T)

WALES: J P R Williams; L T D Daniel, P Bennett, S J Dawes, I Hall; B John,
G O Edwards (captain); D B Llewelyn, V C Perrins, D Williams, W D Thomas,
T G Evans, W D Morris, T M Davies, D Hughes
Scorers *Tries*: Daniel, Llewelyn, Dawes, Morris *Conversions*: Edwards (2), Daniel

SCOTLAND: I S G Smith; M A Smith, J N M Frame, C W W Rea,
A J W Hinshelwood; I Robertson, R G Young; J McLauchlan, F A L Laidlaw,
A B Carmichael, P K Stagg, P C Brown, W Lauder, J W Telfer (captain), R J Arneil
Replacement G L Brown for P C Brown (42 mins)
Scorers *Try*: Robertson *Penalty Goal*: Lauder *Dropped Goal*: Robertson

Referee D P d'Arcy (Ireland)

CAP 10 28 February 1970, Twickenham

England 13 (2G 1PG) Wales 17 (1G 1DG 3T)

ENGLAND: R Hiller (captain); M J Novak, J S Spencer, D J Duckham, P M Hale; I R Shackleton, N C Starmer-Smith; C B Stevens, J V Pullin, K E Fairbrother, A M Davis, P J Larter, A L Bucknall, R B Taylor, B R West
Scorers *Tries*: Duckham, Novak *Conversions*: Hiller (2) *Penalty Goal*: Hiller

WALES: J P R Williams; S J Watkins, S J Dawes, W H Raybould, I Hall; B John, G O Edwards (captain); D B Llewelyn, J Young, D Williams, W D Thomas, T G Evans, W D Morris, T M Davies, D Hughes
Replacement R Hopkins for Edwards (62 mins)
Scorers *Tries*: Davies, John, Hopkins, J P R Williams *Conversion*: J P R Williams *Dropped Goal*: John

Referee R Calmet (France) replaced by R F Johnson (England) (39 mins)

CAP 11 14 March 1970, Lansdowne Road, Dublin

Ireland 14 (1G 1PG 1DG 1T) Wales 0

IRELAND: T J Kiernan (captain); A T A Duggan, F P K Bresnihan, C M H Gibson, W J Brown; B J McGann, R M Young; S Millar, K W Kennedy, P O'Callaghan, W J McBride, M G Molloy, R A Lamont, K G Goodall, J F Slattery
Scorers *Tries*: Duggan, Goodall *Conversion*: Kiernan *Penalty Goal*: Kiernan *Dropped Goal*: McGann

WALES: J P R Williams; S J Watkins, S J Dawes, W H Raybould, K S Hughes; B John, G O Edwards (captain); D B Llewelyn, J Young, D Williams, W D Thomas, T G Evans, W D Morris, T M Davies, D Hughes

Referee G C Lamb (England)

CAP 12 4 April 1970, Cardiff Arms Park

Wales 11 (1G 2PG) France 6 (2T)

WALES: J P R Williams; J L Shanklin, S J Dawes (captain), A J L Lewis, R Mathias; P Bennett, G O Edwards; D J Lloyd, J Young, D B Llewelyn, W D Thomas, I S Gallacher, W D Morris, T M Davies, J Taylor
Replacement W H Raybould for Shanklin (65 mins)
Scorers *Tries*: Morris *Conversion*: J P R Williams *Penalty Goals*: J P R Williams (2)

FRANCE: P Villepreux; J Cantoni, A Marot, J-P Lux, J-M Bonal; L Paries, M Puget; J Iracabal, R Benesis, J-L Azarete, E Cester, J-P Bastiat, P Biemouret, B Dauga, C Carrere (captain)
Scorers *Tries*: Cantoni, Bonal

Referee K D Kelleher (Ireland)

CAP 13 16 January 1971, Cardiff Arms Park

Wales 22 (2G 1PG 2DG 1T) England 6 (1PG 1T)

WALES: J P R Williams; T G R Davies, S J Dawes (captain), A J L Lewis, J C Bevan; B John, G O Edwards; D B Llewelyn, J Young, D Williams, W D Thomas, M G Roberts, W D Morris, T M Davies, J Taylor
Scorers *Tries*: T G R Davies (2), Bevan *Conversions*: Taylor (2)
Penalty Goal: J P R Williams *Dropped Goals*: John (2)

ENGLAND: P A Rossborough; J P A G Janion, C S Wardlow, J S Spencer, D J Duckham; I D Wright, J J Page; D L Powell, J V Pullin, K E Fairbrother, P J Larter, B F Ninnes, A L Bucknall (captain), R C Hannaford, A Neary
Scorers *Try*: Hannaford *Penalty Goal*: Rossborough

Referee D P d'Arcy (Ireland)

CAP 14 6 February 1971, Murrayfield

Scotland 18 (4PG 2T) Wales 19 (2G 1PG 2T)

SCOTLAND: I S G Smith; W C C Steele, J N M Frame, C W W Rea, A G Biggar; J W C Turner, D S Paterson; J McLauchlan, F A L Laidlaw, A B Carmichael, A F McHarg, G L Brown, N A McEwan, P C Brown (captain), R J Arneil
Scorers *Tries*: Carmichael, Rea *Penalty Goals*: P C Brown (4)

WALES: J P R Williams; T G R Davies, S J Dawes (captain), I Hall, J C Bevan; B John, G O Edwards; D B Llewelyn, J Young, D Williams, W D Thomas, M G Roberts, W D Morris, T M Davies, J Taylor
Scorers *Tries*: Taylor, John, Edwards, T G R Davies *Conversions*: Taylor, John
Penalty Goal: John

Referee M H Titcomb (England)

CAP 15 13 March 1971, Cardiff Arms Park

Wales 23 (1G 2PG 1DG 3T) Ireland 9 (3PG)

WALES: J P R Williams; T G R Davies, S J Dawes (captain), A J L Lewis,
J C Bevan; B John, G O Edwards; D B Llewelyn, J Young, D Williams,
W D Thomas, M G Roberts, W D Morris, T M Davies, J Taylor
Scorers *Tries*: T G R Davies (2), Edwards (2) *Conversion*: John *Penalty Goals*: John
(2) *Dropped Goal*: John

IRELAND: B J O'Driscoll; A T A Duggan, F P K Bresnihan, C M H Gibson
(captain), E L Grant; B J McGann, R M Young; R J McLoughlin, K W Kennedy,
J F Lynch, W J McBride, M G Molloy, M L Hipwell, D J Hickie, J F Slattery
Scorer *Penalty Goals*: Gibson (3)

Referee R F Johnson (England)

CAP 16 27 March 1971, Stade Colombes, Paris

France 5 (1G) Wales 9 (1PG 2T)

FRANCE: P Villepreux; R Bourgarel, R Bertranne, J-P Lux, J Cantoni; J-L Berot,
M Barrau; J Iracabal, R Benesis, M Lasserre, W Spanghero, C Spanghero,
P Biemouret, B Dauga, C Carrere (captain)
Scorers *Try*: Dauga *Conversion*: Villepreux

WALES: J P R Williams; T G R Davies, S J Dawes (captain), A J L Lewis,
J C Bevan; B John, G O Edwards; D B Llewelyn, J Young, D Williams,
W D Thomas, M G Roberts, W D Morris, T M Davies, J Taylor
Scorers *Tries*: Edwards, John *Penalty Goal*: John

Referee J Young (Scotland)

CAP 17 15 January 1972, Twickenham

England 3 (1PG) Wales 12 (1G 2PG)

ENGLAND: R Hiller (captain); J P A G Janion, M C Beese, D J Duckham,
K J Fielding; A G B Old, J G Webster; C B Stevens, J V Pullin, M A Burton,
A Brinn, C W Ralston, P J Dixon, A G Ripley, A Neary
Scorer *Penalty Goal*: Hiller

WALES: J P R Williams; T G R Davies, R T E Bergiers, A J L Lewis, J C Bevan;
B John, G O Edwards; D J Lloyd (captain), J Young, D B Llewelyn, W D
Thomas, T G Evans, W D Morris, T M Davies, J Taylor
Scorers *Try*: J P R Williams *Conversion*: John *Penalty Goals*: John (2)

Referee J Young (Scotland)

CAP 18 5 February 1972, Cardiff Arms Park

Wales 35 (3G 3PG 2T) Scotland 12 (1G 2PG)

WALES: J P R Williams; T G R Davies, R T E Bergiers, A J L Lewis, J C Bevan;
B John, G O Edwards; D J Lloyd (captain), J Young, D B Llewelyn, W D Thomas,
T G Evans, W D Morris, T M Davies, J Taylor
Replacement P Bennett for J P R Williams (26 mins)
Scorers *Tries*: Edwards (2), T G R Davies, Taylor, Bergiers *Conversions*: John (3)
Penalty Goals: John (3)

SCOTLAND: A R Brown; W C C Steele, J N M Frame, J M Renwick, A G Biggar;
C M Telfer, D S Paterson; J McLauchlan, R L Clark, A B Carmichael, I A Barnes,
G L Brown, N A McEwan, P C Brown (captain), R J Arneil
Replacement L G Dick for Biggar (43 mins)
Scorers *Try*: Clark *Conversion*: P C Brown *Penalty Goals*: P C Brown, Renwick

Referee G A Jamison (Ireland)

CAP 19 25 March 1972, Cardiff Arms Park

Wales 20 (4PG 2T) France 6 (2PG)

WALES: J P R Williams; T G R Davies, R T E Bergiers, A J L Lewis, J C Bevan;
B John, G O Edwards; D J Lloyd (captain), J Young, D B Llewelyn, W D Thomas,
T G Evans, W D Morris, T M Davies, J Taylor
Replacement D L Quinnell for T M Davies (78 mins)
Scorers *Tries*: T G R Davies, Bevan *Penalty Goals*: John (4)

FRANCE: P Villepreux (captain); B Duprat, J Maso, J-P Lux, J Sillieres; J-L Berot,
M Barrau; J Iracabal, R Benesis, J-L Azarete, C Spanghero, A Esteve, J-C Skrela,
B Dauga, P Biemouret
Scorer *Penalty Goals*: Villepreux (2)

Referee M H Titcomb (England)

CAP 20 2 December 1972, Cardiff Arms Park

Wales 16 (4PG 1T) New Zealand 19 (5PG 1T)

WALES: J P R Williams; T G R Davies, R T E Bergiers, J L Shanklin, J C Bevan;
P Bennett, G O Edwards; G Shaw, J Young, D B Llewelyn, W D Thomas
(captain), D L Quinnell, W D Morris, T M Davies, J Taylor
Scorers *Try*: Bevan *Penalty Goals*: Bennett (4)

NEW ZEALAND: J F Karam; B G Williams, D A Hales, R M Parkinson,
G B Batty; R E Burgess, S M Going; J D Matheson, R W Norton, K Murdoch,
H H Macdonald, P J Whiting, A J Wyllie, A R Sutherland, I A Kirkpatrick
(captain)
Replacement A I Scown for Wyllie (72 mins)
Scorers *Try*: Murdoch *Penalty Goals*: Karam (5)

Referee R F Johnson (England)

CAP 21 20 January 1973, Cardiff Arms Park

Wales 25 (1G 1PG 4T) England 9 (2PG 1DG)

WALES: J P R Williams; T G R Davies, R T E Bergiers, A J L Lewis (captain),
J C Bevan; P Bennett, G O Edwards; G Shaw, J Young, D J Lloyd, W D Thomas,
D L Quinnell, W D Morris, T M Davies, J Taylor
Scorers *Tries*: Bevan (2), T G R Davies, Edwards, Lewis *Conversion*: Bennett
Penalty Goal: Taylor

ENGLAND: S A Doble; A J G Morley, P Warfield, P S Preece, D J Duckham;
A R Cowman, J G Webster; C B Stevens, J V Pullin (captain), F E Cotton,
P J Larter, C W Ralston, J A Watkins, A G Ripley, A Neary
Replacement G W Evans for Warfield (32 mins)
Scorer *Penalty Goals*: Doble (2) *Dropped Goal*: Cowman

Referee G Domercq (France)

CAP 22 3 February 1973, Murrayfield

Scotland 10 (1G 1T) Wales 9 (3PG)

SCOTLAND: A R Irvine; W C C Steele, I R McGeechan, I W Forsyth,
D Shedden; C M Telfer, D W Morgan; J McLauchlan (captain), R L Clark,
A B Carmichael, A F McHarg, P C Brown, N A McEwan, G M Strachan,
J G Millican
Scorers *Tries*: Telfer, Steele *Conversion*: Morgan

WALES: J P R Williams; T G R Davies, R T E Bergiers, A J L Lewis (captain),
J C Bevan; P Bennett, G O Edwards; G Shaw, J Young, D J Lloyd, W D Thomas,
D L Quinnell, W D Morris, T M Davies, J Taylor
Scorers *Penalty Goals*: Bennett (2), Taylor

Referee F Palmade (France)

235

CAP 23 10 March 1973, Cardiff Arms Park

Wales 16 (1G 2PG 1T) Ireland 12 (1G 2PG)

WALES: J P R Williams; T G R Davies, R T E Bergiers, A J L Lewis (captain),
J L Shanklin; P Bennett, G O Edwards; G Shaw, J Young, P D Llewellyn,
W D Thomas, M G Roberts, W D Morris, T M Davies, J Taylor
Scorers *Tries*: Shanklin, Edwards *Conversion*: Bennett *Penalty Goals*: Bennett (2)

IRELAND: A H Ensor; T O Grace, R A Milliken, C M H Gibson, A W McMaster;
B J McGann, J J Moloney; R J McLoughlin, K W Kennedy, J F Lynch,
W J McBride (captain), K M A Mays, J F Slattery, T A P Moore, S A McKinney
Scorers *Try*: Gibson *Conversion*: McGann *Penalty Goals*: McGann (2)

Referee T F E Grierson (Scotland)

CAP 24 24 March 1973, Parc des Princes, Paris

France 12 (3PG 1DG) Wales 3 (1DG)

FRANCE: J-M Aguirre; J-F Phliponeau, J Maso, C Badin, J Cantoni; J-P Romeu,
M Pebeyre; J Iracabal, R Benesis, J-L Azarete, W Spanghero (captain), E Cester,
J-C Skrela, O Saisset, P Biemouret
Scorer *Penalty Goals*: Romeu (3) *Dropped Goal*: Romeu

WALES: J P R Williams; T G R Davies, R T E Bergiers, A J L Lewis, J L Shanklin;
P Bennett, G O Edwards (captain); G Shaw, J Young, P D Llewellyn,
W D Thomas, M G Roberts, J Taylor, T M Davies, T P David
Replacement J J Williams for Lewis (41 mins)
Scorer *Dropped Goal*: Bennett

Referee D P d'Arcy (Ireland)

CAP 25 10 November 1973, Cardiff Arms Park

Wales 24 (4PG 3T) Australia 0

WALES: J P R Williams; T G R Davies, R T E Bergiers, K S Hughes, J J Williams;
P Bennett, G O Edwards (captain); G Shaw, R W Windsor, P D Llewellyn,
A J Martin, D L Quinnell, W D Morris, T M Davies, T P David
Replacement R C Shell for Edwards (81 mins)
Scorers *Tries*: T G R Davies, Morris, Windsor *Penalty Goals*: Bennett (4)

AUSTRALIA: R L Fairfax; O G Stephens, R D l'Estrange, G A Shaw, J J McLean;
G C Richardson, J N B Hipwell; R Graham, M E Freney, J L P Howard,
S C Gregory, G Fay, M R Cocks, A A Shaw, P D Sullivan (captain)

Referee K A Pattinson (England)

CAP 26 19 January 1974, Cardiff Arms Park

Wales 6 (1G) Scotland 0

WALES: J P R Williams; T G R Davies, K S Hughes, I Hall, J J Williams;
P Bennett, G O Edwards (captain); G Shaw, R W Windsor, P D Llewellyn,
A J Martin, D L Quinnell, W D Morris, T M Davies, T J Cobner
Scorers *Try*: Cobner *Conversion*: Bennett

SCOTLAND: A R Irvine; A D Gill, I R McGeechan, J M Renwick, L G Dick;
C M Telfer, A J M Lawson; J McLauchlan (captain), D F Madsen,
A B Carmichael, A F McHarg, G L Brown, N A McEwan, W S Watson, W Lauder

Referee R F Johnson (England)

CAP 27 2 February 1974, Lansdowne Road, Dublin

Ireland 9 (3PG) Wales 9 (1G 1PG)

IRELAND: A H Ensor; V A Becker, R A Milliken, C M H Gibson, P J Lavery;
M A M Quinn, J J Moloney; R J McLoughlin, K W Kennedy, J F Lynch,
W J McBride (captain), M I Keane, J F Slattery, T A P Moore, S M Deering
Scorer *Penalty Goals*: Ensor (3)

WALES: J P R Williams; C F W Rees, I Hall, A A J Finlayson, J J Williams;
P Bennett, G O Edwards (captain); G Shaw, R W Windsor, W P J Williams,
A J Martin, G A D Wheel, W D Morris, T M Davies, T J Cobner
Scorers *Try*: J J Williams *Conversion*: Bennett *Penalty Goal*: Bennett

Referee K A Pattinson (England)

CAP 28 16 February 1974, Cardiff Arms Park

Wales 16 (3PG 1DG 1T) France 16 (3PG 1DG 1T)

WALES: J P R Williams; T G R Davies, I Hall, A A J Finlayson, J J Williams;
P Bennett, G O Edwards (captain); G Shaw, R W Windsor, W P J Williams,
I R Robinson, D L Quinnell, W D Morris, T M Davies, T J Cobner
Scorers *Try*: J J Williams *Penalty Goals*: Bennett (3) *Dropped Goal*: Edwards

FRANCE: J-M Aguirre; R Bertranne, J Pecune, J-P Lux, A Dubertrand; J-P Romeu,
J Fouroux; A Vaquerin, R Benesis, J Iracabal, E Cester (captain), A Esteve,
J-C Skrela, C Spanghero, V Boffelli
Scorers *Try*: Lux *Penalty Goals*: Romeu (3) *Dropped Goal*: Romeu

Referee N R Sanson (Scotland)

CAP 29 18 January 1975, Parc des Princes, Paris

France 10 (2PG 1T) Wales 25 (1G 1PG 4T)

FRANCE: M Taffary; J-F Gourdon, C Dourthe, R Bertranne, J-P Lux; J-P Romeu, J Fouroux (captain); A Vaquerin, A Paco, J-L Azarete, G Senal, A Esteve, O Saisset, J-P Bastiat, V Boffelli
Replacements J Cantoni for Gourdon (44 mins); J-C Skrela for Saisset (44 mins)
Scorers *Try*: Gourdon *Penalty Goals*: Taffary (2)

WALES: J P R Williams; T G R Davies, R W R Gravell, S P Fenwick, J J Williams; J D Bevan, G O Edwards; A G Faulkner, R W Windsor, G Price, A J Martin, G A D Wheel, T J Cobner, T M Davies (captain), T P Evans
Scorers *Tries*: Fenwick, Cobner, Price, T G R Davies, Edwards
Conversion: Fenwick *Penalty Goal*: Fenwick

Referee K A Pattinson (England)

CAP 30 15 February 1975, Cardiff Arms Park

Wales 20 (1G 2PG 2T) England 4 (1T)

WALES: J P R Williams; T G R Davies, R W R Gravell, S P Fenwick, J J Williams; J D Bevan, G O Edwards; A G Faulkner, R W Windsor, G Price, A J Martin, G A D Wheel, T J Cobner, T M Davies (captain), T P Evans
Replacement D L Quinnell for Wheel (25 mins)
Scorers *Tries*: Fenwick, T G R Davies, J J Williams *Conversion*: Martin
Penalty Goals: Martin (2)

ENGLAND: A M Jorden; P J Squires, K Smith, P S Preece, D J Duckham; M J Cooper, J G Webster; C B Stevens, P J Wheeler, F E Cotton (captain), N E Horton, C W Ralston, J A Watkins, R M Uttley, A Neary
Replacements S J Smith for Webster (20 mins); J V Pullin for Wheeler (44 mins)
Scorer *Try*: Horton

Referee A M Hosie (Scotland)

CAP 31 1 March 1975, Murrayfield

Scotland 12 (3PG 1DG) Wales 10 (2PG 1T)

SCOTLAND: A R Irvine; W C C Steele, J M Renwick, D L Bell, L G Dick; I R McGeechan, D W Morgan; J McLauchlan (captain), D F Madsen, A B Carmichael, A F McHarg, G L Brown, M A Biggar, D G Leslie, N A McEwan
Scorers *Penalty Goals*: Morgan (3) *Dropped Goal*: McGeechan

WALES: J P R Williams; T G R Davies, R W R Gravell, S P Fenwick, J J Williams;
J D Bevan, G O Edwards; A G Faulkner, R W Windsor, G Price, A J Martin,
M G Roberts, T J Cobner, T M Davies (captain), T P Evans
Replacements P Bennett for Bevan (26 mins); W R Blyth for Fenwick (37 mins)
Scorers *Try*: Evans *Penalty Goals*: Fenwick (2)

Referee J R West (Ireland)

CAP 32 15 March 1975, Cardiff Arms Park

Wales 32 (3G 2PG 2T) Ireland 4 (1T)

WALES: J P R Williams; T G R Davies, R T E Bergiers, R W R Gravell,
J J Williams; P Bennett, G O Edwards; A G Faulkner, R W Windsor, G Price,
A J Martin, G A D Wheel, T J Cobner, T M Davies (captain), T P Evans
Scorers *Tries*: T G R Davies, Edwards, J J Williams, Faulkner, Bergiers
Conversions: Bennett (3) *Penalty Goals*: Bennett (2)

IRELAND: A H Ensor; T O Grace, R A Milliken, C M H Gibson, A W McMaster;
W M McCombe, J J Moloney; R J McLoughlin, K W Kennedy, R J Clegg,
W J McBride (captain), M I Keane, J F Slattery, W P Duggan, M J A Sherry
Scorer *Try*: Duggan

Referee J Saint Guilhem (France)

CAP 33 20 December 1975, Cardiff Arms Park

Wales 28 (3G 1PG 1DG 1T) Australia 3 (1PG)

WALES: J P R Williams; J J Williams, R W R Gravell, S P Fenwick, C F W Rees;
J D Bevan, G O Edwards; A G Faulkner, R W Windsor, G Price, A J Martin,
G A D Wheel, T J Cobner, T M Davies (captain), T P Evans
Scorers *Tries*: J J Williams (3), Edwards *Conversions*: Fenwick (2), Martin
Penalty Goal: Fenwick *Dropped Goal*: Bevan

AUSTRALIA: P E McLean; P G Batch, R D l'Estrange, G A Shaw, L E Monaghan;
J C Hindmarsh, J N B Hipwell (captain); J E C Meadows, P A Horton,
R Graham, R A Smith, G Fay, J K Lambie, G Cornelsen, A A Shaw
Replacements G K Pearse for Lambie (14 mins); R G Hauser for Hipwell
(39 mins)
Scorer *Penalty Goal*: McLean

Referee D P d'Arcy (Ireland)

CAP 34 17 January 1976, Twickenham

England 9 (3PG) Wales 21 (3G 1PG)

ENGLAND: A J Hignell; P J Squires, A W Maxwell, D A Cooke, D J Duckham; M J Cooper, M S Lampkowski; F E Cotton, P J Wheeler, M A Burton, W B Beaumont, R M Wilkinson, M Keyworth, A G Ripley, A Neary (captain)
Replacement P S Preece for Squires (30 mins)
Scorer *Penalty Goals*: Hignell (3)

WALES: J P R Williams; T G R Davies, R W R Gravell, S P Fenwick, J J Williams; P Bennett, G O Edwards; A G Faulkner, R W Windsor, G Price, A J Martin, G A D Wheel, T J Cobner, T M Davies (captain), T P Evans
Scorers *Tries*: J P R Williams (2), Edwards *Conversions*: Fenwick (3)
Penalty Goal: Martin

Referee G Domercq (France)

CAP 35 7 February 1976, Cardiff Arms Park

Wales 28 (2G 3PG 1DG 1T) Scotland 6 (1G)

WALES: J P R Williams; T G R Davies, R W R Gravell, S P Fenwick, J J Williams; P Bennett, G O Edwards; A G Faulkner, R W Windsor, G Price, A J Martin, G A D Wheel, T J Cobner, T M Davies (captain), T P Evans
Scorers *Tries*: J J Williams, Edwards, Evans *Conversions*: Bennett (2)
Penalty Goals: Bennett (3) *Dropped Goal*: Fenwick

SCOTLAND: A R Irvine; W C C Steele, J M Renwick, A G Cranston, D Shedden; I R McGeechan, D W Morgan; J McLauchlan (captain), C D Fisher, A B Carmichael, A F McHarg, G L Brown, M A Biggar, G Y Mackie, D G Leslie
Scorers *Try*: Irvine *Conversion*: Morgan

Referee A Cuny (France)

CAP 36 21 February 1976, Lansdowne Road, Dublin

Ireland 9 (3PG) Wales 34 (3G 4PG 1T)

IRELAND: A H Ensor; T O Grace (captain), P J Lavery, C M H Gibson, A W McMaster; B J McGann, D M Canniffe; P A Orr, J L Cantrell, P O'Callaghan, M I Keane, R F Hakin, S M Deering, W P Duggan, S A McKinney
Replacement L A Moloney for Lavery (24 mins)
Scorer *Penalty Goals*: McGann (3)

WALES: J P R Williams; T G R Davies, R W R Gravell, S P Fenwick, J J Williams;
P Bennett, G O Edwards; A G Faulkner, R W Windsor, G Price, A J Martin,
G A D Wheel, T P David, T M Davies (captain), T P Evans
Scorers *Tries*: T G R Davies (2), Bennett, Edwards *Conversions*: Bennett (3)
Penalty Goals: Bennett (3), Martin

Referee N R Sanson (Scotland)

CAP 37 6 March 1976, Cardiff Arms Park

Wales 19 (5PG 1T) France 13 (1G 1PG 1T)

WALES: J P R Williams; T G R Davies, R W R Gravell, S P Fenwick, J J Williams;
P Bennett, G O Edwards; A G Faulkner, R W Windsor, G Price, A J Martin,
G A D Wheel, T P David, T M Davies (captain), T P Evans
Replacement F M D Knill for Price (35 mins)
Scorers *Try*: J J Williams *Penalty Goals*: Bennett (2), Fenwick (2), Martin

FRANCE: M Droitecourt; J-F Gourdon, R Bertranne, J Pecune, J-L Averous;
J-P Romeu, J Fouroux (captain); G Cholley, A Paco, R Paparemborde, M Palmie,
J-F Imbernon, J-P Rives, J-P Bastiat, J-C Skrela
Replacement J-M Aguirre for Droitecourt (40 mins)
Scorers *Tries*: Gourdon, Averous *Conversion*: Romeu *Penalty Goal*: Romeu

Referee J R West (Ireland)

CAP 38 15 January 1977, Cardiff Arms Park

Wales 25 (2G 2PG 1DG 1T) Ireland 9 (3PG)

WALES: J P R Williams; T G R Davies, S P Fenwick, D H Burcher, J J Williams;
P Bennett (captain), G O Edwards; G Shaw, R W Windsor, G Price, A J Martin,
G A D Wheel, T P Evans, J Squire, R C Burgess
Replacement D L Quinnell for Evans (68 mins)
Scorers *Tries*: J P R Williams, T G R Davies, Burgess *Conversions*: Bennett (2)
Penalty Goals: Bennett (2) *Dropped Goal*: Fenwick

IRELAND: F Wilson; T O Grace (captain), A R McKibbin, J A McIlrath,
D StJ Bowen; C M H Gibson, R J M McGrath; P A Orr, P C Whelan,
T A O Feighery, M I Keane, R F Hakin, S M Deering, W P Duggan,
S A McKinney
Replacement B O Foley for Hakin (40 mins)
Scorer *Penalty Goals*: Gibson (3)

Referee N R Sanson (Scotland)

CAP 39 5 February 1977, Parc des Princes, Paris

France 16 (1G 2PG 1T) Wales 9 (3PG)

FRANCE: J-M Aguirre; D Harize, R Bertranne, F Sangalli, J-L Averous; J-P Romeu, J Fouroux (captain); G Cholley, A Paco, R Paparemborde, M Palmie, J-F Imbernon, J-P Rives, J-P Bastiat, J-C Skrela
Scorers *Tries*: Harize, Skrela *Conversion*: Romeu *Penalty Goals*: Romeu (2)

WALES: J P R Williams; T G R Davies, S P Fenwick, D H Burcher, J J Williams; P Bennett (captain), G O Edwards; G Shaw, R W Windsor, G Price, A J Martin, D L Quinnell, T J Cobner, J Squire, R C Burgess
Replacement G L Evans for Davies (49 mins)
Scorer *Penalty Goals*: Fenwick (3)

Referee A M Hosie (Scotland)

CAP 40 5 March 1977, Cardiff Arms Park

Wales 14 (2PG 2T) England 9 (3PG)

WALES: J P R Williams; T G R Davies, S P Fenwick, D H Burcher, J J Williams; P Bennett (captain), G O Edwards; C Williams, R W Windsor, G Price, A J Martin, G A D Wheel, T J Cobner, D L Quinnell, R C Burgess
Scorers *Tries*: J P R Williams, Edwards *Penalty Goals*: Fenwick (2)

ENGLAND: A J Hignell; P J Squires, B J Corless, C P Kent, M A C Slemen; M J Cooper, M Young; R J Cowling, P J Wheeler, F E Cotton, W B Beaumont, N E Horton, P J Dixon, R M Uttley (captain), M Rafter
Scorer *Penalty Goals*: Hignell (3)

Referee D I H Burnett (Ireland)

CAP 41 19 March 1977, Murrayfield

Scotland 9 (1G 1DG) Wales 18 (2G 2PG)

SCOTLAND: A R Irvine; W B B Gammell, J M Renwick, A G Cranston, D Shedden; I R McGeechan (captain), D W Morgan; J McLauchlan, D F Madsen, A B Carmichael, I A Barnes, A F McHarg, M A Biggar, D S M MacDonald, W S Watson
Scorers *Try*: Irvine *Conversion*: Irvine *Dropped Goal*: McGeechan

WALES: J P R Williams; T G R Davies, S P Fenwick, D H Burcher, J J Williams; P Bennett (captain), G O Edwards; C Williams, R W Windsor, G Price, A J Martin, G A D Wheel, T J Cobner, D L Quinnell, R C Burgess
Scorers *Tries*: J J Williams, Bennett *Conversions*: Bennett (2) *Penalty Goals*: Bennett (2)

Referee G Domercq (France)

CAP 42 4 February 1978, Twickenham

England 6 (2PG) Wales 9 (3PG)

ENGLAND: A J Hignell; P J Squires, B J Corless, P W Dodge, M A C Slemen; J P Horton, M Young; B G Nelmes, P J Wheeler, M A Burton, W B Beaumont (captain), N E Horton, R J Mordell, J P Scott, M Rafter
Scorer *Penalty Goals*: Hignell (2)

WALES: J P R Williams; T G R Davies, R W R Gravell, S P Fenwick, J J Williams; P Bennett (captain), G O Edwards; A G Faulkner, R W Windsor, G Price, A J Martin, G A D Wheel, J Squire, D L Quinnell, T J Cobner
Scorer *Penalty Goals*: Bennett (3)

Referee N R Sanson (Scotland)

CAP 43 18 February 1978, Cardiff Arms Park

Wales 22 (1PG 1DG 4T) Scotland 14 (2PG 2T)

WALES: J P R Williams; T G R Davies, R W R Gravell, S P Fenwick, J J Williams; P Bennett (captain), G O Edwards; A G Faulkner, R W Windsor, G Price, A J Martin, G A D Wheel, T J Cobner, D L Quinnell, J Squire
Scorers *Tries*: Edwards, Gravell, Fenwick, Quinnell *Penalty Goal*: Bennett *Dropped Goal*: Bennett

SCOTLAND: B H Hay; W B B Gammell, J M Renwick, A G Cranston, D Shedden; I R McGeechan, D W Morgan (captain); J McLauchlan, C T Deans, N E K Pender, A F McHarg, A J Tomes, M A Biggar, D S M MacDonald, C B Hegarty
Replacement C G Hogg for Shedden (8 mins)
Scorers *Tries*: Renwick, Tomes *Penalty Goals*: Morgan (2)

Referee J R West (Ireland)

CAP 44 4 March 1978, Lansdowne Road, Dublin

Ireland 16 (3PG 1DG 1T) Wales 20 (4PG 2T)

IRELAND: A H Ensor; C M H Gibson, A R McKibbin, P P McNaughton, A C McLennan; A J P Ward, J J Moloney (captain); P A Orr, P C Whelan, E M J Byrne, M I Keane, H W Steele, S A McKinney, W P Duggan, J F Slattery
Scorers *Try*: Moloney *Penalty Goals*: Ward (3) *Dropped Goal*: Ward

WALES: J P R Williams; T G R Davies, R W R Gravell, S P Fenwick, J J Williams;
P Bennett (captain), G O Edwards; A G Faulkner, R W Windsor, G Price,
A J Martin, G A D Wheel, J Squire, D L Quinnell, T J Cobner
Scorers *Tries*: Fenwick, J J Williams *Penalty Goals*: Fenwick (4)

Referee G Domercq (France)

CAP 45 18 March 1978, Cardiff Arms Park

Wales 16 (1G 2DG 1T) France 7 (1DG 1T)

WALES: J P R Williams; J J Williams, R W R Gravell, S P Fenwick, G L Evans;
P Bennett (captain), G O Edwards; A G Faulkner, R W Windsor, G Price,
A J Martin, G A D Wheel, J Squire, D L Quinnell, T J Cobner
Scorers *Tries*: Bennett (2) *Conversion*: Bennett *Dropped Goals*: Edwards, Fenwick

FRANCE: J-M Aguirre; D Bustaffa, R Bertranne, C Belascain, G Noves; B Vivies,
J Gallion; G Cholley, A Paco, R Paparemborde, F Haget, M Palmie, J-P Rives,
J-P Bastiat (captain), J-C Skrela
Scorers *Try*: Skrela *Dropped Goal*: Vivies

Referee A Welsby (England)

CAP 46 11 June 1978, Ballymore, Brisbane

Australia 18 (1G 4PG) Wales 8 (2T)

AUSTRALIA: L E Monaghan; P G Batch, A G Slack, M Knight, P J Crowe;
P E McLean, R G Hauser; S C Finnane, P A Horton, S J Pilecki, D W Hillhouse,
G Fay, A A Shaw (captain), M E Loane, G Cornelsen
Scorers *Try*: Crowe *Conversion*: McLean *Penalty Goals*: McLean (4)

WALES: J P R Williams; T G R Davies, R W R Gravell, S P Fenwick, J J Williams;
W G Davies, D B Williams; A G Faulkner, R W Windsor, G Price, A J Martin,
G A D Wheel, T J Cobner (captain), D L Quinnell, J Squire
Replacement S M Lane for Squire (78 mins)
Scorers *Tries*: T G R Davies, D B Williams

Referee R T Burnett (Australia)

CAP 47 17 June 1978, Sydney Cricket Ground

Australia 19 (3PG 2DG 1T) Wales 17 (2PG 1DG 2T)

AUSTRALIA: L E Monaghan; P G Batch, A G Slack, M Knight, P J Crowe; P E McLean, R G Hauser; S C Finnane, P A Horton, S J Pilecki, D W Hillhouse, G Fay, A A Shaw (captain), M E Loane, G Cornelsen
Scorers *Try*: Loane *Penalty Goals*: McLean (3) *Dropped Goals*: Monaghan, McLean

WALES: A J Donovan; T G R Davies (captain), R W R Gravell, S P Fenwick, J J Williams; W G Davies, T D Holmes; A G Faulkner, R W Windsor, G Price, A J Martin, G A D Wheel, S M Lane, C E Davis, J P R Williams
Replacements S J Richardson for Price (5 mins); G L Evans for Donovan (36 mins)
Scorers *Tries*: T G R Davies, Holmes *Penalty Goals*: W G Davies (2)
Dropped Goal: W G Davies

Referee R G Byres (Australia)

CAP 48 11 November 1978, Cardiff Arms Park

Wales 12 (4PG) New Zealand 13 (3PG 1T)

WALES: J P R Williams (captain); J J Williams, R W R Gravell, S P Fenwick, C F W Rees; W G Davies, T D Holmes; A G Faulkner, R W Windsor, G Price, A J Martin, G A D Wheel, P J Ringer, D L Quinnell, J Squire
Scorers *Penalty Goals*: Davies (3), Fenwick

NEW ZEALAND: C J Currie; S S Wilson, B J Robertson, W M Osborne, B G Williams; O D Bruce, D S Loveridge; B R Johnstone, A G Dalton, W K TeP Bush, A M Haden, F J Oliver, L M Rutledge, G A Seear, G N K Mourie (captain)
Replacement B J McKechnie for Currie (5 mins)
Scorers *Try*: Wilson *Penalty Goals*: McKechnie (3)

Referee R C Quittenton (England)

CAP 49 20 January 1979, Murrayfield

Scotland 13 (3PG 1T) Wales 19 (1G 3PG 1T)

SCOTLAND: A R Irvine; K W Robertson, J M Renwick, I R McGeechan (captain), B H Hay; J Y Rutherford, A J M Lawson; J McLauchlan, C T Deans, R F Cunningham, A J Tomes, A F McHarg, M A Biggar, I K Lambie, G Dickson
Scorers *Try*: Irvine *Penalty Goals*: Irvine (3)

WALES: J P R Williams (captain); H E Rees, R W R Gravell, S P Fenwick,
J J Williams; W G Davies, T D Holmes; A G Faulkner, R W Windsor, G Price,
A J Martin, G A D Wheel, P J Ringer, D L Quinnell, J Squire
Scorers *Tries*: Holmes, Rees *Conversion*: Fenwick *Penalty Goals*: Fenwick (3)

Referee F Palmade (France)

CAP 50 3 February 1979, Cardiff Arms Park

Wales 24 (2G 4PG) Ireland 21 (2G 3PG)

WALES: J P R Williams (captain); H E Rees, R W R Gravell, S P Fenwick,
J J Williams; W G Davies, T D Holmes; A G Faulkner, R W Windsor, G Price,
A J Martin, G A D Wheel, P J Ringer, D L Quinnell, J Squire
Replacement S M Lane for Wheel (46 mins)
Scorers *Tries*: Martin, Ringer *Conversions*: Fenwick (2) *Penalty Goals*: Fenwick (4)

IRELAND: R M Spring; T J Kennedy, A R McKibbin, P P McNaughton,
A C McLennan; A J P Ward, C S Patterson; P A Orr, P C Whelan,
G A J McLoughlin, M I Keane, H W Steele, C C Tucker, M E Gibson, J F Slattery
(captain)
Scorers *Tries*: McLennan, Patterson *Conversions*: Ward (2)
Penalty Goals: Ward (3)

Referee A M Hosie (Scotland)

CAP 51 17 February 1979, Parc des Princes, Paris

France 14 (2PG 2T) Wales 13 (3PG 1T)

FRANCE: J-M Aguirre; J-F Gourdon, R Bertranne, C Belascain, G Noves;
A Caussade, J Gallion; A Vaquerin, A Paco, R Paparemborde, F Haget, A Maleig,
J-P Rives (captain), A Guilbert, J-L Joinel
Scorers *Tries*: Gourdon (2) *Penalty Goals*: Aguirre (2)

WALES: J P R Williams (captain); H E Rees, D S Richards, S P Fenwick,
J J Williams; W G Davies, T D Holmes; A G Faulkner, R W Windsor, G Price,
A J Martin, B G Clegg, P J Ringer, D L Quinnell, J Squire
Scorers *Try*: Holmes *Penalty Goals*: Fenwick (3)

Referee D I H Burnett (Ireland)

CAP 52 17 March 1979, Cardiff Arms Park

Wales 27 (2G 1DG 3T) England 3 (1PG)

WALES: J P R Williams (captain); H E Rees, D S Richards, S P Fenwick,
J J Williams; W G Davies, T D Holmes; S J Richardson, A J Phillips, G Price,
A J Martin, M G Roberts, P J Ringer, D L Quinnell, J Squire
Replacement C Griffiths for J P R Williams (60 mins)
Scorers *Tries*: Rees, Richards, Ringer, Roberts, J J Williams *Conversions*: Fenwick,
Martin *Dropped Goal*: Davies

ENGLAND: A J Hignell; P J Squires, R M Cardus, P W Dodge, M A C Slemen;
W N Bennett, P Kingston; C E Smart, P J Wheeler, G S Pearce, W B Beaumont
(captain), N E Horton, A Neary, J P Scott, M Rafter
Scorer *Penalty Goal*: Bennett

Referee J-P Bonnet (France)

CAP 53 1 November 1980, Cardiff Arms Park

Wales 3 (1PG) New Zealand 23 (2G 1PG 2T)

WALES: J P R Williams; H E Rees, D S Richards, S P Fenwick (captain),
R A Ackerman; W G Davies, T D Holmes; C Williams, A J Phillips, G Price,
D L Quinnell, A J Martin, P J Ringer, G P Williams, J Squire
Replacements E T Butler for Squire (21 mins); P J Morgan for Rees (80 mins)
Scorer *Penalty Goal*: Fenwick

NEW ZEALAND: D L Rollerson; S S Wilson, B J Robertson, W M Osborne,
B G Fraser; N H Allen, D S Loveridge; R C Ketels, H R Reid, G A Knight,
A M Haden, G Higginson, G N K Mourie (captain), M G Mexted, M W Shaw
Scorers *Tries*: Mourie, Fraser, Allen, Reid *Conversions*: Rollerson (2)
Penalty Goal: Rollerson

Referee J R West (Ireland)

CAP 54 17 January 1981, Cardiff Arms Park

Wales 21 (1G 4PG 1DG) England 19 (5PG 1T)

WALES: J P R Williams; R A Ackerman, D S Richards, S P Fenwick (captain),
D L Nicholas; W G Davies, D B Williams; I Stephens, A J Phillips, G Price,
C E Davis, G A D Wheel, J R Lewis, G P Williams, J Squire
Scorers *Try*: Davis *Conversion*: Fenwick *Penalty Goals*: Fenwick (4)
Dropped Goal: Davies

ENGLAND: W H Hare; J Carleton, C R Woodward, P W Dodge, M A C Slemen; J P Horton, S J Smith; F E Cotton, P J Wheeler, P J Blakeway, W B Beaumont (captain), M J Colclough, M Rafter, J P Scott, D H Cooke
Replacement A Sheppard for Cotton (15 mins)
Scorer *Try*: Hare *Penalty Goals*: Hare (5)

Referee J B Anderson (Scotland)

CAP 55 7 February 1981, Murrayfield

Scotland 15 (2G 1PG) Wales 6 (2PG)

SCOTLAND: A R Irvine (captain); S Munro, J M Renwick, K W Robertson, B H Hay; J Y Rutherford, R J Laidlaw; J Aitken, C T Deans, N A Rowan, W Cuthbertson, A J Tomes, J H Calder, J R Beattie, D G Leslie
Scorers *Tries*: Irvine (pen try), Tomes *Conversions*: Renwick (2)
Penalty Goal: Renwick

WALES: J P R Williams; R A Ackerman, D S Richards, S P Fenwick (captain), D L Nicholas; W G Davies, D B Williams; I Stephens, A J Phillips, G Price, C E Davis, G A D Wheel, J R Lewis, G P Williams, J Squire
Replacement G Evans for Nicholas (40 mins)
Scorer *Penalty Goals*: Fenwick (2)

Referee D I H Burnett (Ireland)

Index